Social Mobility in the 19th and 20th Centuries

Europe and America in Comparative Perspective

Social Mobility in the 19th and 20th Centuries

Europe and America in Comparative Perspective

Hartmut Kaelble

ST. MARTIN'S PRESS
New York

For Brigitte

English translation © Berg Publishers 1986
Original German contributions © Vandenhoeck and Ruprecht,
Göttingen 1983

All rights reserved. For information, write: Scholarly &
Reference Division, St. Martin's Press, Inc., 175 Fifth Avenue,
New York, NY 10010

First published in the United States of America in 1986

Printed in Great Britain

ISBN 0-312-73448-4

Library of Congress Cataloging-in-Publication Data

Kaelble, Hartmut
Social Mobility in the 19th and 20th centuries.
Bibliography: p.
Includes index.
1. Social classes—Europe—History.   2. Equality—
History. I. Title.
HN380.Z9S64413   1985   305.5'094   85—13415

Contents

Tables

Introduction

This book reflects increased interest in comparative historical study of social mobility. The author attempts to open up new perspectives on the old question of whether social mobility increased, decreased or remained stable during the emergence of modern industrial society, raising four questions rarely posed before — at least by historians.

Firstly, the book discusses the concept of an upheaval in social mobility: the idea that the almost static traditional pre-industrial European societies gave way to a unique golden age of new and unlimited opportunities during the industrialisation process, directly leading to our present high level of social mobility. Alternatively, has twentieth-century bureaucratisation caused a decline in social mobility? Does the empirical evidence support these ideas or should we rather view the industrial revolution as a period of crisis preceding modern, substantial rates of social mobility?

Secondly, the starting-point of the comparative debate on social mobility, which opened some twenty-five years ago, has, so far engaged contemporary observers and sociologists rather than historians: that is, the idea of a high rate of social mobility in the new, open, egalitarian American society and, correspondingly, a low rate in the old, class-ridden, elitist European societies, especially during industrialisation. The European image of an America in which at any moment the servant may become master (de Tocqueville), a perfectly fluid society (Marx), poses a crucial question: if social mobility was in fact substantially higher in America than in Europe, emergence of modern industrial society cannot have been the only factor involved. The author does not wish to underrate the features that industrialising America and industrialising Europe had and have in common; neither will he neglect the differences, but rather seek to explain them.

Thirdly, the author deals with a topic of special concern to historians of Germany, an interest in the development of social mobility in Germany having provided the initial impulse for this study: the argument that Nazism in Germany was centrally rooted in a society which, compared with American and other West European societies, was more authoritarian, more rigidly stratified, more influenced by traditional values and expectations and less liberal, modern or mobile than America or other West European societies. In developing rather than rejecting this argument, the author tries to show the areas in which German society was less

1

mobile and those where it shared a more general European or even Atlantic pattern. This is not the place to discuss exactly how the development of social mobility in Germany paved the way for the rise of Nazism; rather, the book examines one of the major elements in the non-Western path taken by German social history.

Finally, the study seeks to show what factors, apart from industrialisation, were significant for long-term changes in social mobility. This is not to ignore the important role of economic development, but rather to bring other important influences (demographic change, migration, family structure, changes of attitude, political structures) into the debate. Without pretending to offer definitive answers the author discusses why and when these factors played an important role and the evidence of their effects.

In raising these questions, the comparative method is specifically confined to Western societies in a similar stage of economic development. Only in this sense does comparison seem fruitful. Moreover, unlike many historical studies, the book does not simply show differences, but the author has sought out similarities in order to find out which were more significant in various historical eras. Not only the rates of social mobility are compared, but also its changes and dynamics, and explanations are also attempted: the book therefore deals with the differences between social mobility in America and Europe and with even more interest, in how these differences developed and whether it was the contrasts or the similarities which intensified during the nineteenth and twentieth centuries. This dynamic approach to the comparison of social mobility is shared by only a few other studies in this field.[1]

There are four chapters. Chapter 1 gives a perspective of society as a whole, dealing with the upward social mobility of manual workers and a downward mobility into manual occupations. The basic question here is whether, for workers, America proved to be the land of unlimited opportunities; this is discussed through a comparison of European and American cities, since our knowledge of nineteenth- and early twentieth-century working class mobility comes almost exclusively from urban studies. The comparison concentrates on the pre-1914 period, as urban studies are still rare for the years from 1914 onwards. It is complemented by a brief summary of our present knowledge about changes in social mobility in twentieth-century Europe and America, gleaned from sociologically-based studies of whole societies. Chapter 2 covers a question of specific importance for a growing proportion of Europeans and Americans in recent years: the *educational opportunities* in secondary and higher education. Again, the question of a more closed European society with less egalitarian educational institutions is discussed and a comparison made with American education. The chapter also tries to ascertain whether all European educational institutions (at least in the larger countries) strongly resembled each other, or whether we find, especially during the first thirty years of the twentieth century, a specifically *German* development of educational opportunities differing from the more continuously democratic West European path. The background to these comparisons is the question of the impact of industrialisation on higher education: how forceful was it and, conversely, how far was the expansion of higher education independent of economic development? An answer may be found in a discussion of later periods of changing relationships between education and the economy. Chapter 3 deals with a still more specific question which, nevertheless, has a marked symbolic effect on the evaluation of social mobility in industrial societies: the open or exclusive nature of the social origins of the *business elites*. Once again, we compare long-term trends in the nineteenth and twentieth centuries in America and Europe, covering four major European countries, France, Britain, Sweden and Germany, the business elites of other European countries having so far not been sufficiently investigated. The impact of social and cultural changes other than industrialisation; the existence of a more 'open' society in America; the particular development of Germany; and the possible existence of a golden age of the classic early-industrial self-made man: these are the main questions investigated by this comparison.

Chapter 4 is a *generalising synthesis* of the three preceding comparative chapters and of non-comparative research on other aspects of the subject. In it are discussed the chief influences on social mobility in the nineteenth and twentieth centuries, that is, changes in occupational structure, capitalism, migration, demographic transition, family structures, government intervention, differing attitudes. Moreover, it shows how the effect of these factors was modified in the long progress from a pre-industrial society to the initial industrial revolution, thereafter to a second industrialisation and, finally, to the present post-industrial society. The author hopes to encourage the comparative analysis of social mobility by presenting a framework which helps to disclose the similarities and differences in social mobility in America and Europe. This framework is not purely theoretical; it comprises and refers to much empirical research. In conclusion, the four major questions of the introduction are reiterated. The comprehensive answers which are given are not to be regarded as final but are intended to stimulate further studies. Fruitful comparative research is a dialogue among specialists rather than the endeavour of the lonely scholar.

Several characteristics of the book should be mentioned here. Firstly, it is largely an analysis of secondary sources, using published contemporary statistical materials. To a larger degree, however, it is based on thorough, time-consuming, sometimes pioneering studies by other historians or by sociologists, published too early for comparative secondary research.[2] In some respects, it extends the scope of other comparative studies by including more countries or by covering longer periods. Thus comparison is pushed as far as possibile by standing, as it were, on others' shoulders. The text also includes some material drawn and revised from previously published articles; since these articles were written according to a plan, it makes sense to integrate them here.[3] Finally, the book is the product of a period when the author was able to travel in order to carry out his research. So the basic ideas it contains were discussed with colleagues at Yale University, Syracuse University, Rutgers University, St Antony's College, Oxford, in Fernand Braudel's seminar, at the universities of Lyon, Nanterre, Stockholm, Uppsala, at congresses at Maryland University, the Maison des Sciences de l'Homme in Paris, the Erasmus University in Rotterdam, the University of Manchester, in Edinburgh, at the University of Bielefeld, in Freiburg, at the Max-Planck-Institut in Göttingen, in the Reimers Foundation in Bad Homburg and, most especially, in our Berlin research group on the history of modernisation. I have received important suggestions from Peter Flora, Roy Hay, Arnold Heidenheimer, Bill Hubbard, Konrad Jarausch, Arthur Imhof, Jürgen Kocka, Peter Lundgreen, Fred Marquardt, Hans-Jürgen Puhle, Bo Öhngren; I am grateful for all their advice, criticism and interest. I am also grateful to Heike Siesslack, who found her way through what was often a puzzle rather than a manuscript, as well as to Ruth Stanley, who translated parts of the second chapter into English, to Juliet Standing, who corrected my English, to Maureen Roycroft, to Andrea Schmelz, and to Rüdiger Hohls, who collected the data for the troublesome tables 2.2 and 2.11. The book is printed with the financial help of the Ernst-Reuter-Gesellschaft der Förderer und Freunde der Freien Universität Berlin (e.V.).

I dedicate this book to my wife, who tolerated more than ten immobile years in the service of social mobility research.

1 Social Mobility of the Common Man

The opportunities available to ordinary people are a major and fascinating topic which, for the last twenty years, has been the new social historians' central theme in the history of social mobility. However, they have rarely considered this topic as a history of the average person's imagination, influenced by famous examples of self-made men. In general, it is the unspectacular and modest steps upwards or downwards in society that historians deal with: a small farmer's son becoming a well-to-do master artisan, the cottage worker a white-collar employee in a textile factory, the shopkeeper's son becoming a labourer. It is a world in which what matters is the step from poverty to security, from enforced instability to settled living conditions, from an endless series of individual life crises to a long-term perspective of planning of the individual life, from control by others to independence, from marginality to respectability. Many historians have been puzzled by the social mobility of ordinary individuals because of the ambiguity of ascent and descent and some have even abandoned the topic in despair. In any case, it is a world very different from the history 'from above' to which we turn in later chapters, in which social mobility has to do with wealth, power, higher education, with spectacular success or dramatic descent. Social mobility of the commonalty exists in a world apart. Even if all wealth and power stemmed from the lower social classes, this would barely affect the life and social mobility of ordinary people, simply because they form such a large section in any society while the rich and powerful are only a tiny proportion of the population.

The history of social mobility is informative in two respects. Firstly, it tells us whether all modern societies can offer the ordinary individual the same basic chances of upward mobility while presenting the same danger of descent, or whether some societies have been more promising than others. So in this chapter we compare the United States, during the nineteenth and early twentieth centuries the most spectacularly promising of all societies, with the earlier European society. We ask whether the situation arose from a mentality specific to the ordinary American or from the availability of opportunities in American society.

Secondly, studying the history of ordinary people will teach us about

5

progress or decline, the increase, stagnation or even the blocking of
chances for social mobility in the history of industrialisation and industrialised societies. This history of the long-term changes in social mobility
is considered to have three major turning points: the Industrial Revolution and its consequences for social mobility; the second industrialisation; and the postwar emergence of the welfare state and the tertiary
society. Long-term social mobility is a topic on which we have far too
little knowledge, either for a comparative perspective or for individual
countries. There is no base as yet for presenting comparative arguments,
but two possibilities emerge: we can point to a few isolated studies and
present some preliminary results, as briefly set out at the end of this
chapter. Conclusions may also be drawn (as attempted in Chapter 4) from
circumstantial evidence concerning factors which influence social mobility.

North American and European Cities in the Nineteenth and Early-Twentieth Centuries

'There is still a class of menials and a class of masters, but these classes are
not always composed of the same individuals, still less of the same
families; and those who command are not more secure of perpetuity than
those who obey — At any moment a servant may become a master, and
he aspires to rise to that condition.'[1] This view of social mobility in North
America by Alexis de Tocqueville in 1840 has been the predominant
perception almost to the present. Only after the Second World War did
two basically different arguments emerge. On the one hand, historians of
social mobility in nineteenth-century American and European cities, such
as Boston, Marseilles and Bochum, came to the tentative conclusion that
rates of upward social mobility were in fact higher in the United States
than in Europe and that this was especially true for upward mobility from
the working-class into non-manual occupations. In effect, their assessments corroborated the assertion which de Tocqueville had made more
than a century ago.[2] The explanation for these differences, historians
argued, was to be found in the values of the European working class: a
strong traditional commitment to occupational heredity, or the beginnings of class consciousness, kept European workers from using chances
of social ascent into non-manual occupations much more than American
workers. On the other hand, Seymour M. Lipset and Reinhard Bendix
have claimed that social mobility becomes similarly high in all societies,
once a certain degree of industrialisation and economic expansion has
been reached.[3] The idea behind this argument is that rates of social
mobility depend on economic development and changes of occupational
structure, both of which follow the same basic pattern in Europe and

North America. Whilst the empirical evidence for this assessment depends on post-1945 studies of social mobility in America and Europe, there are grounds for projecting the argument back to the late nineteenth century. Firstly, if economic development does lead to similar mobility rates, this effect should have emerged by the end of the era of industrialisation. Secondly, studies of the trend of social mobility in the United States as well as in various European countries show the same long-term stability of rates of social mobility since the late nineteenth century.[4] Hence, if rates of social mobility were similar after the Second World War, and if the long-term trend was similar too, mobility rates at the end of the era of industrialisation cannot have differed much.

The proliferation of local, mostly urban, historical studies in recent years has produced new evidence on social mobility in America and Europe during the nineteenth century. A comparative analysis of the data on social mobility in these studies can be attempted now, focusing upon the opportunities of the ordinary individual, rather than on access to élites or to the middle class.[5] Our basic interest is a contribution to a discussion of historical factors of social mobility, rather than the progressiveness or backwardness of any society. The comparative analysis is used to check which of the two main positions on social mobility outlined above — whose contrasts may have been somewhat overemphasised — comes nearest to the nineteenth-century reality. We also discuss which of the two lines of explanation of social mobility (that is, the argument about the values and mentalities of nineteenth-century workers, or the connections made between industrialisation and subsequent occupational change) are more helpful for making comparisons between American and European society in the nineteenth century.

There is still no possibility of exploring and comparing rates of social mobility of these societies at national level. Perhaps this possibility will never emerge for the nineteenth century as a whole. Even a comparison based on detailed city studies has to face many difficulties. Firstly, the cities chosen for investigation were not selected systematically for comparative purposes, and important urban types — the big industrial city, the administrative centre (large or small) and the non-industrial centre in agrarian areas — have been investigated either too rarely or not at all. Secondly, the available studies are often restricted to different types of social mobility where comparison is not possible — to career mobility or mobility between generations, to overall rates of social mobility or to social ascent within or out of the working class. Hence, for each type of mobility, a reduced number of city studies is available. Thirdly, definitions of occupations and social classes vary in these studies and many of them use, though with variations, definitions of social class which conceal rather than help to follow up important changes of mobility. They do not always distinguish the petty bourgeoisie from white-collar employees, for example, or modern industrial working-class occupations from traditional agrarian or proto-industrial workers, or the small self-employed artisan from the lower sectors of the business community.[6] Fourthly, different populations are dealt with: sometimes certain groups are explicitly excluded, such as women, blacks, or transient migrants; sometimes the exclusion is hidden behind the choice of sources. Finally, many of the available studies are narrowly descriptive, yielding insufficient information on important factors in social mobility such as occupational structure and change, demographic development, migration, urbanisation, mobility barriers and channels, or economic and political institutions affecting social mobility.

Despite these problems, the available studies do allow for some quantitative comparisons to be made, which is crucial for this topic, enabling us to deal with graduated differences rather than with basic contrasts. In any case, to wait for more numerous and more sophisticated studies does not seem to make much sense. Further expensive and time-consuming projects of primary research may well represent wasted effort unless they can yield more innovative conclusions than might emerge from a comparison of the research already done. The latter ought to be attempted first. Here, the initial part of this chapter presents some descriptive conclusions about the contrasts and similarities of social mobility between American and European cities. This involves a somewhat complicated comparison, distinguishing between various aspects of social mobility. The basic distinction is that of mobility between generations, fathers and sons,[7] and that of career mobility, that is, mobility within one life cycle. In each case they are dealt with first in terms of overall rates of social mobility, thereafter in terms of the social ascent of workers' sons (and workers), and downward mobility into the working class and manual occupations. The second part of the chapter is concerned with giving explanations for the findings.

Rates of social mobility compared

The first, perhaps astonishing, conclusion to derive from the available research on social mobility between the generations in nineteenth-century cities is that no clear American pattern of the overall rate of social mobility emerges. There is no indication from the many studies of mobility rates between various social classes that the proportion of inhabitants who left the social class of their fathers was larger in America than in Europe (Table 1.1).* Moreover, no distinct American pattern emerges even if

*Studies of Americans in: Boston; Poughkeepsie (New York); Waltham (Massachusetts); Steelton (Pennsylvania). European studies include: Denmark (Copenhagen); Britain (London); France (Toulouse); Austria (Graz); Netherlands (Rotterdam, Eindhoven); Sweden (Västerås, Halmstad, Örebro); Germany (Cologne, Bielefeld, Berlin, Ludwigshafen).

Table 1.1 Social mobility between generations in European and North American cities 1830–1920 (mobile individuals)

	Boston USA	Walt-ham USA	Pough-keepsie USA	Steel-ton USA	In-diana-polis USA	Hamil-ton Can.	Copen-hagen Dk.	Swed-ish cities	SE Lon-don UK	Col-ogne Germ.	Eus-kirchen Germ.	Lud-wigs-hafen Germ.	Tou-louse Fr.	Rotter-dam Neth.	Eind-hoven Neth.	Graz Aus.	Biele-feld Germ.	Borg-horst Ger.	Berlin Germ.
	1	2	3	4	5	6	7	8	9	10	11	12	13	14	15	16	17	18	19

1. Proportion of mobile individuals

	1	2	3	4	5	6	7	8	9	10	11	12	13	14	15	16	17	18	19
1830	—	—	—	—	—	—	—	—	—	—	—	—	42	—	—	—	—	—	—
1840	—	—	—	—	—	—	—	—	—	52	45	—	—	—	—	—	—	—	62
1850	—	—	—	—	—	20[a]	39	—	32[a]	—	—	—	—	53	25	—	—	—	—
1860	—	—	46	—	—	28[a]	—	—	—	—	—	—	—	—	—	—	—	—	57
1870	—	55	—	—	—	—	—	—	33[a]	44	44	—	52	54	—	62	49	—	—
1880	54	—	—	—	—	—	26	—	—	—	—	58[c]	—	—	—	—	—	—	55
1890	—	—	—	49	—	—	—	58	—	—	—	—	—	—	32	—	—	—	—
1900	56	—	—	—	—	—	—	—	—	—	—	—	—	49	—	—	—	32	—
1910	—	—	—	—	35	—	—	—	—	55	46	—	—	—	—	55	—	—	56
1920	—	—	—	—	—	—	—	—	—	—	—	—	—	—	34	—	—	—	—

Continued on page 10

Table 1.1 *continued*

2. Relation of upward mobility to downward mobility[b]

	Boston USA	Waltham USA	Pough-keepsie USA	Steel-ton USA	In-diana-polis USA	Hamil-ton Can.	Copen-hagen Dk.	Swed-ish cities	SE Lon-don UK	Col-ogne Germ.	Eus-kirchen Germ.	Lud-wigs-hafen Germ.	Tou-louse Fr.	Rotter-dam Neth.	Eind-hoven Neth.	Graz Aus.	Biele-feld Germ.	Borg-horst Ger.	Berlin Germ.
	1	2	3	4	5	6	7	8	9	10	11	12	13	14	15	16	17	18	19
1830	—	—	—	—	—	—	—	—	—	—	—	—	0.6	—	—	—	—	—	0.6
1840	—	—	—	—	—	—	—	—	—	1.3	0.6	—	—	—	—	—	—	—	0.5
1850	—	—	—	—	—	1.1[a]	0.5	—	1.3[a]	—	—	—	—	0.9	0.3	—	—	—	—
1860	—	—	—	—	—	1.5[a]	—	—	—	—	—	—	—	—	—	0.4	—	—	—
1870	—	—	—	—	—	—	—	—	1.5[a]	0.7	1.2	—	0.6	0.3	—	—	1.4	—	0.5
1880	—	1.0	2.4	—	—	—	—	—	—	—	—	—	—	—	—	—	—	—	—
1890	1.0	—	—	—	—	—	1.2	—	—	—	—	0.7[c]	—	—	1.3	—	—	—	—
1900	—	—	—	2.1	—	—	—	2.3	—	—	—	—	—	1.4	—	—	—	—	—
1910	2.1	—	—	—	0.9	—	—	—	—	0.7	0.8	—	—	—	—	0.7	—	0.6	0.6
1920	—	—	—	—	—	—	—	—	—	—	—	—	—	—	0.2	—	—	—	—

[a]Three classes only
[b]Upwardly mobile to downwardly mobile individuals. Over 1: upward mobility predominates; below 1: downward mobility predominates.
[c]Not including the agricultural sector; had it been included the downward trend would have been even more marked.

upward and downward social mobility are seen in relation to each other. At first glance, the available research seems to indicate that de Tocqueville's view is corroborated and that the Americans who did not remain in the social class of their fathers moved up somewhat more frequently and descended somewhat more rarely than the Europeans (Table 1.1). Upward social mobility seems to have predominated more often and been more visible in North America than in Europe. However, it should be stressed that the evidence is ambivalent, at the least. The difference might be due to the better quality of the sources used in studies of most American cities but, leaving this problem aside, it can be argued that the relationship of upward to downward mobility in almost half the American cases is less favourable than in the corresponding number of European ones.

This leads us to a second less surprising, but very important conclusion on social mobility *between generations*: the extensive *variety* of social mobility on both sides of the Atlantic. This is perhaps most clear for mobility across the line between working-class and white-collar occupations (Table 1.2). There are very low rates of social ascent of working-class

Note to Table 1.1:

With the exception of Hamilton and South-East London, the table gives mobility rates between four social classes: middle class, lower-middle class, skilled workers, unskilled workers. If more classes were investigated, mobility rates were recalculated in order to allow crude comparisons. Any comparison, however, has to be made carefully, since definitions of the four classes vary. Structural mobility or any indicator of social mobility was not calculated, since the marginal distribution of the standard mobility table in local studies does not indicate occupational change: too many of the fathers on whose occupations the tables are based lived elsewhere. Calculated from: Boston: S. Thernstrom, *The Other Bostonians* (Harvard UP, Cambridge, Mass., 1973), p. 89; Waltham: H. M. Gitelman, *Workingmen of Waltham* (Johns Hopkins UP, Baltimore, 1974), p. 66 (sample 1850–80); Poughkeepsie: C. and S. Griffen, *Natives and Newcomers* (Harvard UP, Cambridge, Mass., 1978), p. 67; Steelton: J. Bodnar, *Immigration and Industrialization* (University of Pittsburgh Press, Pittsburgh, 1977), p. 134 (three small samples — 1888, 1896, 1905); Indianapolis: J. C. Tully et. al., 'Trends in Occupational Mobility in Indianapolis', in *Social Forces*, vol. 49 (1970–1), p. 193; Hamilton: M. Katz, *The People of Hamilton, Canada West* (Harvard UP, Cambridge, Mass., 1975), p. 166; Copenhagen: T. Rishoy, 'Metropolitan Social Mobility, 1850–1950: The Case of Copenhagen', in *Quantity and Quality*, vol. 5 (1971), pp. 136ff.; Swedish cities: S. Akerman, 'Swedish Migration and Social Mobility: the Tale of Three Cities', in *Social Science Hist.*, vol. 1 (1977); South-East London: G. Crossick, *An Artisan Elite in Victorian Society. Kentish London 1840–1880* (Croom Helm, London, 1978), pp. 113f., 122f. (Table 1.1 contains rough approximations calculated from tables which cover only particular social classes.); H. Daheim, 'Berufliche Intergenerationen–Mobilität in der komplexen Gesellschaft', in *Kölner Zeitschrift für Soziologie*, vol. 16 (1964), pp. 117ff.; R. Mayntz, *Soziale Schichtung und sozialer Wandel in einer Industriegemeinde* (Enke, Stuttgart, 1958), pp. 66, 68 (for 1870–1914); Toulouse: R. Aminzade and R. Hodson, 'Social Mobility in a mid-19th-Century French City, in *American Sociological Review*, vol. 47 (1982), pp. 447f.; Rotterdam and Eindhoven: H. von Dijk, J. Visser and E. Wolst, 'Regional Differences in Social Mobility Patterns in the Netherlands between 1830 and 1940', in *Journal of Social History*, vol. 17 (1984), Table 1; Graz: W. H. Hubbard, 'Social Mobility and Social Structure in Graz, 1875–1910', in *Journal of Social History*, vol. 17 (1984), Table 2; Bielefeld and Borghorst: J. Kocka et al., *Familie und soziale Plazierung* (Westdeutscher Verlag, Opladen, 1980), p. 371 (Bielefeld 1830–1910; Borghorst 1880–1911); Berlin: data from a study in progress by Ruth Federspiel (1825–7, 1855–71, 1882–4, 1890–7).

Table 1.2 *Social mobility between generations in North American and European cities 1825–1914 (%)*

	Upward mobility from manual and non-manual positions			Downward mobility from non-manual positions	Proportion employed in non-manual positions
	from working-class background	from skilled workers	from unskilled workers[a]		
	1	2	3	4	5
North America					
Newburyport 1860	—	—	7	—	—
Newburyport 1870	—	—	10	—	—
Hamilton 1850[e]	5	6	2	28	24
Hamilton 1860[e]	14	14	15	6	30
New Orleans 1870	—	—	21	—	—
Poughkeepsie 1880	26	29	19	11	42
Newburyport 1880	—	—	8	—	—
Boston ca. 1890	41	37	43	20	59
Boston ca. 1910	41	43	39	17	55
Indianapolis 1910	21	23	19	40	39
Europe					
Berlin (D) 1825	20	25	19	31	38
Toulouse (F) 1830	10	9	11	13	47
Euskirchen (D) 1833–40	8	11	6	59[c]	20
Cologne (D) 1833–40	10	11	7	47[b]	24
Marseilles (F) 1850	14	—	—	—	—
Copenhagen (DK) 1850	21	25	—	33	44

SE London (GB)	1851–3	20	19	21	29	35
Eßlingen (D)	1846–70	—	45	—	—	—
Berlin (D)	1855	19	17	20	34	22
Graz (AU)	1869	11	9	12	72	57
Toulouse (F)	1872	13	13	12	60	50
Euskirchen (D)	1870–7	18	19	16	24[c]	34
Cologne (D)	1870–7	15	19	12	47[b]	30
SE London (GB)	1873–5	13	22	1	31	25
Graz (AU)	1880	9	8	10	49	63
Berlin (D)	1885	11	23	10	24	30
Berlin (D)	1905–07	15	14	15	34	21
Euskirchen (D)	1906–13	17	21	10	45[c]	29
Cologne (D)	1906–13	18	23	14	43[b]	36
Bochum (D)	1900	12	10–18	6	—	25[d]
Swed. cities (S)	1910	27	40	21	36	36
Ludwigshafen (D)	1876–1914	9	11	5	58	17
Eßlingen (D)	1870–1914	—	39	—	—	—
Bielefeld (D)	1830–1910	18	22[f]	19	44[g]	31
Borghorst (D)	1880–1911	16	19[f]	9	49[g]	29

[a] Semi-skilled workers included in 'unskilled workers'
[b] 'Downward mobility' from farmers: 27 per cent in 1833–40, 25 per cent in 1870–7, 13 per cent in 1906–13
[c] 'Downward mobility' from farmers: 45 per cent in 1833–40, 14 per cent in 1870–7, 20 per cent in 1906–13
[d] 1880
[e] Son's first job
[f] Social ascent of cottage workers: 20 per cent in Bielefeld, 25 per cent in Borghorst
[g] Downward mobility from farmers: 66 per cent in Bielefeld, 68 per cent in Borghorst

AU = Austria; D = Germany; DK = Denmark; F = France; GB = Great Britain; S = Sweden

sons in the German cities of Ludwigshafen and Euskirchen as well as in
the North American cities of Newburyport and Hamilton, while very
high rates of social ascent obtain not only in the American city of Boston
but also in the German city of Eßlingen (for skilled workers at least), the
Danish city of Copenhagen and the Swedish cities of Västerås, Halmstad
and Örebro. It is interesting that this variety is not directly related to the
degree of industrialisation. The two most typical, rapidly expanding
industrial cities among the cases investigated (Bochum and Ludwigshafen in Germany), do not show the high rates of social mobility which
one might expect. On the contrary, they are among the cities with the
poorest chances of social ascent, related to the small lower-middle classes
of the purely industrial city (Table 1.2). These variations cast doubt on
whether there is any clear and homogeneous European or American
pattern of social ascent between generations. To de Tocqueville, some
American cities must have been disappointing, while some European
cities must have appeared like little Americas.

A third perhaps surprising, conclusion is that a distinct North American pattern existed for downward rather than for upward mobility. It
appears that downward mobility from white-collar family background to
working class was much more frequent in European cities than in American ones. The difference is unusually clear-cut, at least among the cities
which were explored (Table 1.2, col. 4). Only two North American cities
come close (but in only one year) to the European rates of downward

Note to Table 1.2:

Newburyport: S. Thernstrom, *Poverty and Progress: Social Mobility in a Nineteenth-Century City*
(Harvard UP, Cambridge, Mass., 1964), Table 5 (for comparison with the other studies,
mostly based on marriage registers and therefore tending to relate to men in their late
twenties, I have used Thernstrom's data concerning sons aged 20–30, so that for example
social mobility of 1860 relates to those born in 1830–39); Hamilton: Katz, *People of Hamilton*,
p. 144; Poughkeepsie: Griffen, *Natives and Newcomers*, p. 67 (son's last job); Boston: Thernstrom, *The Other Bostonians*, p. 89 (son's last job); Indianapolis: Tully et al., 'Trends in
Occupational Mobility in Indianapolis', p. 192; New Orleans: D. T. Kearns, 'The Social
Mobility of New Orleans Laborers 1870–1900' (PhD thesis, Tulane University, 1977), p. 102;
Toulouse: Aminzade and Hodson,'Social Mobility in a Mid-19th-Century French City', pp.
447f.; Euskirchen: Mayntz, *Soziale Schichtung und sozialer Wandel in einer Industriegemeinde*,
pp. 154ff.; Cologne: Daheim, 'Berufliche Intergenerationen–Mobilität in der komplexen
Gesellschaft', pp. 117ff.; Copenhagen: Rishoy, 'Metropolitan Social Mobility 1850–1950: the
Case of Copenhagen', pp. 136f.; Eßlingen: H. Schomerus, *Die Arbeiter der Maschinen-Fabrik
Eßlingen* (Klett-Cotta, Stuttgart, 1977), p. 276 (machine-building workers only); Bochum:
D. Crew, 'Definitions of Modernity: Social Mobility in a German Town, 1880–1901', in *Journal
of Social History*, vol. 7 (1973–4), p. 61; Marseilles: W. H. Sewell, 'Social Mobility in a
Nineteenth-Century European City ' in *Journal of Interdisciplinary History*, vol. 7. (1976), p. 211;
Swedish cities: S. Akerman, 'Swedish Migration and Social Mobility: the Tale of Three
Cities'; Ludwigshafen: W. von Hippel, 'Regionale und soziale Herkunft der Bevölkerung
einer Industriestadt', in W. Conze and U. Engelhardt (eds.) *Arbeiter im Industrialisierungs-
prozeß* (Klett-Cotta, Stuttgart, 1979), pp. 67f.; London: Crossick, *An Artisan Elite in Victorian
Society*, pp. 113f., 122f.; Bielefeld and Borghorst: Kocka et. al., *Familie und soziale Plazierung*,
pp. 11, 364, 371; Graz: Hubbard, 'Social Mobility and Social Structure in Graz, 1857–1910',
Table 2; Berlin: data from a study in progress by Ruth Federspiel.

mobility — Hamilton, Canada, which led the investigator, Michael Katz, to suppose that Canada as a nineteenth-century country was different from the 'American' pattern, and early-twentieth-century Indianapolis. All other American cities which have been investigated (and also Hamilton in another year) show much lower rates of downward mobility than the European cities. *It might have been the low danger of descending from the father's social class rather than the promise of social ascent which characterised American cities.*[8] This would fit neither de Tocqueville's view nor the interpretation by Bendix and Lipset.

The comparison of career mobility in American and European cities yields partly different conclusions. To begin with overall rates of mobility between various social classes, only eleven studies of this aspect exist so far. Once again, there is no clear American pattern. In American as well as in European cities, between 17 and 25 per cent of the population moved within one decade between the four social classes which can be compared so far, that is, between unskilled and semi-skilled workers, skilled workers, the lower-middle class, and the middle class, without any clear relationship between rapid industrialisation and high rates of mobility (Table 1.3). Although two North American cases have somewhat higher rates of mobility, one of them is Canadian and the other, Steelton, Pennsylvania, had the lowest rate ever in a different year. By chance, three of the available studies cover seaports. Even in these cities with a similar economic structure no distinctly American pattern emerged: between 1830 and 1860 Rotterdam had about the same rates of career mobility as Boston and Philadelphia. This is still true if upward and downward career mobility are followed separately. Upward social mobility predominated in American as in European cities (with the qualification that the social mobility of migrants is unknown on either side of the Atlantic). Even the precise relation of upwardly mobile individuals to downwardly mobile ones was not more favourable in North American cities (Table 1.3).

The conclusions are somewhat different if we turn to career mobility across the line between the working class and the lower-middle and middle class. At first glance the available research supports the view of de Tocqueville. The chances of social ascent for workers were *clearly higher* in American cities than in European ones (Table 1.4). In almost all European cities 10 per cent or less of the workers reached lower-middle-class (rarely middle-class) positions within ten years.* In most American cities 10 per cent and more of workers reached these positions during one decade.† This is probably what was in the mind of those social historians

---

*Preston, 5 per cent; Bochum, 8 per cent; Rotterdam, 7 per cent (average); Eindhoven, 8 per cent (average); Oskarsham, 10 per cent; Graz, 19 per cent (average, making this the exception)
†Boston, 11 per cent (average); South Bend, 12 per cent (average); Hamilton, 16 per cent;

Table 1.3 *Career mobility in European and North American cities, 1820–1930 (mobile individuals)*

Year	Philadelphia (USA)	Boston (USA)	Poughkeepsie (USA)	Waltham (USA)	Warren (USA)	Steelton (USA)	Hamilton (Canada)	Rotterdam (Netherlands)	Bochum (Germany)	Graz (Austria)	Eindhoven (Netherlands)
	1	2	3	4	5	6	7	8	9	10	11
1. Proportion of mobile individuals											
1820–30	14	—	—	—	—	—	—	—	—	—	—
1830–40	19	11	—	—	—	—	—	10	—	—	—
1840–50	15	10	—	—	—	—	—	—	—	—	—
1850–60	20	16	22	17	—	—	—	18	—	—	7
1860–70	—	—	24	22	—	—	27	—	—	22	—
1870–80	—	—	23	17	—	—	—	14	—	23	—
1880–90	—	21	—	—	—	28	—	—	11	—	—
1890–00	—	—	—	—	22	—	—	—	—	—	14
1900–10	—	—	—	—	—	9	—	—	—	29	—
1920–30	—	—	—	—	—	—	—	—	—	—	19
2. Relation of upward mobility to downward mobility[a]											
1820–30	1.4	—	—	—	—	—	—	—	—	—	—
1830–40	1.9	4.7	—	—	—	—	—	1.6	—	—	—
1840–50	1.4	2.8	—	—	—	—	—	—	—	—	—
1850–60	1.5	5.3	2.8	1.5	—	—	1.9	1.9	—	—	0.9
1860–70	—	—	3.0	2.8	—	—	—	—	—	2.0	—
1870–80	—	—	1.9	2.7	—	—	—	8.7	—	1.3	—
1880–90	—	1.7	—	—	—	3.7	—	—	2.0	—	—
1890–00	—	—	—	—	2.2	—	—	—	—	—	1.8
1900–10	—	—	—	—	—	2.0	—	—	—	1.3	—
1920–30	—	—	—	—	—	—	—	—	—	—	2.2
Average	1.6	3.6	2.6	2.3	2.2	2.8	1.9	4.1	2.0	1.5	1.6

[a]Upwardly mobile to downwardly mobile individuals. Over 1: upward mobility predominates; below 1: downward mobility predominates

who made the assessment that nineteenth-century workers had better opportunities in America than in Europe. The argument seems to be the more important since rates of downward career mobility into manual positions were about the same in American and European cities.[9] Hence,

Atlanta, 11 per cent; New Orleans, 10 per cent (average); Hamilton, 16 per cent; Atlanta, 11 per cent; New Orleans, 10 per cent (unskilled workers only); Omaha, 22 per cent (average); Birmingham, 18 per cent (average); Warren, 16 per cent; Poughkeepsie, 4 per cent (average); Newburyport, 5 per cent (average, unskilled workers only). Poughkeepsie and Newburyport are thus the exceptions.

the somewhat higher rates of chances for social ascent in America were not offset by a stronger danger of social descent.

An even more distinct American pattern emerges from the comparison of social ascent for unskilled and skilled workers on both sides of the Atlantic. At least in the few cases which have been explored, there is rarely much difference between American unskilled and skilled workers in their social ascent across the line between the working class and lower-middle class. Sometimes unskilled workers were even more successful than skilled workers. In European cities, on the contrary, rates of social ascent across that particular line were much lower among unskilled than among skilled workers (Table 1.4, cols 2,3). Hence, if America was the land of promise, this was more true for the unskilled workers (or for skilled people who had become unskilled) than for any other social group.[10] It was hardly true for skilled workers, who moved up into the lower-middle class more often in Europe than in America.

Even if there is a distinct American pattern of higher rates of social ascent, two qualifications still have to be made. Firstly, once again the variety among American cities is so extensive that no consistent American pattern appears. The difference between the most promising American cities (Omaha and Birmingham) and the least promising (Atlanta, Poughkeepsie and Boston — in most years) is so large that the historian is tempted to deal with contrasts within America rather than with anything like a specifically American way of social mobility.

Even more important is the fact that the cities and/or periods with low

Note to Table 1.3

In this Table I have tried to calculate mobility rates between four social classes: unskilled (including semi-skilled) workers, skilled workers, the lower-middle class, the middle class. Structural mobility or any other indicator of social mobility was not computed since the marginal distribution of the standard mobility table of a local study usually does not indicate occupational change, because of the high rates and occupational differentials of migration. (Hence, column 5 of Table 1.4, based on the marginal distribution, should be used with care.) The Table is restricted to career mobility within ten years; only for this time span do we have sufficient studies.

Philadelphia: S. Blumin, 'Mobility and Change in Ante-bellum Philadelphia', in S. Thernstrom and R. Sennet (eds.), *Nineteenth-Century Cities* (Yale UP, New Haven, 1969), pp. 173ff. (rates of mobility between five social classes); Boston: P. R. Knights, *The Plain People of Boston, 1830–1860* (Oxford UP, New York, 1971), pp. 98f.; Thernstrom, *The Other Bostonians*, p. 57; Poughkeepsie: Griffen, *Natives and Newcomers*, p. 60; Waltham: Gitelman, *Workingmen of Waltham*, p. 66; Warren: A. E. Broadman and M. P. Weber, 'Economic Growth and Occupational Mobility in Nineteenth-Century Urban America', in *Journal of Social History*, vol. 11 (1977–8), p. 64 (results are compiled from four cohorts: 1870–80, 1880–90, 1890–1900, 1900–10); Steelton: Bodnar, *Immigration and Industrialization*, p. 70 (second cohort, 1905–15); Hamilton: Katz, *The People of Hamilton*, p. 150; Rotterdam: H. van Dijk, *Rotterdam 1810–1880* (Interbook International, Schiedam, 1976), pp. 152ff.; Bochum: Crew, 'Definitions of Modernity', Table 1 (mobility between three classes only, hence low rate of mobility); Graz: Hubbard, 'Social Mobility and Social Structure in Graz, 1857–1910', Table 1; Eindhoven: van Dijk et. al., 'Regional Differences in Social Mobility Patterns', Table 3 (mobility between six social classes).

Table 1.4 Career mobility across the line between manual and non-manual occupations in European and North American cities, 1830–1930 (outflow percentages in ten years)

| | | Upward mobility from manual to non-manual occupations | | | Downward mobility from non-manual to manual occupations | Proportion of non-manual workers |
| | | from the working class | from unskilled positions | from skilled positions | | |
		1	2	3	4	5
North America						
Boston	1830–40	9	14	4	2	39
Boston	1840–50	7	7	7	0	46
Boston	1850–60	17	15	18	5	29
Poughkeepsie	1850–60	6	6	6	1	35
Newburyport	1850–50	—	5	—	—	—
South Bend	1850–60	14[a]	—	—	—	41
Hamilton	1850–60	16	16	16	15	34
Poughkeepsie	1860–70	4	4	4	8	34
South Bend	1860–70	10[a]	—	—	—	20
Newburyport	1860–70	—	5	—	—	—
Poughkeepsie	1870–80	2	3	2	3	34
Atlanta	1870–80	11	—	—	6	29
New Orleans	1870–80	—	10	—	—	—
Newburyport	1870–80	—	5	—	—	—

South Bend	1870–80	9[a]	—	—	—	18
Boston	1880–90	10	15	6	10	39
Omaha	1880–90	21	—	—	2	40
Birmingham	1890–99	15	12	14[b]	—	—
Birmingham	1899–1909	20	14	24[b]	—	—
Omaha	1900–1910	23	—	—	8	64
Warren	1870–1910	16	15	22	8	39
Europe						
Rotterdam NL	1830–40	5	1	8	11	37
Rotterdam NL	1850–60	13	2	17	13	17
Eindhoven NL	1850–60	1	—	1	1	66
Preston GB	1850–60	5	—	—	—	—
Graz AU	1857–69	22	9	31	12	45
Rotterdam NL	1870–80	10	5	17	7	21
Graz AU	1869–80	16	9	23	12	43
Bochum D	1880–90	8	6	10	4	22
Oskarsham S	1890–1900	10	—	—	—	—
Eindhoven NL	1890–1900	8	3	9	2	47
Graz AU	1900–1910	18	12	22	16	43
Eindhoven NL	1920–30	14	7	15	6	57

a) immigrant workers only
b) without service workers, whose definition is not clear

AU = Austria; D = Germany; GB = Great Britain; NL = Netherlands; S = Sweden.

rates of social ascent in America were close to the European rates. This is true even if one drops the two most deviant cases of Poughkeepsie, New York, with its low 'European' rates of social ascent and Graz, Austria, with its high 'American' rates. For the rest the differences which do occur are small, perhaps even merely technical differences, which do not make a strong point for superior opportunities in American cities.[11] Hence, if there are any spectacular contrasts among nineteenth-century cities, the dividing lines running across America and perhaps also across Europe were as important as the contrast between America and Europe.

To sum up, the bulk of the evidence does not support the view of distinctly superior opportunities in nineteenth-century American cities. Only downward mobility into the working class might have been lower in the US which is, however, not what the idea of superior opportunities really means. A clear American pattern of superior rates of opportunities could be found, if at all, only in a restricted sense, that is, only for career mobility across the line between the working class and the (mostly lower-) middle class. Such a pattern existed to a certain degree for the working class as a whole, though this conclusion is blurred by large variations among American as well as among European cities. The pattern emerges much more distinctly for unskilled American workers when compared to skilled workers. The large gap of opportunities between unskilled and skilled workers in Europe did not exist in America. Subject to the qualification that our knowledge is based on few cases, this is where de Tocqueville's observation in 1840 remained valid throughout the nineteenth century. One ought, nevertheless, to keep in mind that, in America as well as in Europe, the majority of unskilled workers remained in their social class.

Explanation of the findings

We should not be surprised at finding basic similarities between American and European societies since both of them industrialised in about the same situation of the world economy and technological knowledge, and there were strong economic and cultural links between them, not least because of European settlement in America. What needs expla-

Note to Table 1.4:

Table 1.4 is calculated from: Boston: Knights, *The Plain People of Boston*, pp. 98f.; Thernstrom, *The Other Bostonians*, p. 57 (semi-skilled under category 'unskilled'); Newburyport: Thernstrom, *Poverty and Progress*, p. 96; South Bend: D. R. Esslinger, *Immigrants and the City* (Kennikat Press, Port Washington, 1975, p. 82; Hamilton: Katz, *The People of Hamilton*; Atlanta: R. J. Hopkins, 'Occupational and Geographical Mobility in Atlanta, 1870–1896', *J. Southern Hist.*, vol. 34 (1968), pp. 205ff.; Birmingham: P. B. Wortham, 'Working Class Mobility in Birmingham, Alabama, 1880–1914' in T. K. Hareven (ed.) *Anonymous Americans* (Prentice-Hall, Englewood Cliffs, 1971), pp. 194f.; New Orleans: Kearns, 'The Social Mobility of New Orleans Laborers', p. 45; Omaha: H. P. Chudacoff, *Mobile Americans* (Oxford

nation, therefore, is how the differences of social mobility between American and European cities arose. It is still too early to offer any final and definite explanation, since the findings that have been presented may be modified by further studies. It should also be stressed that all differences were a matter of scale, and represented simplifications of marked regional and local variations. Nevertheless some suggestions can be made. A first matter needing to be considered, for instance, is the significance of diverging employment structures and developments in patterns between America and industrialising Western Europe[12]. A comparative history of the labour force exists so far only in an initial stage. It seems, however, that nineteenth-century America witnessed a more rapid change of employment than the industrialising European countries. Change proceeded more slowly even in a notoriously rapid developer such as Germany than in the United States. Moreover, the United States in the second half of the nineteenth century (as well as in the twentieth century) was characterised by a comparatively small industrial sector and a comparatively large service sector, because the active population employed in commerce, banking, transportation, and public utilities was relatively larger in the United States than in West Europe (Table 1.5).[13] Related to the sectoral difference, it appears that the industrial working class was relatively smaller and that the lower-middle class, especially in the service sector, became relatively larger in America than in industrialising Western Europe during the second half of the nineteenth century.[14] Hence, in the nineteenth-century American cities investigated so far, 42 per cent of the labour force was employed in lower-middle class occupations compared to only 29 per cent in European cities.[15] These differences would lead one to expect somewhat diverging patterns of social mobility.

A second important difference between America and industrialising Western Europe lies in the decline of the traditional unskilled worker with his extremely low chances of social ascent. The transition from the pre-industrial and early–industrial day labourer, who did non-mechanised work, to the modern unskilled or semi-skilled worker employed in highly mechanised mass production, appears to have taken place earlier and/or more rapidly in the USA than in Europe. The basic economic precondition of this transition was mechanisation and the emergence of

UP, New York, 1972), pp. 17, 99 (it is not quite clear whether Chudacoff traces mobility across the line between manual and non-manual occupations); Warren: Broadman and Weber, 'Economic Growth and Occupational Mobility', p. 64; Rotterdam: van Dijk, *Rotterdam*, pp. 145ff.; Graz: Hubbard, 'Aspects of Social Mobility in Graz, 1857–1880', Table 11; Bochum: Crew, 'Definitions of Modernity', Table 1; or D. Crew, *Town in the Ruhr. The Social History of Bochum, 1860–1914* (Columbia UP, New York, 1979), Table 3.1; Oskarsham: D. Papp and B. Oehngren, *Arbeterna vid Oskarshamvs varn kring sekeskiftet* (sjöhistorika museet, Stockholm, 1973), p. 30; Eindhoven: data which Henk van Dijk kindly permitted to be included in the Table.

Table 1.5 *Employment structure of the US and Western Europe: industry, commerce and transportation, 1860–1910 (percentage of total active population)*

	Industry		Commerce and transportation	
	USA	Industrialising Western Europe	USA	Industrialising Western Europe
	1	2	3	4
1860	20	36	7	7
1870	23	33	10	8
1880	25	33	12	7
1890	28	35	14	9
1900	30	38	16	11
1910	32	40	20	14

[a]Commerce, banking, insurances, transportation, public utilities (excluding restaurants, which are usually included in French and German statistics, but not in the American ones).
Sources: *Historical Statistics of the United States* (US Bureau of Census, Washington, 1960), p. 74; Bairoch, *Working Population*, pp. 83ff. (for Belgium, Britain, Denmark, the Netherlands, Sweden, Switzerland); Toutain, *Population*, Tables 57, 60, 81, 136-7; Hoffmann, *Das Wachstum*, pp. 204ff. The Table includes those European countries whose industrial sector in 1910 contained some 30 per cent or more of the total active population - that is, Belgium, Britain, Denmark, France, Germany, the Netherlands, Sweden, Switzerland.
For further remarks see n. 12 for this chapter.

standardised mass production.[16] Whatever the reasons for this — the scarcity of labour in general and of skilled labour in particular in the USA, the more innovative American entrepreneur, the more developed trade of mass-produced consumption goods, the more open attitude of the American consumer towards industrial rather than artisanal commodities — the rise of the modern unskilled worker was an important factor of social mobility since his steadier work and life situation was more favourable for using educational and occupational chances and possibilities of social ascent. Therefore more modern unskilled or semi-skilled work might have increased upward social mobility rates, especially from unskilled work into the lower-middle class. Since European 'backwardness' was only a matter of scale and there were substantial variations within the USA as well as among industrialising European countries, this factor brought about only gradual differences of social mobility.

A further important reason for different opportunities in America and Europe might be found by examining life-cycles. Research on age-specific upward and downward mobility during the nineteenth century has only just started and only a few, mostly local urban, studies exist. One might suppose that the somewhat higher occupational opportunities in America applied mainly to the age of about 40 and 50. After that, downward (relative to upward) mobility was probably the same or even stronger than in Europe since a larger proportion of Europeans seem to have retired at that age, and especially since lower-white-collar Europeans were more reluctant to accept occupational downward mobility even under the condition of a deteriorating standard of living.[17]

A final reason for differences between America and Europe is a technical one. Apparent differences in rates of social mobility might depend upon the quality of sources. Marriage licence files, the main source for studies of mobility between generations, underrate the extent of upward social mobility since the generation of sons is explored at an early age, when chances of social ascent still lay ahead. Some studies, such as those of late-nineteenth-century Boston and Poughkeepsie, which found particularly low rates of downward mobility, used sources covering later stages of the life cycle of social mobility.[18]

To sum up, there are various reasons for not explaining the somewhat better career prospects of American urban workers simply by their weaker commitment to trades or to a working-class culture. First of all, there is a basic contradiction in this argument. In Europe those workers committed to corporativist ideas or to class consciousness, and those workers who experienced comparatively little social ascent, comprised different groups. The former, usually skilled workers, were upwardly mobile as often or more frequently than their American counterparts; whilst those European unskilled workers who experienced much less social ascent than their American counterparts often had few commitments to any occupation or to working-class consciousness during most of the century. No doubt the values of European *skilled* workers made an important difference to political and social life in Europe compared with America. However, the impact of this on social mobility is not yet clear.

In any case there are other factors which can be adduced to explain higher rates of social ascent among workers in America. As we have seen, and leaving aside the problem of whether American studies use better sources, employment structures and technological development were more favourable to social ascent in America, especially for the unskilled, and the life cycle of occupational opportunity may have been more distinct in America with similar consequences. Other factors, such as the less rigid and less formalized stratification of American society and the more open attitude of the American middle class towards social success, might have been important as well.[19]

Conclusion

This section departs from two contradictory, albeit tentative, arguments about social mobility in nineteenth-century America and Europe. These arguments have been set against evidence on social mobility in over thirty local urban studies and it turns out that neither is wholly wrong. There is more evidence for the argument that links similarities in rates of social mobility to similar paths of industrialisation. No distinct American pattern of superior social mobility was found for most aspects of mobility between generations and for overall rates of career mobility. However, there was some restricted evidence for the second argument about the superiority of opportunities in nineteenth-century America. Social ascent across the line between the working class and the lower-middle class was somewhat more frequent in the USA, at least for unskilled workers. The argument about differences in values between European and American society may have been a factor explaining this, by pointing to certain differences in the social mobility of ordinary people and even greater variation in access to the middle class and the élite on the two sides of the Atlantic,[20] but the better explanation seems to lie in the more favourable opportunity structures in American society. In respect of the unskilled and semi-skilled worker, America was not simply the land of more promising individuals, but the land of more promise. Apart from restricted trans-Atlantic differences, however, similarities, or at least similarly large variations in the social mobility of the average person were characteristic of societies on both sides of the Atlantic.

These conclusions raise the question of how to explain our expectations that nineteenth-century America was the land of superior opportunities. It might be expected, first, that transatlantic migration was to a large degree a search for better opportunities and we might well ask why this migration happened at all if migrants found the same chances in the United States as in Europe. However, recent research on emigration from Europe has shown that migrants rarely shared the view of de Tocqueville — the overwhelming majority wanted to leave unbearable economic circumstances to find a living, or to earn more money in the same trade, rather than to use chances of social ascent in other occupations.[21] Secondly, one might expect — as did Werner Sombart — that the weakness of socialism in the American labour movement was due partly to better opportunities in America and that European workers were more radical because they had less chance of leaving their proletarian situation. However, social opportunity was just one factor in radical labour movements, and radicalism itself depended on perceptions of social mobility rather than the actual rates of mobility, which are interpreted differently even among today's social scientists, and were not in any case known exactly during the nineteenth century. Finally, one might expect superior opportunities in America due to the 'frontier' — the existence of local societies in the making, without the traditional social barriers of European societies. Among the studies examined in this chapter there was only one

American frontier city (Omaha, Nebraska) and this city showed very high rates of upward social mobility. The rural 'frontier' was omitted altogether.[22] However, if future research does find spectacularly high rates of social mobility in frontier districts, the result will be probably more important for differences within America and between rural Europe and rural America, which was, after all, where a majority of Europeans and Americans lived for most of the nineteenth century. It will probably be much less important for the comparison of urban opportunities, since the studies already undertaken include not only many European-type cities in America but also new, expanding, frontier-type cities in Europe.

Tendencies of Change in the Twentieth Century

'On the whole there has been a steady decline of skilled jobs and a decrease in the worker's chances to get ahead. Social mobility is no longer present.'[23] W. Lloyd Warner's pessimistic view stated shortly after the Great Depression of the 1930s has not really been relinquished in recent years. It survived the boom period of the 1950s and 1960s, informing one school of thought. Even among today's social scientists, the first period of industrialisation is often seen as a 'golden age', in which economic and social success was open to all talents and in which, technically speaking, rates of social mobility rose above the level of pre-industrial societies. There are still some social scientists who believe, with Warner, that the slowing down of basic economic innovations and of occupational change after the first great period of industrialisation, together with the emergence of mass production and large bureaucracies, put an end to the era of the self-made man and blocked social mobility in many ways. In this view, it is the transition from pre-industrial to industrial society, the second industrialisation and the rise of the corporate society which are the periods of major concern for the history of social mobility.

There is a second school of thought, differing in two major respects. On the one hand, industrialisation is not regarded as the major turning-point in the history of social mobility. Rather, based on empirical investigations (as is the other theory), it is argued that rates of social mobility did not necessarily rise during the transition from pre-industrial and industrial society, since they do not appear to differ between contemporary underdeveloped and developed countries. It follows, therefore, that the second industrialisation is not a major turning point either. This school of theory stresses the following as factors of rising social mobility: indirect or direct political and cultural factors; changing government policies in education; occupational change owing to the rise of the welfare state; changing structures of political values and mentalities. According to this school, it is the emerging welfare state and the rise of non-elitist political cultures which produced the major turning point in the history of social mobility, above all in the postwar era.[24]

When discussing the main arguments of the two major schools of theory, we have to explore three crucial demarcations or turning-points: the supposed rise in social mobility during the transition from pre-industrial to industrial societies; the estimated stabilisation or even decline of social mobility after the major period of industrialisation and during the rise of corporate societies; the estimated rise of social mobility during the emergence of the modern welfare state and the postwar non-elitist political cultures. There will be a return to these questions in Chapter 4, with a discussion of long-term changes in conditions and factors bearing on social mobility. Here we shall concentrate on available studies of the long-term trend of social mobility and dealing with successive turning-points.

Our present knowledge of the historical changes effected in social mobility rates by the industrialisation of Europe and America is very limited. Most researches in this period cover either one point in time or a comparatively short period, rather than the long-term trends (see Tables 1.2, 1.4). Only two long-term studies of nineteenth-century social mobility in industrialising communities are available, one dealing with Westphalian communities and the other with Dutch communities.[25] They document two directions of change which do not coincide with the idea of a golden age of social success during an industrial revolution.

One study covers the German city of Bielefeld in Westphalia, a small commercial and artisan centre about 1830, at the beginning of the period investigated. It industrialised during the second half of the nineteenth century, mainly into textiles and engineering. By 1910 it was a prospering industrial city, where rates of social mobility between generations had not as yet changed. In the old commercial and artisan town they had been relatively high, with downward social mobility always predominant. The Industrial Revolution did not lead to an increase in social ascent between generations. The second work covers the Dutch city of Eindhoven. In 1850 it was a small market town; it industrialised in the second half of the nineteenth century, mainly into tobacco, textiles. Upward social mobility between fathers and sons increased initially from 7 per cent in 1850 to 18 per cent in 1890, but fell back to 7 per cent by 1920. As in Bielefeld, there was no long-term increase of social mobility between generations during industrialisation. Downward social mobility between generations appears to have predominated.[26] In the case of Eindhoven, career mobility was also investigated. Notably, there was a distinct increase in upward career mobility, from about 3 per cent in 1850–60 to 9 per cent in 1890–1900 and up to 13 per cent in 1920–30. Upward clearly predominated over downward career mobility at the end of the period (Table 1.3).[27] Thus, in Eindhoven the impact of industrialisation appears to have been ambiguous. As before, sons, in early adulthood at least, rarely did better than their fathers and often did worse. By comparison with his father's social situation, a son was unlikely to find that industrial-isation had led to improvement. What did change during the Industrial Revolution was a person's occupational career within his own lifetime. The chances of upward social mobility measured against an earlier social position continually improved. Compared to other more mixed cities, however, the level of upward career mobility in industrial Eindhoven remained modest even at its peak. Altogether, industrialising Eindhoven and Bielefeld do not appear to have become gold-mines of social mobility. It is possible that there are many other cities like this in Europe and America; Eindhoven and Bielefeld might well reflect the strictly indus-trial-urban type of change of social mobility during massive industrialis-ation.[28]

There is also one study of an industrialising village, Borghorst, again in the German region of Westphalia. About 1830 it was an agricultural village with a flourishing cottage industry based on linen. During the second half of the nineteenth century Borghorst industrialised and be-came a factory community based mainly on cotton spinning and weaving. Its population had almost tripled by 1910. In Borghorst, the rates of upward social mobility between generations increased decisively, from 6 per cent (1830-59) to 15 per cent (1880–1911). This expansion of social mobility, however, should not be seen as the entry to a golden age; Borghorst simply reached the normal level of nineteenth-century cities (Table 1.2). Social ascent remained even less frequent than in Bielefeld, the other case-study in the same region.[29] Borghorst might well be an example of a second type of long-term change of social mobility in industrialising agricultural or proto-industrial regions, although it is still far too early to generalise.

Another way of answering the question as to how social mobility changed during nineteenth-century industrialisation is by comparing contemporary non-industrialised and industrialised communities. For this we can in fact use studies of short-term social mobility rates — though it should be noted that few of the communities investigated fall into simple categories of industrial or non-industrial. Once again, the 'golden age' idea is not borne out. The representative cases of industrial cities so far explored — the Dutch city of Eindhoven (1890 and 1920), Bochum in the Ruhr (1900), Ludwigshafen in the upper Rhine valley (1876–1914), the Westphalian city of Bielefeld (1830–1910) — clearly do not have generally higher rates of social mobility than the representative cases of pre-industrial cities — Toulouse in south-western France (1830 and 1872), the Rhenish city of Cologne in the 1830s, the Danish capital city Copenhagen (1850) (Tables 1.1 and 1.2). Again one must be careful about generalising from these few cases. However, the evidence so far available falls short of the usual assessments of the considerable effect of industrial revolution on upward social mobility, although these might be true in the narrow sense of a comparison between pre-industrial villages and industrial communities.[30] Such a comparison is on much less firm ground if the major urban areas of nineteenth-century industrialising Europe are concerned.

What do we know about the second turning point after the industrial revolution proper? Did rates of social mobility stagnate or even decline when a certain level of industrialisation had been achieved? Once again, studies of the long-term changes in communities or in whole societies are far from abundant. Rather than drawing general conclusions, we can discuss only isolated examples and shall begin with cases of stagnation, going on to examples of decline.

Very few studies show social mobility rates distinctly levelling off from rise to stagnation. Perhaps the clearest is a study of Germany as a whole, based upon a West German enquiry of 1974, which compares different age groups in order to reconstruct the historical evolution of social mobility rates. The oldest groups were born between 1850 and 1879, the youngest between 1940 and 1949. The study shows that, after a clear rise of upward social mobility rates from 21 per cent among those born in 1880s to 35 per cent among those born in the 1920s, social mobility stagnated. The author of the study, however, does not interpret these findings as a structural turn from rising social mobility rates during industrial revolution to stagnating social mobility rates thereafter. He regards the postwar reconstruction and the economic boom of the 1950s and 1960s as the major factors from which those born in the 1920s derived so much profit. A consistent finding was that the older the age cohort, the less was the degree of upward mobility, whereas the younger groups rose at about the same rate as those born in the 1920s.[31] In any case, we would feel considerable doubt as to whether the life stories of people born during the 1880s and after could tell us very much about social mobility during the Industrial Revolution, which is considered to have ended in Germany on the eve of the First World War, or even in the early 1870s.

Many more researches show a decline in the rates of social mobility during some period in the twentieth century: studies of the Danish city of Aarhus (1949); of the Danish capital Copenhagen (comparing social mobility in 1850, 1890, 1950); of the North American city of Boston (showing declining rates of career mobility for the 1930s as compared to the 1910s); on France (showing declining rates of occupational mobility in the 1930s as compared to the 1920s); on England and Wales (1949) (also showing a slight diminution of social mobility rates among those born in the 1910s and 1920s compared to those born about the turn of the century).[32] While this is an impressive list of studies showing an international decline in social mobility rates, do they document a turning point in the history of social mobility? Two considerations incline us to scepticism. It is highly probable that this decline in social mobility was a short-term development lasting only one or two decades. It appeared to be definite only in those studies produced immediately after the Second World War when the decline was still recent. Later studies during the 1970s have clearly shown that rates of social mobility regained at least their previous level.[33] Moreover, it has been argued that their decline was an aftermath of such events as the Great Depression and the Second World War, rather than the consequence of long-term structural changes. This is the argument put forward by the most carefully-researched study and cannot therefore be easily put aside.[34] In fact, no one has so far satisfactorily connected this decline with long-term structural changes occurring at the end of the industrial revolution proper. Again, one should not generalise too quickly; however, the available studies often show no distinct change at all, so that the evidence for a second turning-point is not very strong.[35]

The third line of demarcation has been the subject of numerous retrospective sociological studies. All authorities appear to agree that there was a long-term increase in the rates of upward social mobility between generations in the developed countries, especially after the Second World War. Studies of the USA, Britain, France, Sweden and Germany document this.[36] The main reason is the change of occupational structure, especially the expansion of white-collar employment, the professions and highly-qualified positions in business and public administration. Theories differ concerning the precise reasons for this shift, especially on the impact of educational changes and altered methods of recruitment for the higher white-collar positions. It is debatable, therefore, whether all these changes were related to specific structural shifts such as the rise of the welfare state and the egalitarian government intervention. One might also ask whether this long-term upswing in social mobility rates is a development limited in time and in fact already terminated by the recent economic depression. Nevertheless, if there is any well-documented turning point, in the history of social mobility, it is this last one.

No doubt the conclusions reached here are not based on a great deal of evidence. According to our present state of knowledge, however, the idea of three major turning-points in the history of social mobility has not been strongly supported by empirical research. The first scission, that is, the rise in social mobility owing to the industrial revolution, might be more limited than one would expect. So far it has been borne out, if at all, only by studies of industrialising agricultural regions and communities rather than by the industrialising urban world. The latter formed an important part of pre-industrial European societies and was an important regional base of industrialisation. The second turning–point, from the rise in social mobility rates during the industrial revolution to their stagnation or even decline after the industrial revolution proper, is only superficially supported by several studies which show declining rates of social mobility, especially during the interwar period. The predominating interpretation regards short-term events such as the Great Depression and the Second World War as the major factor, rather than long-term structural changes in European societies. So this scission is probably the least clear-cut. The third turning-point, leading to rising rates of upward social mobility in welfare or post-industrial societies, is supported by excellent retrospective sociological studies of the most important Western countries. For no other demarcation does such a wealth of evidence exist. However, interpretations vary, so that the upward movement is ascribed, on the one hand, to purely occupational changes and, on the other, to the rise of the welfare state and the egalitarian culture often seen behind changes in occupation. There is little doubt that our knowledge of each scission has improved during recent years. But the interpretation which I hope to substantiate in Chapter 4 from other perspectives might yet be amended after further research.

2 Opportunities in Higher Learning

There is little doubt that during the nineteenth and the first half of the twentieth centuries educational opportunities in secondary schools and in higher learning had played little part in the life of ordinary individuals. Immediately after the Second World War, it was still only a small proportion of young European adults who went to secondary schools or on to universities. The average person's sons or daughters seldom attended these institutions. None the less, the historian of social mobility cannot ignore the topic. Firstly, past events have largely moulded today's educational opportunities, when higher learning is no longer marginal — about one-quarter of young Europeans and about one-third of young American adults now attend universities. The historical processes work in many ways; national differences in educational levels have deep roots. To discover the reasons for this, we must research into the past. Moreover, the observable national differences of contemporary educational institutions were shaped in specific historical circumstances. The decentralised American system of higher education, the *grandes écoles* in France, the prestige of Oxford and Cambridge can be understood and explained only with the aid of the historian. Merely to consider present educational policies will not lead very far — the social differences controlling opportunities of learning are also a product of historical circumstances. Today's relatively good educational chances for women in France are founded upon a long tradition of liberal access dating back to the late nineteenth century, so that contemporary policy cannot fully explain it. The relatively high proportion of working-class children at British universities is the culmination of a long tradition dating back to reforms before the First World War; the present British educational system does not account for the situation. Generally speaking, the opportunities present in to-day's mass higher education cannot be put into context without a knowledge of their historical development.

More importantly, it appears that higher education had an increasing impact on social mobility at a time when only a very small proportion of young people attended such an institution. During the nineteenth and early-twentieth centuries, higher education became more and more a precondition not only for academic careers and for higher administration, the jurisdiction and the professions, but also for business careers. It gradually became an accepted route to positions of high prestige, high income, security, sometimes even of real power and absolute wealth. Hence any study of social mobility during the nineteenth and early twentieth centuries cannot ignore the development of educational opportunities. Higher education is not yet a commonplace of everyone's life: but middle-class success and failure cannot be fully understood without a knowledge of the history of higher learning.

The comparative history of educational opportunities has become a flourishing topic among historians.[1] More substantial comparative research has been done in this field than in any other branch of social history. This chapter builds upon such research, although without attempting to summarise the manifold questions and answers involved. Instead it seeks answers to three particular questions. Firstly, the object is to show how educational opportunities changed over the long term from pre-industrial societies through early industrialisation and thence to the period of welfare societies, which did not fully emerge until the postwar era after a long and important period of transition. This division of educational history into periods can be based on much empirical evidence from recent research. Secondly, an attempt is made to compare European development with its American counterpart. The same questions are asked as in Chapter 1: Was American society more promising? Did it offer more educational opportunities? Though the picture is more optimistic than for ordinary people's possibilities of social mobility, America does not hold the centre stage as much as in Chapter 1. Historical research on educational opportunities in America is surprisingly rare in contrast to the work on most European countries (often carried out by American scholars). Finally, in comparing European societies, the author traces a remarkably consistent European pattern and shows that conclusions drawn by Fritz Ringer in comparing Germany with France and England are upheld even when many more European countries are included. At the same time, the German experience is discussed, especially the dramatically negative impact of the Nazi regime on educational opportunities. The two aspects are closely intertwined. If there is any specifically German experience, then it should be singled out from the background of the general European development. If there is a European pattern, the German experience is a crucial test of its consistency.

The present chapter has certain limits which have been set by its comparative approach. Firstly, it will *not* show how important education was for the careers of the European and American middle classes in the nineteenth and twentieth century.[2] It is clear that access to executive positions in large enterprises and to senior posts in administration, the professions and the academic world did not depend simply on educational opportunities. Even after graduation there were other important barriers to be surmounted and channels to be negotiated. It is also clear that the weight given to education in the career structure varied from country to country. An international comparison of careers of former university graduates would be a fascinating topic! However, sufficient research is not yet available from which to draw comparative conclusions (except for the business élite, to which we will return). Secondly, the chapter deals with the inequality of educational *opportunities* rather than with the inequality of education. More precisely, it does not investigate how educational opportunities for young people were translated into variation of education among all adults. We have to take into account the fact that it takes a long time for increasing rates of university attendance among the young to become increasing rates of higher education for the total population. Many factors are involved. We may speak of rising student ratios in prewar Europe, but the consequences of this might not be visible in European societies as a whole until after the Second World War. Similarly with the educational explosion of the 1960s and 1970s, the corresponding increase in the proportion of university graduates among adults will become fully visible only in future decades. This time-lag between the educational opportunities available and the differences of education in society as a whole is crucial for social mobility but cannot be treated here, owing to a lack of historical research as a basis for comparison.[3] Finally, the multinational comparison which is undertaken here imposes certain demands on space. Many important and fascinating differences between pairs or trios of countries cannot be demonstrated or explained in a single short chapter. Very high priority has been given to the European pattern of educational opportunities which, with few exceptions, has largely been a neglected area of historical research. Clarification of this area of educational history will, it is hoped, more than above for any necessary compression.

The chapter has two sections, the first dealing with the nineteenth century and up to 1914, the other covering the rest of the twentieth century. The first section starts with a general discussion on historical periods of educational opportunities, thereafter dealing in greater detail with the European pattern and the factors shaping it. The second section also begins with some general remarks on periods of educational opportunities, then goes on to more detailed discussions of the specifically European pattern for the pre-, inter- and postwar periods.

A Conceptual Framework

Current historical and sociological research on nineteenth-century educational opportunities in Europe has reached the point where it can benefit from a conceptual framework covering the definition and general determinants of educational opportunity and its long-term changes of pattern during the nineteenth and twentieth centuries. Since these theoretical components are closely interwined, all are dealt with briefly at the outset.

The term 'educational opportunities' can be variously employed. With regard to post-primary education, it seems most appropriate to define it in terms of the proportion of children of different social or occupational classes who obtain secondary or higher education; similar definitions could be used for the regional, sexual, or ethnic distribution of educational opportunities not covered here. Relevant to this definition, therefore, are the origin of students and the overall development of the enrolment levels in post-primary education. Educational opportunity thus defined also embraces closely-related structural changes, often neglected in historical studies.[4] The only disadvantage of the definition is the reduction of a very complex phenomenon to a few statistics. Therefore, two distinct dimensions of educational opportunities are employed in this essay: social distribution (the social origin of students in relation to the social structure of a society) and magnitude (the volume of enrolment figures in relation to respective age cohorts — sometimes also called 'student ratio' or 'relative attendance').[5] This distinction is appropriate also because the time series are less determined by estimated data.

Four determinants warrant examination for their role in shaping the magnitude and distribution of educational opportunities in modern societies. They are: (1) variations in the demand for highly-trained manpower due to economic development and the growth of public bureaucracy, with its attendant effect on the social prestige of education and occupational mobility; (2) variable class perceptions of the utility of higher education as a guarantor of social status, shaped by class differentials in information and in the financial resources available for education, as well as by the prevalent cultural values and their conformity with educational inequality; (3) the permeability of educational institutions to a broad social range of students, the availability of financial support for them, and the related social consequences stemming from competition and conflict over the social distribution of post-primary education; (4) the changing role of the government, its educational goals and underlying interests, and its capacity to implement them.

Obviously, one chapter of a larger study can touch only lightly upon such complex determinants, but it is clear that their impact on educational opportunities varied widely as modern society developed. From the standpoint of historical analysis these determinants operated to produce a definable pattern, constituting three successive eras of educational opportunities.[6] They differ from the eras of social mobility to be discussed in Chapter 4, since the history of educational opportunities pursued its own course.

The era of charity opportunities

Although industrialisation may have got under way, European post-primary education during this period was rarely linked to economic development. Industrial innovation was not usually triggered by scientific research, nor was the qualified labour force in the economy trained in institutions of secondary and higher education. The major traditional markets for university graduates were the church, some professions and public administration; this market was small in relation to the total work-force and showed no long-term expansionary tendencies. Short-term fluctuations predominated. Therefore, only a very small proportion of a given cohort received secondary and higher education. The chief variable governing cross-national differences in the social prestige of higher education and its role in facilitating occupational mobility was the status of the higher civil service. Sections of the European nobility and the traditional elites recognised higher education as a channel for mobility into the highest positions in the church and to some extent in public administration. In the long run this awareness might have increased the demand for higher education. In lower- and lower-middle-class families, limitations in information and income precluded substantial investments in the secondary or higher education of children. However, an uncoordinated charity system for low-income students did exist, sustained by churches, small private foundations, individual notables, family connections and academics. At some universities, the job market for students was quite favourable.

The comparative lack of competition in secondary and higher education inhibited the formalisation of the educational system, making it easier to transfer between educational institutions. To be sure, in the absence of systematic government intervention in favour of non-privileged groups, educational opportunities were of limited magnitude, a matter of chance and charity. Nevertheless, contingent on the strength of demand for higher education from the nobility and the educated classes, this environment could produce a relatively high proportion of students from families below the middle classes, such as master artisans, dependent artisans, traditional white-collar employees and farmers.

The era of competitive opportunities

This transitional era could be divided into two periods, the first characterised by fluctuating enrolment, followed by a second period of gradual long-term growth. To simplify, however, we shall join the two periods into a single category.

During this era, the links between education and the industrialisation process intensified. Scientific research began to contribute to industrial innovation, especially in iron and steel manufacture, but later in the chemical and electronics industries as well. Even more important was the rising industrial demand for university graduates. The proportion of university graduates rose steadily among both business leaders and, to a lesser extent, executives. In some countries, this demand for university graduates was reinforced by the expansion of public administration and the higher ranks of the civil service. Therefore, enrolment figures in relation both to the population and to educational investments started to rise slowly in the later part of this era, though the proportion of respective age cohorts attending secondary and higher education remained small until 1914. The demand for higher education among the traditional upper classes increased in response to the growing recognition of education as a gateway to well-paid and prestigious positions, and perhaps also because of a rise in relative family size. Secondary and higher education began to gain recognition as a transmitter of social status, though it was still not as important as it was to become in the second half of the twentieth century relative to property ownership. The demand for higher education among the lower-middle class expanded as well, partly because of declining economic prospects for small artisans and partly in response to the greater number of ambitious lower-grade civil servants. Rising demand made secondary and higher education more competitive. This was one reason for the greater formalisation of access to post-primary education, especially regarding the separation of primary and secondary education, and the declining permeability of institutions of post-primary education. Even where the relevant policy was not tightened, scholarships for gifted students from the lower classes became scarcer because of stronger competition or, later on, because of an increasing number of enrolments.

Government policy aimed primarily at financing the expansion of secondary and higher education, upgrading the quality of teaching and research, and modernising the curricula to meet new social and economic needs. The non-privileged social classes lacked sufficient political influence to counteract the growing trend toward educational inequality. All these factors led to static or deteriorating educational opportunities for the lower classes. Educational opportunities improved mainly for the petty bourgeoisie and sometimes for the lower grade of white-collar workers. This limited growth in educational opportunities was a by-product of rising student enrolments, rising standards of living and changing occupational prospects for the lower-middle classes, rather than a result of deliberately egalitarian government reforms.

The era of welfare opportunities
This era is one of transition, characterised by growing government intervention and by a further increase in the demand for university gradu-

ates in business. Because of this gradual change, we shall subdivide it into a preparatory experimental era and a fully-established era of welfare opportunities. University graduates gradually came to dominate managerial and executive positions, at least in large corporations. Among white-collar employees, new markets emerged for university-trained skills in such fields as scientific management and marketing. The expansion of public administration and professional services further reinforced demand for highly-educated manpower, causing student enrolments to rise more sharply than before. The expansion of education led to a rising demand for teaching staff. As university graduates became a significant part of the labour force, filling relatively well-paid, secure and prestigious positions, secondary and higher education gradually became the major route to the upper-middle class and to the élite. Hence it became the main instrument of status inheritance and social ascent, although the pattern varied from country to country. Broad social awareness of this development intensified competition for secondary and higher education, particularly inasmuch as educational institutions were still characterised by the high formalisation of access and low permeability typical of the era of competitive opportunities.

The most important characteristic of the era of welfare opportunities is the change in political structure and in educational policy goals. Political systems emerged from a long and contradictory period of transition with decision-making processes dominated by three groups: the bureaucracy, organised labour and organised big business. In contrast to former eras, some politically influential groups were composed of members who were not highly educated. Such prospective or actual changes in the power structure generated three new and interrelated educational policy goals, all tied to the issues of welfare state policy. The first was a policy of active provision for sufficient educational facilities through the expansion of educational investment and teaching staffs. The two additional goals centred on the reduction of educational inequality, either by extending, modernising and equalising basic education, or by opening up post-primary education through scholarship programmes, tuition reduction and more flexible access rules.

In contrast to the unsystematic options of the era of charity opportunities, the new educational entitlements were often recognised as constitutional or at least legal rights. Even so, educational opportunities improved only slowly, magnitude usually changing more measurably than did social distribution. Changes in access were most noticeable in secondary education, much less so in higher education and least of all in entry to the professions. Indeed, the emergence of welfare opportunities in education was a very slow and sometimes even strongly regressive process. The range of contrasting Western European political systems during the first half of the twentieth century ensured that the era of transition to welfare opportunities was a period of highly variable educational policy in which a common pattern of educational opportunities was hard to discern.

The above is an abbreviated account of the three eras of educational opportunities. A fuller account of the much more differentiated historical reality of nineteenth-century educational opportunities now follows, the twentieth-century era of welfare opportunities being dealt with in the next section. Starting with a detailed description of common features and differences in the magnitude as well as the social distribution of educational opportunities, the account will then consider the major historical factors bearing on the change of educational opportunities: the labour market for university graduates; social class differences in the demand for higher education; the permeability of institutions in secondary and higher education; and educational policy by the governments up to 1914. We shall concentrate on Western Europe, referring to the United States as the major non-European point of comparison.

Opportunities in Nineteenth-Century Higher Education

Common features in European patterns of educational opportunities
The most striking comparative finding of the nineteenth-century history of our chosen topic is that the similarity of educational opportunities in higher and related secondary education throughout Europe is much more distinct than one might expect. It was Fritz Ringer who first drew our attention to this historical fact in his comparison of France and Germany.[7] In a more comprehensive investigation of a greater number of countries, we attempt to reaffirm this argument, dealing first with the magnitude and thereafter with the social distribution of educational opportunities, the two main dimensions defined above.

One common European characteristic concerns developments in the magnitude of post-primary education during the nineteenth century, as measured by the relationship of the enrolment figures to the respective age cohorts. Most available European data cover only the last decades before 1914 for a rather wide range of mostly industrialising countries.[8] Such data show that enrolments in secondary and higher education increased slowly but distinctly and continuously (Tables 2.1, 2.2). Hence, in all countries, the chances for children and young adults to acquire secondary and higher education improved, although in fact in almost all European countries only a very small minority of any given cohort entered secondary and higher education. The change of magnitude occurred at such a low level that the majority of nineteenth-century citizens might well not have noticed it. Furthermore, the limitation of data to the period between about 1870 and 1914 seems to be crucial. Investigations attempting to reach further back show that growth in the magnitude of educational opportunities was not consistent throughout the whole nineteenth century. Studies of France, England, and Germany conclude that the take-off in higher education occurred in the 1870s and 1890s. Hence, it was only in the latter part of the era of competitive opportunities that educational opportunities seem to have expanded at all.[9]

Just as there are common features in the pattern of enrolment growth, so are there similarities in enrolment levels reached before the First World War. In most European countries a strikingly similar proportion of school-age youth in fact attended institutions of secondary and higher education; the percentage receiving some secondary education clustered between 2 per cent and 3 per cent (Table 2.1). Only Portugal and Romania had a far lower secondary schooling ratio and so give an impression of the less-developed European countries, for which data are scarce. Furthermore, in most countries, about 1 per cent of young adults attended institutions of higher learning (Table 2.2). Therefore, the prevailing scholarly impression that significant differences existed among industrialising European countries is not supported by the available data.

It is interesting that the larger European countries to which the attention of the historian is usually drawn show very similar magnitudes of educational opportunities of somewhat more than 1 per cent of the respective age cohort around 1910. This applies to Britain, France, Italy, Spain, Germany, the Netherlands and Belgium. To be sure, in late nineteenth-century peripheral European countries such as Norway, Sweden, Portugal, Greece and Romania the magnitude of educational opportunities was often much lower. In Switzerland, on the other hand, with its peculiar role in European education and its high proportion of foreign students, student ratio was high by European standards. Therefore strict statistical measurement does not show strong convergence. Similarities between the important European countries is none the less surprisingly distinct before 1914.

Moreover, a peculiarly European pattern of educational opportunities, as against that of the United States, had already emerged by 1914. The magnitude of opportunities at European secondary schools and universities fell behind that in American secondary and higher learning (Tables 2.1, 2.2). The crucial difference has lasted throughout the ensuing period. No doubt this statistical finding has different meanings for the period before 1914 and that after 1945. Institutions of higher education were often badly defined in the United States. The standard of American universities often lagged behind the European one. Nevertheless, even before 1914 the American lead is important not only because it was a pre-condition for later and higher magnitudes of opportunities in America. It might have also been a more open gateway to the upper middle

Table 2.1 Opportunities in European and North American secondary education, 1840–1910: students related to respective age cohorts (10 to 19 inclusive)

	Aus.	Bel.	Den.	Fin.	France	Ger.	Britain		Hun.	Italy	N'lands	Nor.	Port.	Rom.	Swed.	Switz.	USA
							Eng.	Scot.									
	(1)	(2)	(3)	(4)	(5)	(6)	(7)	(8)	(9)	(10)	(11)	(12)	(13)	(14)	(15)	(16)	(17)
1840	.	.	.	.	.	.	.	.	.	.	(0.2)[h]	.	.	.	0.9[m]	.	.
1850	.	.	.	.	.	.	.	.	.	.	(0.3)[h]	.	.	.	0.9[m]	.	.
1860	.	1.3[b]	.	.	.	.	.	.	.	.	(0.3)[h]	.	.	.	.	.	.
1870	1.1[a]	1.8[b]	.	.	.	2.3	.	.	3.0[f]	0.4[g]	(0.2)[h]	1.1[i]	.	.	1.7[m]	.	2.0
1880	1.6	2.5	.	.	2.4	2.6	.	.	1.1	0.5[g]	0.9	2.8	.	.	1.6[m]	4.7	2.5
1890	1.5	2.3	.	2.1	2.4	2.5	.	.	1.3	0.7[g]	1.1	2.8	0.4	.	1.9[m]	6.1[k]	3.5
1900	1.9	2.4	1.4[c]	2.6	2.5	2.7	1.4[e]	1.9[l]	1.6	1.4[g]	1.2	2.9	0.5	0.5	2.3[m]	7.8	6.3
1910	2.8	2.5	2.6[c]	4.1	2.6	3.2[d]	2.4[e]	2.2[l]	1.8	2.4[g]	1.7	3.0	1.0	0.5	0.5	10.0	8.6

a. 1869
b. 1856,1866
c. 1901; 1911
d. 1911
e. 1901/05, 1911 (state and state-aided schools only)
f. 1869
g. 1871, 1881, 1891, 1901, 1911 (1901, 1911 including training schools for teachers)
h. 1849, 1859, 1869, 1879, 1889, 1899, 1909 (in brackets: only parts of secondary education)
i. 1875 (without private schools)
k. 1888
l. 1901, 1911
m. 1843, 1853, 1862, 1881–85, 1891–95, 1901–05, 1911–15

class than was available in Europe.[10]

There are also shared European aspects of the social distribution of educational opportunities in secondary institutions leading to higher education. To be sure, long-term changes in the social origins of secondary-school students are still unclear and have rarely been investigated even in recent research. However, the few social scientists who have entered this field reach similar conclusions. T. W. Bamford demonstrated that during the first half of the nineteenth century the aristocracy and the professions became more dominant in the English public schools, which in turn became more important for access to the university. Theodore Zeldin and Robert Anderson hold that in French secondary education, which had been almost comprehensive during the Second Empire, the proportion of pupils from the lower and lower-middle classes had decreased by the beginning of the twentieth century. In a case study of the academic high school (*Gymnasium*) of the German town Minden, Margret Kaul argues that Prussian secondary education before 1848 was competitive and socially open, rather than elitist as it later became. In another case study on secondary education in nineteenth-century Berlin, Detlev K. Müller also argues that Prussian education deteriorated from a socially open, comprehensive school system into a much more formalised, exclusive institution with primary and secondary education largely becoming strictly separated. Müller's assessment has not been fully accepted by other scholars. In fact, his unique long-term time series on the social origin of students in the last grade of secondary education (*Abiturienten*) supports his pessimistic view only until about the 1880s. Up to this time, the proportion of lower-middle-class students dwindled, while general enrolment levels stagnated, in what has been described as the early period of competitive opportunities. However, in the last decades before 1914, the share of students with this background expanded again, along with expanding enrolment levels for the final grades of secondary education.[11]

Note to Table 2.1

For the use of the data compare the note to Table 2.2. Data on secondary school pupils is seldom broken down further. In view of this gap, the Table in almost every case relates to *all* such pupils and not merely to those whose secondary education was preparatory to university entry. Cols. 1–4, 7–16: B. R. Mitchell, *European Historical Statistics 1750–1970* (Macmillan, London, 1975), pp. 29ff., 750ff.; cols. 5–6: Fritz Ringer, *Education and Society in Modern Europe* (Indiana Univ. Press, Bloomington, 1979); other calculations for France: V. Isambert-Jamati, *Crises de la société, crises de l'enseignement* (Presses univ. de France, Paris, 1970), p. 377; J. Maillet, 'L'évolution des effectifs de l'enseignement secondaire de 1803 à 1961' in *La scolarisation en France depuis un siècle* (Mouton, Paris, 1974), pp. 129ff.; J.-C. Toutain, *La population de la France*, p. 238; col. 15: L. Jörberg, 'Some Notes on Education in Sweden in the 19th Century', *Annales Cisalpines d'histoire sociale*, vol. 2 (1971), pp. 70f.; col 17: *The Statistical History of the United States* (Basic Books, New York, 1976), p. 379 (highschool graduates in % of persons 17 years old).

Table 2.2 *Opportunities in European and North American higher education, 1840–1978: students related to respective age cohorts (20 to 24 inclusive)*

Country	1840	1850	1860	1870	1880	1890	1900	1910	1920	1930	1940	1950	1960	1970	1978
	(1)	(2)	(3)	(4)	(5)	(6)	(7)	(8)	(9)	(10)	(11)	(12)	(13)	(14)	(15)
Austria	0.90	0.70	0.48	0.71	0.68	0.85	1.06	3.77	[1]4.30	3.87	2.29	4.55	7.86	11.50	21.62
Belgium	0.50	0.48	0.62	0.65	0.99	1.04	0.89	1.25	1.36	1.54	2.46	3.07	9.09	18.48	25.79
Bulgaria							0.16	0.65[1]	1.26	1.26	[2]2.38	4.87	10.56	14.80	18.09
Switzerland					0.70	0.90	1.40	2.16	1.99	1.83	[1]2.71	3.67	5.80	8.24	16.74[1]
Czechoslovakia									2.23	2.21	[3]2.77	3.94	10.49	10.44	16.07
Germany					0.55	0.77	0.89	1.22	2.05	1.96	1.06	4.39	6.31	13.53	25.46
East Germany												2.18[1]	9.91	13.90	10.26
Denmark			0.65	[2]0.88	0.99[3]			(1.45)	(2.27)	2.59	2.31	6.18	9.16	18.04	28.14
Spain						0.23[3]	0.21	1.21	1.30	1.66	1.72	2.07	3.90	8.56	[1]24.08
Ireland									1.65	1.88	2.44	4.27	8.95	13.77	18.32
France	0.31	0.32	0.27	0.43	0.42	0.62	0.93	1.32	1.50	2.31	3.46	4.34	7.39	15.81	24.11
Finland			0.30	0.40	0.58	1.06	1.15	1.19	1.16	2.01	2.63	4.25	7.25	13.43	20.97
UK						0.73	0.79	1.31	1.96	1.89	1.89	2.86	8.88	14.14	[1]19.40
Greece								0.29[2]	0.38	1.40	(1.15)	2.76[5]	3.96	12.57	18.06
Hungary			0.35[1]	0.20	0.28	0.37[1]	0.62	1.62	2.20[3]	2.07[2]	[2]1.67	3.39	6.64	10.34	11.72
Italy			0.45	0.53	0.50	0.76	1.02	1.05[1]	1.64[1]	1.25	3.99	3.56	6.52	16.97	27.46
Norway		0.40	0.47	0.70	0.46	1.03	0.74	0.81	0.76	1.97[2]	2.17	3.29	6.84	15.94	24.58
Netherlands	0.58	0.38	0.23	0.41	0.46	0.74	0.69	1.05	1.53	2.58	3.35	7.65	13.13	19.51	28.29
Portugal							0.25	0.241[1]	0.58	0.90	1.42	1.71	3.23	7.98	10.89[1]
Poland								0.88[1]	1.44[1]	1.52	[3]1.74	5.95	9.13	11.19	17.89[1]
Romania							1.05	[2]0.88	0.94	1.74	[3]1.85	3.41	4.57	10.04	10.77[1]
Sweden	0.58			0.50	0.60	[2]0.91	[2]0.65		[2]2.12	1.69	1.99	3.68	9.02	21.32	35.56
Yugoslavia									1.00[3]	1.10	[2]1.51	3.88	8.88	15.72	23.02[1]
Europe total			(0.46)	(0.56)	(0.58)	0.71	0.88	1.23	1.60	1.77	2.07	3.76	7.30	13.83	21.47
West Europe total			(0.46)	(0.63)	(0.63)	0.75	0.92	1.24	1.64	1.81	2.14	3.63	6.93	14.51	23.83

			1.10	1.60	1.80	2.30	2.90	4.70	7.20	9.10	16.50	20.50	30.60	40.00
USA														
Europe variation coefficient	(37.1)	(32.4)	(35.1)	(39.6)	(42.2)	37.2	45.6	65.0	50.8	33.2	33.5	34.1	30.8	26.1	30.5
West Europe variation coefficient			(35.1)	(33.6)	(39.1)	34.7	41.8	65.5	55.3	34.3	35.3	36.4	32.8	27.1	24.3
West Europe without Spain, Greece or Portugal — variation coefficient										29.5	29.9	29.5	22.4	22.0	19.9

The relative openness of secondary education during the last decades before 1914 is supported by studies focused on one point in time rather than on long-term change. As far as all grades of secondary education are concerned, the majority of secondary students came from the lower-middle class — that is, from families of small independent artisans, shopkeepers, white-collar employees, lower civil servants — and small farmers. This has been shown for a London grammar school as well as for *Gymnasien* in Hessen, Baden, and in various German cities such as Berlin, Breslau, Hanover, and Bochum (Tables 2.3, 2.4, 2.5). To be sure, children of these social groups did not have fully equal chances. If the social origin

Note to table 2.2:

Superscript numbers refer to the years which vary from those in the table heading. Varying years of data collection are noted to the left of the number, in those cases in which the year referred to was *before* the year in the heading. They are noted to the right of the number, when the year of collection was later than the year which appears in the heading. All European countries apart from very small ones, such as Luxembourg, Iceland, Vatican City and Malta, and the semi-European countries, such as the Soviet Union and Turkey, have been included in the table. Western Europe was defined in the modern sense as all Europe except the communist Eastern European countries. The figures for Austria before 1910 relate to the entire Empire, after 1910 they should be seen as reflecting the territory of the later Republic. Until 1900 the figures for Denmark concern only the University of Copenhagen (for 1910 and 1920 figures for all Danish universities were extrapolated from data for the years 1915 and 1925). Until 1910 the figures for Great Britain reflect only England and Wales. After 1910 the figures for Hungary relate to the present-day territorial area. The variation coeffecients are in parentheses for the period before 1890, because no data is available for a large number of countries for the nineteenth century. Figures on the number of students were chosen for years closest to those mentioned in the tables. The number of 20–24-year-olds was interpolated in cases in which data was not otherwise available. The interpolations for the postwar years are particularly doubtful. The figures for the years 1920 and 1950 should therefore be interpreted with care. The definition of institutions of higher education cannot be satisfactorily standardised for so many countries over so long a period. Depending on the country and the period, different institutions were seen as institutions of higher learning, alongside the actual universities. Most important of all is the fact that no differentiation was made between the types of institutions of higher education in compiling the figures for the number of students in many major countries. It is therefore impossible to make reliable calculations in retrospect on the basis of the sources used here by employing a standardised definition. For this reason the term 'institution of higher education' reflects the use common to each country and period. This must be taken into consideration when interpreting the data in terms of international variations and historical change. Statistically, it is extremely important whether or not the institutions for training teachers were seen as institutions of higher education. In those cases in which data was available, the percentage of institutions dedicated to teacher training was particularly high. 1950 in: DK (24%), NL (25%); 1960 in: B (18%), DK (33%), GB (13%), NL (40%), N (35%); 1970 in: D (13%), DK (20%), GB (21%), NL (30%), N (16%); S always stayed around 10%. It must, however, be emphasised that the percentages for AU, CH, CSR, DDR, E, F, I, P, PL, R cannot be determined. Parallels can be found for the academicisation of other courses of professional training. Others have taken a different approach: P. Flora, *Quantitative Historical Sociology* (Mouton, The Hague, 1977), pp. 56f.; R. Schneider, 'Die Bildungsentwicklung in den westeuropäischen Staaten, 1870–1979', *Zeitschrift für Soziologie*, vol. 10 (1982); Mitchell, *European Historical Statistics*, pp. 777ff. All three employ a stricter definition. Table 2.2 should be seen not as an improvement, but as a complement. Of decisive importance for the questions dealt with in this chapter is the fact that both Flora's and Mitchell's data demonstrate a growing tendency towards similarity. (The appropriate variation coefficients were calculated as a means of checking our data.) Schneider's data, however, indicate a

of students is related to the social structure as a whole, the children of farmers, white-collar employees (except for lower civil servants in Germany) — and maybe even the children of the petty bourgeoisie, were still underrepresented when compared to the children of the middle class (Table 2.4). To a lesser extent, this is also true for secondary-school graduates, though the social distribution of educational opportunities seems to have been more unequal at that level than among secondary students overall (Table 2.3). Among graduates from Prussian secondary schools between 1875 and 1899, students were almost equally divided into sons of the lower-middle class and sons of the middle class. Probably

---

marked tendency towards the reappearance of differences. The development in individual countries — particularly England, France, Belgium and the Netherlands — in respect of comparative levels of attendance at institutions of higher education differs greatly in table 2.2 and in Flora's and Mitchell's data. This is dependent primarily upon the definition of an institution of higher education. A further problem concerning table 2.2 is the determination of the age group to which the number of students should be related. With the exception of the USA, the age group 20–24-year-olds was used for all countries and all periods. This is surely too schematic. Within the framework at hand, however, it was impossible to collect reliable data concerning historical change and international differences in the length of time spent studying. Other, fully justified, calculations using different age cohorts (Ringer, *Education and Society in Modern Europe*, pp. 54, 148) could not be included in table 2.2, because an international comparison would then have been impossible.

Sources: general sources (in cases in which data varied, the most recent published source was used): demographic data (age cohort 20–24-year-olds): Mitchell, *European Historical Statistics*, pp. 39ff.; *Demographic Yearbook*, vol. 1961, 1962, 1963, 1971, 1972, 1979 (UN, New York, 1962–80); *Demographic Yearbook, Special Issue: Historical Supplement* (UN, New York, 1979; Number of students: Mitchell, *European Historical Statistics*, pp. 772ff; *World Survey of Education*, vol. 4 *Higher Education* (UNESCO, Paris, 1966); *Second Conference of Ministers of Education of European Member States, 26 November–3 December 1973, Final Report* (UNESCO, Paris, 1974), appendix, statistical tables, pp. 6ff.; *Annuaire international d'Éducation et d' Enseignement* (Bureau international d'Éducation, Geneva), vol. 1934, pp. 243, 413, vol. 1939, pp. 108, 310, vol. 1939, p. 300; *Statistical Yearbook UNESCO*, vol. 1977, pp. 324ff., vol. 1980, pp. 413ff, (UNESCO, Paris, 1978, 1981); F. Edding, *Internationale Tendenzen in der Entwicklung der Ausgaben für Schulen und Hochschulen* (Kiel, 1958), Appendix. Additionally, for individual countries: percentage of students taken directly from Flora, *Quantitative Historical Sociology*, pp. 56ff. For CH 1880; AU 1840, 1850, EIR 1860–1990; S 1870. 1880; B 1830; number of students: Denmark 1910–1930; *Danmarks Statistik: Statistiks Åarbog* 1921, pp. 158ff.; 1928, pp. 135ff.; 1932, pp. 145ff.; Italy 1910–1930: *Annuario Statistico Italiano, Seconda Serie*, vol. II, 1913, pp. 87ff.; vol. 9, 1922–1925, pp. 89ff.; *Terza Serie*, vol. 6, 1932, pp. 108ff.; Austria 1910–1920; *Österreichische Statistik*, N. F., vol. 11, part 2, pp. 2ff.; *Statistisches Handbuch für die Republik Österreich*, Jg. 2, 1921, pp. 121ff.; Spain 1920: *Anuario Estadistico de España*, vol. 8, 1912–1922, pp. 366f.; Poland 1930: K. Hartmann, *Hochschulwesen und Wissenschaft in Polen* (Metyner, Berlin–Frankfurt a.M., 1962), p. 13; Czechoslovakia 1920: *Statistische Übersicht der Cechoslovakischen Republik* (compiled by the Statistischen Staatsamte, Prague, 1930), pp. 234ff.; Hungary 1910–1930: *Ungarisches Statistisches Jahrbuch*, N.F., vol. 18, 1910, pp. 354ff.; *Magyar Statisztikai Szemle*, II. Evfolyam 1924, pp. 268ff.; USA 1890–1980: *The Statistical History of the US*, p. 282; *Statistical Abstract of the US*, vol. 102 (1982), pp. 27, 160 (another definition); Britain: R. A. Lowe, taken from K. H. Jarausch (ed.), *The Transformation of Higher Learning* (Klett-Cotta, Stuttgart, 1983), Introduction; data compiled and calculated by Rüdiger Hohls. Time series from a preliminary earlier version of this section were unfortunately published in Jarausch (ed.) *The Transformation of Higher Learning*, p. 16. The series on American student ratios which was printed under my name was misunderstood in that book. It was neither related to the 20–24-year-olds, nor computed by me. It was taken (as annotated) from a publication by Daniel Bell, who in turn used OECD statistics.

Table 2.3 Social origins of secondary school students in France, England and Germany, 1864–1908, by %

	France Secondary Graduates 1864/65	England Public Schools 1801–1850	England Grammar Schools 1884–1900	England Grammar Schools 1904–1918	Württemberg Secondary Graduates 1873	Prussia Secondary Graduates 1875–1899	Hessen 1891/2	Hessen 1904	Baden 1908
	(1)	(2)	(3)	(4)	(5)	(6)	(7)	(8)	(9)
Higher civil servants	12[a]				11[c]	19	26[a]	32[a]	10[i]
Professionals	18[a]	21	13	11	30[g]		5	5	4
Large landowners	17[b]	38				2			
Businessmen	13		10	20	21	23	52	43	
Petty bourgeois	15	3	35[d]	22		10			35
Farmers	12				13	10	8	9	6

Lower civil servants	—[a]				18	23	—[a]	—[a]	24
White collar employees	2	2[e]	17	24		3	7[h]	10[h]	3
Workers	8	25	11	15		0		9	9
Others	4		13	8	8	10	9		9
No answer						0			
Total	100	100[f]	100	100	100	100	100	100	100
No. of cases	12,605	25,931	517	873	659	85,034	8,649	15,860	12,962

a. all civil servants in category 'higher civil servants' including clergy (1%)
b. proprietaires, rentiers
c. only higher civil servants in public administration
d. including formen whose proportion is not given
e. lower classes
f. including 'titled' (12%)
g. including clergy (16%)
h. category not fully clear. Could also be white-collar employees only.

this also applies to the Württemberg graduates of 1873 and the French secondary graduates of 1865–66 (Table 2.3). This finding too is consistent with what has been defined above as the later part of the era of competitive opportunities.

Just as in secondary schools, the social distribution of higher education also manifested common patterns and changes. During the first half of the nineteenth century, higher education was dominated by the children of landed aristocrats, professionals, merchants and higher civil servants. Sons of the lower-middle class were relatively rare. This has been shown for Cambridge and for Oxford in England, for the *école centrale* and the *école polytechnique* in France, for the German universities of Heidelberg, Berlin and Halle, and for Württemberg students (Table 2.5).[12] There are indications that this was the final stage in a long-term early-modern process of growing exclusiveness in European higher education. (Lawrence Stone and C. A. Anderson have demonstrated this process clearly for Oxford and Cambridge. It might be that there was a similar process in Germany,[13] which again would accord with the transition from charity opportunities to early competitive opportunities.) A few cases deviate distinctly from the general pattern just described. The most important is the University of Glasgow, whose structure is probably typical of other Scottish universities. A study by W. M. Mathew established that educational opportunities at that university between 1740 and 1839 were exceptionally well distributed. The proportion of students from aristocratic and large landowning families was low and tended to decline. The proportion of students from the working class, especially from families of skilled artisans and small masters, was high (25 per cent), even by the standards of modern European higher education. The proportion of farmers' sons fell, but still remained at the rather high level of 15 per cent. In addition to the University of Glasgow, less spectacular cases are the *écoles des arts et métiers* in France, including the *conservatoire national des arts*

Note to table 2.3:

Col. 1: P. J. Harrigan, 'The Social Origins Ambitions and Occupations of Secondary Students in France during the Second Empire' in L. Stone (ed.), *Schooling and Society* (Johns Hopkins Univ. Press, Baltimore, 1976), p. 210 (all students likely to graduate in the next two years); col. 2: T. W. Bamford, 'Public Schools and Social Class', *British Journal of Sociology*, vol. 12 (1961), p. 229; col. 3 and 4: J. Floud, F. M. Martin and A. H. Halsey, 'Educational Opportunity and Social Selection in England', *Transaction of the Third World Congress on Sociology* (London, 1954), vol. 2, p. 198 (case study of the London area); col. 5: *Statistik der Universität Tübingen* (Stuttgart, 1877), p. 51; col. 6: H. Kaelble, 'Chancengleichheit und akademische Ausbildung in Deutschland, 1910–1960', *Geschichte und Gesellschaft*, vol. 1 (1975), pp. 142–143; col. 7: *Statistisches Handbuch des Großherzogtums Hessen* 1 (1903), pp. 142–143 (schools included: *Gymnasien, Realgymnasien, Oberrealschulen, Realschulen, Progymnasien*); col. 8: *Mitteilungen der großherzogl. hess. Zentralstelle für die Landesstatistik*, 35 (1905), pp. 12–15 (schools included as above); col. 9: *Badische Schulstatistik*, vol. 2 (Karlsruhe, 1914), p. 139 (schools included as in col. 7 with the exception of *Realschulen*).

Table 2.4 *Social distribution of opportunities for secondary school students in France, England, and Germany, 1864–1918*

	France Secondary Graduates 1864/65	Prussia Secondary Graduates 1875–99	Hessen 1891/92	1904	Baden 1908	England Grammar Schools 1904–18
	(1)	(2)	(3)	(4)	(5)	(6)
Higher civil servants	1.00[b]		3.25[b]	3.67[b]	3.35	
Professionals	6.00	6.74	6.37	6.00	4.56	11.00
Large landowners	—[a]	—[a]	—[a]		—[a]	
Businessmen						
Petty bourgeois	4.59	2.36	3.47	2.93	2.80	4.16
Farmers	0.34	0.75	0.49	0.36	0.35	
Lower civil servants	—[b]	3.83	—[b]	—[b]	3.45	
White-collar employees	0.13[(?)]	0.79			0.55	1.40
Workers	0.20	0.01	0.12	0.18	0.17	0.20

a. included in category 'farmer'.
b. all civil servants included in category 'higher civil servants'

et métiers in Paris. Only one-third to one-seventh of the students stemmed from families of landowners, businessmen and professionals; the overwhelming majority came from the lower-middle class (Table 2.5).[14]

In the second half of the nineteenth century, the social distribution of educational opportunities in higher education seems to have changed. In the countries investigated so far this change had several common aspects. The traditional economic and educational élites became less visible. The proportion of students from families of large landowners and from the

Note to table 2.4:

The recruitment index expresses the relationship between the social origin of students and the occupation of their fathers. The index is calculated in a very simple way:

$$i = \frac{s}{f}$$

i = recruitment index; s = proportion of students stemming from fathers with a certain occupation (%); f = proportion of the members of that occupation among the employed population (%). The purpose of the index is only to measure, not to judge or to explain the distribution of educational opportunities. The basic idea of the index is that students from a certain family background have full educational chances if their proportion of the student body is the same as the proportion of their fathers' occupation among the employed population. In this case the index is 1. If the index is less than 1, this indicates low chances; if the index is more than 1, this indicates privileged chances. If the index falls or rises

clergy declined. In countries with strong bureaucratic traditions, such as France and Prussia, the same is true for the children of top bureaucrats. Students from the rising economic élite of businessmen increased. Furthermore, higher education became somewhat more open to the sons of the petty bourgeoisie and also some lower-grade white-collar employees. These changes have been shown for Oxford students, for students of the *école des arts et métiers* and of the *école polytechnique* in France (the *école centrale* being an exception), for students of Prussian universities, and for Württemberg students (Table 2.5). These changes do not merely reflect alterations in occupational structure. Rather, they represent distinct reductions in the inequality of educational opportunities (Table 2.6). The timing and strength of this trend varied strongly from country to country, but no country so far studied remained untouched by this common pattern.[15]

The changes in social distribution that did occur ought to be qualified in various respects. The distribution of opportunities changed only for limited segments of the population; for some social classes, opportunities in higher education improved very slowly or not at all. This is especially true for unskilled and skilled workers, for peasants and, partly, also for white-collar employees. Large differences in educational opportunities appear to have persisted. The prototypical rank order of educational opportunities had started at the top with the children of higher civil servants and professionals, followed by the children of businessmen, then the petty bourgeoisie and sometimes lower civil servants; children of peasants and white-collar employees trailed by a clear margin, with the children of workers at the bottom of the ladder. This order of priority was somewhat modified in the middle ranks, rather than completely transformed, before 1914 (Table 2.6). What had occurred was an extension of educational privileges, rather than a general democratisation of higher education.

The limits of the change in European educational opportunities are clarified once again if compared with conditions in Scottish universities. In spite of strong pressure to erect stronger barriers between primary and

---

towards 1, this indicates improving educational opportunities or a reduction of educational privileges. The reverse trend is indicated if the index moves away from 1. Table 2.4 is based on data from table 1.1 and on occupational structure data from the following sources: col. 1; France 1866: Toutain, *La population de la France*, Tables 66, 67,148, 154; col. 2; Prussia 1895: *Statistik des Deutschen Reichs*, vol. 104; col. 3; Hessen 1895: ibid.; col. 4–5; Hessen and Baden 1907: ibid., vol. 205; col. 6; England and Wales 1911: A. H. Halsey (ed.), *Trends in British Society since 1900* (St. Martin's Press, London, 1972), p. 113; for individual German cities cf. D. K. Müller, *Sozialstruktur und Schulsystem* (Vandenhoeck & Ruprecht, Göttingen, 1977), p. 523; *Mitteilungen des Statistischen Amts der Stadt Hannover*, 18 (1912), no. 3, p. 7; Crew, 'Definitions of Modernity', p. 64; H. Titze, *Die Politisierung der Erziehung* (Athenäum, Frankfurt, 1973), p. 203; M. Kraul, *Gymnasium und Gesellschaft im Vormärz* (Vandenhoeck & Ruprecht, Göttingen, 1980);

Table 2.5: *Social origins of university students in England, France, and Germany during the nineteenth century* (%)

	England				France					Germany				
	Cambridge		Oxford		Ecole polytechnique		Ecole centrale			Students from Württemberg			Prussia	
	1800–1849	1850–1899	1877	1910	1815–1840	1860–1875	1829–1875	1870–1899	1900–1925	1835–1844	1871–1881	1901–1911	1886–1887	1911–1912
	(1)	(2)	(3)	(4)	(5)	(6)	(7)	(8)	(9)	(10)	(11)	(12)	(13)	(14)
Higher civil servants	2	3	49[a]	48[a]						18[e]	9[e]	8[e]		
Professionals	51[b]	54[b]			32	26	12	16	25	27[g]	25[g]	21[g]	21[f]	21[f]
Large landowners	31	19	40[c]	15[c]	30[d]	19[d]	29[d]	31[d]	25[d]	1	1	1	9	1
Businessmen	6	15	7	21	14	16	36	31	28	3	6	11		12
Petty bourgeoisie			2	7	4	12	6	7	5	23	17	17		24
Farmers					2	6	2	2	2	7	14	10	4	9
Lower civil servant					21	28	13	10	14	21	21	25		27
Lower white-collar										0	1	3	2	3

Continued on page 52

Table 2.5: *Continued*

	England				France					Germany				
	Cambridge		Oxford		Ecole poly-technique		Ecole centrale			Students from Württemberg			Prussia	
	1800–1849	1850–1899	1877	1910	1815–1840	1860–1875	1829–1875	1870–1899	1900–1925	1835–1844	1871–1881	1901–1911	1886–1887	1911–1912
	(1)	(2)	(3)	(4)	(5)	(6)	(7)	(8)	(9)	(10)	(11)	(12)	(13)	(14)
Workers			0	1			3	2	1	0	1	3	0	2
No answer			2	5									0	
Total	100	100	100	100	100	100	100	100	100	100	100	100	100	100
No. of cases	319	352	418	1,030						818	1,724	3,051	13,571	24,218

a. including clergy (1870: 28% 1910: 17%)
b. including clergy (1800–49: 32%, 1850–99: 31%, 1937–38: 7%)
c. mainly aristocrats without specification of occupation
d. "rentiers-propriétaires"
e. administration and army only
f. including clergy (1886/87: 7%, 1911/12: 4%)
g. including clergy (1835/40: 14%, 1871/81: 14%, 1901/11: 10%)

secondary education and to establish more élitist access to higher learning, the Scottish educational system kept its egalitarian tradition. As has been demonstrated by R. D. Anderson, the social structure of Glasgow students became even more open after the first third of the nineteenth century. In 1910, about one-third of the Glasgow students came from mostly skilled working-class families.[16] Scotland, however, seems to be a unique exception to the predominant European pattern of much lower educational opportunities.

Whether social distribution in America of educational opportunities differed from this European pattern is not yet fully clear, as very little research has been carried out on this aspect of American higher learning. A few isolated studies indicate the existence of two tendencies which did not exist in Europe. The first was a distinct embourgeoisement of the social origins of American university students in the late nineteenth century, at a time when European universities became somewhat less dominated by the upper and middle classes. American students from higher white-collar backgrounds, especially from families of professional men, increased more rapidly than students from lower-middle- and lower-class families, as shown by Richard Angelo in a study of students at the University of Pennsylvania. Christopher Jenks and David Riesman drew similar, more general, conclusions from circumstantial evidence. A major reason might have been the growing attractiveness of East Coast universities to Americans who would previously have chosen to attend European universities. The second, long-term, more important and more stable tendency was the accessibility of American universities, which were much more open than those in Europe. It seems that students at American universities (at least after the Civil War) came from blue-collar and farming families to a larger extent than at European universities. Almost every fifth student at the University of Pennsylvania in the 1890s was a blue-collar worker's son. Materials on the social origins of American professionals in the early twentieth century, collected by Pitirim Sorokin, also lead us to conclude that higher education in the United States was

Note to table 2.5:

The table covers only institutions whose students have been investigated at not less than two different points of time. Col. 1–2: H. Jenkins, D.C. Jones, 'Social Class of Cambridge University Alumni of the 18th and 19th Centuries', *British Journal of Sociology*, vol. 1 (1950), p. 99; col. 3–4: L. Stone, 'The Size and Composition of the Oxford Student Body 1580–1910', idem (ed.), *The University and Society* (Princeton Univ. Press, Princeton, 1974), p. 103; col. 5–9: M. Lévy-Leboyer, 'Le patronat français a-t-il été malthusien?', *Le mouvement social*, no. 88 (1974), p. 25; col. 9–13: idem, 'Innovation and Business Strategies in 19th- and 20th-Century France' in E. G. Carter et. al. (eds.), *Enterprise and Entrepreneurs in 19th- and 20th-Century France* (Johns Hopkins Univ. Press, Baltimore, 1976), p. 104ff. (English version has a better temporal grouping of the data for the 19th century); col. 10–12: A. Reinhardt, *Das Universitätsstudium der Württemberger seit der Reichsgründung* (Tübingen, 1918), p. 27ff. col. 13–14: *Preussische Statistik*, vol. 102, p. 68; vol. 236, p. 141.

Table 2.6 Social distribution of opportunities in universities in England, France, and Germany, 1850–1913 (recruitment index)

	England		France				Germany				
	Cambridge	Oxford	Écoles des arts et mét.	École centrale		École polytechnique	Students from Würt.		Prussia		Bavaria
	1850–1899	1910	1860–1875	1870–1899	1900–1925	1860–1875	1871–1881	1901–1911	1886–1887	1911–1912	1913
	(1)	(2)	(3)	(4)	(5)	(6)	(7)	(8)	(9)	(10)	(11)
Higher civil servants }	57.00	48.00					15.00	9.67	10.50	7.00	7.00
Professionals }											9.00
Large landowners											
Businessmen	2.24	6.41	2.94	5.11	8.29	2.77	1.64	2.15	2.43	3.00	2.67
Petty bourgeoisie											
Farmers			1.10	0.08	0.09	0.25	0.61[a]	0.71[a]	0.93[a]	0.91[a]	0.46
Lower civil servants }			1.06	0.59	1.17	1.75	5.25	5.00	1.13	4.50	3.80
White-collar employees }							1.00	0.60	1.00	0.40	0.50
Workers							0.02	0.06	0.00	0.03	0.11

a. Large landowners plus farmers. Farmers only: Würt. 1871–1888: 0.61; Würt. 1901–11: 0.71; Prussia 1886/87: 0.29; Prussia 1911/12: 0.82.

more accessible to the sons of the lower classes than was the case in Europe. Regardless of exceptional European institutions such as the Scottish universities, this seems to indicate the existence of a comparatively egalitarian long-term educational tradition in the United States.[17]

These common European characteristics should not overshadow the existence of significant cross-national variability. The brief enumeration of such differences offered here is suggestive rather than comprehensive and points to the necessity for further research. Regional differences are a case in point.[18] These differences are so pronounced as to raise doubts about the validity of any comparison limited to the national level, especially for secondary education. It is also apparent that the relative opportunities for various social classes differ cross-nationally and over time. For example, sons of artisanal workers were less limited in their opportunities in France during the 1860s than was the case elsewhere, while sons of lower civil servants enjoyed a comparatively favourable position in German secondary and higher education. To class and regional variations should be added sizeable differences in the sexual distribution of educational opportunities; although the percentage of school-age males obtaining post-primary education was relatively similar from country to country, the comparable percentage of females varied significantly.[19] It also appears, though data is scarce, that the undeveloped parts of Europe differed markedly from the industrialising ones. Finally, there are indications of substantial variability in the role of higher education for occupational mobility. The available data for the period before 1914 do not permit the application of modern methods of measuring the impact of education, but the diverging patterns of recruitment for the professions, higher civil servants, teachers on various levels and businessmen indicate that the impact of higher education on European career patterns varied distinctly from country to country.[20]

One should add that the common and diverging characteristics described cover only some of the dimensions of educational opportunities. When information becomes available, it will be of great interest to compare other aspects, such as the contrast between rural and urban educational opportunities and the educational chances of ethnic, religious, national and regional minorities.

Note to table 2.6:

For the calculation of the index see table 2.4; for social origin of students cf. table 2.7; for occupational structure in col. 1–2 (England and Wales 1911): Halsey, *Trends in British Society*, p. 113; col. 3–6 (France 1866, 1886, 1906): Toutain, *Population*, Tables 58, 67, 75, 85, 149, 155; col. 7 (Württemberg 1882): *Statistik des Deutschen Reichs*, vol. 4 (NF); col. 8–11 (Württemberg, Bavaria 1907): ibid., vol. 205; col. 9 (Prussia 1882): ibid., vol. 4 (NF); col. 10 (Prussia 1907): ibid., vol. 204 — Only parts of table 2.5 could be used, since information on occupational structure is not always available. The recruitment index is to be used very carefully, because information on occupational structure is rarely directly comparable in different countries or at different points in time.

To sum up: the nineteenth century seems to have been a period in which educational opportunities showed definite cross-national similarities over time in industrialising Europe and a clear contrast between Europe and the United States. There are indications that the first part of the century was a period of growing inequality in the social distribution of educational opportunities, probably as a final stage in a process that had started in previous centuries. This period was also characterised by small and stagnant enrolments. As such it could be considered as the transition from charity opportunities to competitive opportunities. Generally, information is far too inexact for us to draw any final conclusions or to pinpoint the precise time of the change. Much more research is needed. In the last decades before 1914 the trend seems to have reversed; the social distribution of educational opportunities seems to have become somewhat less unequal, while the magnitude of educational opportunities began a slow growth. However, the beneficiaries of this modest advance were limited to the lower-middle class; the lower classes were excluded from it.

Determinants of Educational Opportunities

The common features just described in nineteenth-century Europe would hardly have existed had they not been generated by common determinants. Four such major determinants were identified in conjunction with the proposed conceptual framework at the beginning of this essay: the demand for higher education by the traditional upper classes and educational élites, especially in the first part of the nineteenth century; the permeability of educational institutions; the demand for university graduates; and the role of the government. Changes in these determinants are closely related to the industrialisation process but also, in contrast to events in new nations such as the United States, to enduring pre-industrial and pre-capitalist remnants in European societies.

Socially differential perceptions of the utility of higher education.
Most scholars agree that the demand for higher and related secondary education by traditional élites such as the landed aristocracy, the clergy, the professionals and, in countries with strong bureaucratic traditions, the higher civil servants and by the educated middle class, was strong and even increased somewhat up to the nineteenth century. This reflects a situation in which meritocratic liberalism was more widely accepted, while the position of traditional élites was threatened by the process of industrialisation. This threat is an important reason why educational opportunities in Europe differed from those in new nations such as the

United States.

For nineteenth-century Germany, various studies testify to the strength of this demand from the traditional leaders in the economic and educational sectors. Karl-Ernst Jeismann points to the eagerness of the rising educational élite to preserve their privileges, in contravention of the original purposes of educational reforms in the early nineteenth century. Konrad Jarausch emphasises that the limited broadening of recruitment in the 1820s and 1830s was reversed in the 1840s, a time of crisis in the job market for trained manpower. Detlev Müller holds that it was political pressure from the educated middle class that made Prussian secondary education shift from an early 'comprehensive' strategy to a socially exclusive strategy during the later nineteenth century. Fritz Ringer argues that higher education was the main instrument for the pre-industrial or early industrial élites to transfer high social status to their children in an industrial society. Though there is marked dissent among scholars about the evolution of educational opportunities in Germany, they do agree on the strong impact of educational demand, especially from these traditional élites.[21] Hence during the period of stagnation both in student enrolments and in the academic job market, a substantial proportion of students came from those classes. Furthermore, the privileged classes faced a growing rather than diminishing demand for higher education from other social classes: the rising industrial bourgeoisie sought higher education for social prestige as well as for economic advancement; the lower civil servants sought jobs within the strict formalisation of occupational advancement in German bureaucracy; occupational groups such as shopkeepers, artisans and peasants, whose economic position was endangered by industrialisation, sought to compensate for economic decline by higher education, as has been shown by John Craig.[22] As long as student enrolments and jobs for university graduates failed to increase, these converging demands for higher education could only intensify competition and increase political pressure from the privileged classes for the limitation of educational opportunities.

Research on England is even more controversial. There is a consensus on the strong educational demand from the upper and middle classes, but dissent about the specific class from which the demand came most vigorously. Nicholas Hans and Brian Simon argue that it was the rising industrial bourgeoisie who most strongly demanded higher education for their children and who were thus instrumental in bringing about a reduction in the proportion of students from the lower classes and a shift from charity opportunities to competitive opportunities. Other scholars come to opposite conclusions. T. W. Bamford finds that it was the nobility and the professionals who increasingly predominated among the pupils of the top public schools in the first half of the nineteenth century, as the public school became integrated into the life of the English aristocracy.

Lawrence Stone argues that the numbers of students from the lower classes started to diminish much earlier than the period of the Industrial Revolution and that it was the clergy and the nobility rather than the industrial bourgeoisie who profited from the process. Only in the 1860s did the aristocratic character of Oxford reach its peak. The contrasting situation at the Scottish universities supports this position. To be sure, there were several reasons for the extraordinarily open access to Scottish post-primary education; one was the absence of the Scottish aristocracy from regional universities and their strong preference for the aristocratic style of life at English universities.[23]

The permeability of educational institutions.
A second major determinant of educational opportunity during the nineteenth century was a complex of institutional changes that reduced the permeability of higher education. These included a gradual separation of primary and secondary education and a clear differentiation among institutions of post-primary education according to their role for social mobility. Scholarships for students from low-income families became scarcer; access to higher education became more competitive and formalised. Though the impact of these changes varies from country to country, they seem to have had some importance everywhere, reinforcing rather than alleviating the inequality of educational opportunities.

For France, recent studies by Robert Anderson and by Patrick Harrigan show that secondary education was used not only by the upper classes for the preservation of their social status, but also by the lower-middle classes as a means of social ascent. Scholarship policy favoured families that had served the state, rather than low-income families, but the modest school fees seem to have been within the reach even of artisanal workers. However, in the view of Robert Anderson and Theodore Zeldin, French secondary education retained its almost comprehensive character only until the Second Empire, when educational reforms led to a stronger separation of primary and secondary education and to more marked differences within secondary education. Harrigan shows that the social origins of pupils in the *lycées*, who had access to the *grandes écoles*, were more élitist than those in the *enseignement special*, which was introduced in the 1860s and did not lead to higher education. Zeldin even argues that, as a consequence of these and other reforms, the overall social structure of pupils in French secondary education became more exclusive in the decades before 1914 for reasons that are still unclear. Differences in higher education were even more pronounced. Graduation from the universities, which were open to everybody who could pay the fees and who had passed the *baccalauréat*, did not necessarily pave the way for occupational success. However, access to the *grandes écoles*, which were a channel to higher positions in public administration, business, and the professions, had become highly competitive during the early nineteenth century.[24]

Studies dealing with Germany reveal similar institutional changes beginning some decades earlier. From the 1830s on, primary and secondary education by and large became distinct sectors with diminishing possibilities of transition from the one to the other. Furthermore, secondary education was gradually subdivided into separate branches with different curricula stratified by occupational career and social class. Scholars, including Max Weber, agree on the negative consequences of these institutional changes for the social distribution of educational opportunities. Distinct contrasts in the social recruitment of pupils emerged within secondary education; *Gymnasien* affording access to higher education and to the higher ranks of the civil service and the professions were more socially élitist than other institutions of secondary education.

Moreover, access to higher education became more formalised and competitive, though in a different sense than in France. In the first place, the access routes to university education underwent a transformation. Starting with the first crisis in the academic job market in the 1830s and 1840s, access to universities was gradually limited to graduates from the *Gymnasien*, with their strong emphasis on classics. This change was motivated by the desire to relate education and occupational careers more closely and by the fear that an excess of university-trained manpower would threaten occupational prospects for the children of the educated social classes. Although access to universities was extended in the late nineteenth century to graduates of other secondary schools with a somewhat stronger emphasis on modern languages and science, only a small percentage of secondary pupils entered higher education. It may also be that university scholarship policies became less favourable for educational opportunities. In the decades before 1914, the proportion of university students receiving scholarships in Prussia dropped from about 20 per cent in 1887 to 1888, to about 10 per cent in 1911. Furthermore, clear contrasts existed, especially between the socially more élitist law faculty, which was the main channel to prestigious positions in higher administration and the judiciary, and the other sections of the university.

These changes in the university access structure were paralleled by changes in technical education. Access to technical education, which had been rather flexible and open in the first half of the nineteenth century, later adapted to the university system of admittance. This process was reinforced by scholarship policies; as Peter Lundgreen has demonstrated, financial support for low-income students was drastically reduced by the middle of the nineteenth century and replaced by competitive grants. Perhaps the most competitive part was the post-university trainee programme for public administration, the judiciary and secondary teaching.

Especially when there was a surplus of university graduates, competition at this educational level was intense and even seems to have been used as a deterrent to university study.[25]

Studies dealing with English secondary and higher education describe decisive institutional changes leading in the same direction, though with different institutional manifestations. As in France and Germany, primary and secondary education became distinct branches during the nineteenth century, without linkages or possibilities for transition. Certainly, this was a much more gradual and ambiguous process in England because of the extreme decentralisation of the English school system and the strong influence of the local clientele on the curricula. Only in the second half of the century did government intervention in favour of distinct secondary education become more apparent. Furthermore, the emergence of the public school reinforced the demarcation of secondary education. In the late eighteenth and early nineteenth centuries, public schools developed from endowed schools for local educational needs, who took in children from all social classes, to institutions designed to prepare a national, mainly aristocratic, élite for university studies. To this end, public schools became boarding schools with a nation-wide intake, high fees and few free places; they emphasized classics, abolishing all curricula not related to university studies. In spite of considerable variations among public schools, the social structure of the students was clearly different from that of other secondary schools less important for social advancement.

Recent studies also pinpoint institutional changes that brought about the growing exclusiveness of the universities of Oxford and Cambridge. One such change was the growing dominance of access to these two universities by the public schools. An additional obstacle was financial, although the fees and actual cost of living were less prohibitive in this regard than the high cost of maintaining the eccentric aristocratic student lifestyle. Prospective students also confronted a widening gulf between university curricula and the educational expectations of the middle class, as well as university apathy towards raising student enrolments or changing the social structure of the student body. Consequently a marked contrast existed between the social origins of Oxbridge students and those of students at the new civic universities, most of which were founded in the second half of the nineteenth century.[26]

One might question whether these institutional changes abolished a truly comprehensive system; what existed under the *ancien régime* and survived into the early nineteenth century was clearly different from the modern comprehensive school system, above all in its size and in its role as a gateway to occupational mobility. Nevertheless, these institutional changes did contribute to the erection of strong barriers to educational opportunities during the period of slow growth in student enrolment and academic jobs. In fact, they may well have been a response to rising educational competition that generated fears among the upper and educated middle classes of overcrowding in post-primary education and of an excess of trained manpower. As education became more important for social mobility, the need to formalise educational access to higher education also induced institutional change. Hence, in the conception put forward above, one could consider these institutional changes as the transition from the era of charity opportunities to the era of competitive opportunities.

The changing demand for highly-trained manpower
The situation changed markedly when the demand for university-trained manpower started to increase in the last decades before 1914. There are various reasons for this increase. The proportion of university graduates among members of the European business élites as well as among white-collar employees began to rise. Public administration expanded, though at very different rates, throughout Europe. The enlarging private service sector also included a growing number of jobs for university graduates, especially for lawyers and physicians. As a consequence, more teachers in secondary and higher education were needed to train the rising number of future university graduates. These occupations and/or the proportion of university graduates in these occupations expanded more rapidly than the population. To be sure, the expansion was only the beginning of the much more substantial increase which followed the Second World War, but the take-off clearly occurred before 1914.[27]

The expanding demand for university graduates had a distinctive impact on both of the dimensions of educational opportunities discussed here. Firstly, the growth in enrolment figures and hence in the magnitude of educational opportunities has already been shown. Certainly, the growth rates were still low compared to the postwar period and did not coincide precisely with demand; for instance, the over-supply of educated manpower produced a severe crisis in the job market, especially in the 1880s. Nevertheless, the long-term increase in enrolment could not be explained without the rising demand for university graduates. Secondly, the growth in demand exercised an indirect impact on the social distribution of educational opportunities by reducing competition in secondary and higher education. The demand for higher education from the traditional upper classes and educated élites was satisfied more easily, allowing somewhat more open access to secondary and higher education for children of the lower-middle class and also for female graduates.[28]

The role of governments
There are few indications that this limited change in educational oppor-

tunities was the consequence of direct government intervention in favour of a more equal distribution of educational opportunities. Except for the British Education Act of 1902, the educational policies of European government were primarily concerned with adapting educational institutions to the needs of the developing modern societies, rather than with reducing inequality in educational opportunities. Political parties and organisations that influenced or participated in educational policy decisions usually took an élitist rather than an egalitarian view before 1914.

On this point, available research seems in full accord. Studies of France describe the strong preoccupation of educational policy with the exact proportion of classics to more modern subjects in secondary school curricula, with church control of a large sector of secondary education, and with the modernisation and integration of university education into a coordinated system and its relation to the *grandes écoles* and special research institutions. For most of the nineteenth century, equality of educational opportunities seems to have had a low priority for the French political élites. Only at the end of the century did more egalitarian opportunities for the lower-middle classes become a less marginal topic in educational policies and lead to an abolition of fees in state faculties, to a substantial though rapidly declining scholarship programme, to a discussion of the barriers between primary and secondary schools and to the early entrance of women into higher education. Except for the increasing proportion of women students, the effects of these policies in France are unclear.[29] Studies on Germany point to a political debate on the share of classics, sciences and modern languages in the curricula of the secondary level, to the revaluation of institutions of higher technical training and to the development of intra- and extra-university research, above all in the sciences. Especially in the second half of the nineteenth century, those involved in educational decision-making were concerned with the preservation of privilege and the exclusion of the lower– and lower-middle classes, rather than with furthering egalitarian approaches.

Studies on English educational policies also fall into a similar pattern — the debate over classics versus modern topics in the curricula of public schools, grammar schools and the major universities, the relation of university training to the needs and expectations of the business sector, the special English problem of an extremely decentralized system of nonprivate endowed schools and the problem of Anglican control of the most prestigious institutions of secondary and higher education. Once again, the participants in the controversies over the various Education Acts looked at the distribution of educational opportunities from an élitist viewpoint.

The similar orientation of educational policies in these three major European countries stems from several causes. One was the extensive exchange of ideas among educational institutions. Moreover, in all three countries, those institutions confronted the needs of the industrialisation process. It should also be noted that in each case those excluded from educational privileges did not participate or receive consideration in the political decision-making on education before 1914. Furthermore, secondary and higher education were not yet widely regarded by these social classes as instruments of social advancement that ought to be distributed more equally.[30] All this indicates that the limited change of educational opportunities in pre-1914 Europe ought to be considered — in terms of the conception put forward at the beginning — as the last stage in the era of competitive opportunities, with rising demand for university-trained manpower, rather than a period in which purposeful, efficient and egalitarian educational policies led to a reduction of inequality. It is true that the rising demand for university graduates was partly a consequence of the evolution of social policy with subsequent effects on the increase of civil servants, physicians and teaching staffs. However, direct effective government intervention in favour of more equity in educational opportunity was yet to come.

Opportunities in twentieth-century higher education
Little comparative research has yet been done on the history of education in Europe during the course of the twentieth century. While there are a considerable number of recent comparative studies on educational opportunities at the beginning of the century or after the Second World War, none of them has covered the entire period from 1900 until the mid-1980s. There are a number of good reasons for this: generally speaking, the development of the twentieth century as a whole belongs to the interdisciplinary no-man's-land between history and sociology. Many studies by social historians end in 1914, many sociological studies do not begin until 1945. Moreover, a truly comprehensive comparison — even though limited to Western Europe — has to concern itself with an elusive, multilingual literature scattered over many disciplines and with numerous national statistical publications unavailable as a complete set in any single library. Finally — and this is undoubtedly the most important reason for the lack of intensive comparative research — up till now there has been no burning debate, no direct or strong motivation for a *European* comparison of twentieth-century educational history. Despite the high regard in which comparative research is held and its unconditional support in the social sciences, it does not yet form part of the historian's everyday approach.

So far as the history of educational opportunities in twentieth-century Europe is concerned, this need not remain the case. Comprehensive collections of data on the relevant social history have recently been made, at considerable expense; they include information on essential aspects of the long-term development of educational opportunities, thus relieving researchers from the laborious march through national statistics.[31] Furthermore, there has been a clear increase in comparative studies of the subject,[32] although limited in their comparisons; that is, they deal neither with Western Europe as a whole nor with the entire period from 1900 to the present. They are, however, extremely important as a basis for further work. Finally, it is only a small step from the current debate between historians and sociologists to a comparative study of twentieth-century Europe.

At least three questions on the development of educational opportunities emerge from the general trend of the historians' current interest in the present century: (1) whether the deep division in Western Europe during the first half of the twentieth century, between liberal democracies and fascist systems, is a superficial political phenomenon, or does it also reflect a gulf between social structures, to be seen, for example, in the aspect — central to liberal democracies — of equality and equity in educational opportunities? Is such a division the cause of large and growing differences in educational opportunities in Europe, along the line of demarcation between fascism and democracy? (2) Conversely, is the historically unique, close political cooperation in postwar Western Europe a phenomenon of short-term and transient political constellations; or is it founded on a growing and widening similarity and convergence between Western European societies, a convergence also reflected in educational opportunities, which take on added importance? Is there, in fact, a greater similarity of educational opportunities in post-Second World War Western Europe than in the period before 1914, or from 1918 to 1939? (3) Have twentieth-century European societies remained, in comparison with the 'new nations' (above all the United States), more traditional, less mobile, less equal, more élitist? Is this characteristic, ascribed to twentieth-century Europe by social scientists on both sides of the Atlantic, also recognisable in the field of educational opportunities? Or does it reveal itself on closer inspection to be a national or even regional peculiarity? Is Europe in this sense only a geographical concept or is it also one of social history?

This section contains some preliminary theses and reflections on these questions. The definition of educational opportunities, the terms employed and the factors seen as having a central influence on them are those presented at the beginning of the chapter. This section will concentrate on higher education. The following arguments rely almost entirely on secondary material, hardly at all on primary sources. This presents problems, mainly because very little comparative research has been done on the educational policies and educational institutions of twentieth-century Europe. As a first step, however, a secondary analysis appeared to be the most profitable. The following comparison is, in the first instance, intended to shed light on Western European similarities and convergences, since historical research generally tends to ignore them. This does not mean that differences between nations are disregarded; on the contrary, were they to be ignored, such a comparison would run the risk of setting false emphases. The peculiarities of *individual* countries, regions and institutions, however, will remain in the background — the regrettable price of a comparison of many countries which must concentrate upon general characteristics. The history of educational opportunities in the communist countries of Eastern Europe since 1917 and the late 1940s has not been systematically explored, interesting though this would be, since the research findings published in languages accessible to the author are too meagre to allow of a systematic comparison. For the same reason no inter-regional comparisons have been made; here too, both the state of research and the published statistical material are entirely inadequate.

Before 1914: the era of competitive opportunities
The magnitude and social distribution of educational opportunities, that is, enrolments in relation to the respective age cohorts, varied less in Europe before 1914 than one might expect. In most European countries the magnitude of educational opportunities was at the same level of about 1 per cent of the relevant age-group and in all European countries, it began to grow steadily (Table 2.2). The social distribution of educational opportunities also — with a few exceptions — reveals obvious parallels. In most of the European countries for which we possess information, students from the higher classes were in the majority in higher education, students from the petty bourgeoisie (the families of middle-ranking civil servants and white-collar workers) accounted for a further considerable share, while there were only a very few children of lower-class families. As far as we can judge from the very sparse information available, the slight opening of the universities to the lower-middle class in the period before the First World War was also a European phenomenon.

Even before 1914, common causes influenced this common development of educational opportunities. The pressure from the traditional industrial, administrative and educational élites for higher education for their children led in Europe — in contrast to the USA — to strong competition for the available educational opportunities, which had a number of effects (though these cannot be assigned solely to this cause). Educational expansion, and thus the danger of a surplus of university graduates, was not as great in Europe as in the USA. There was a whole series of institutional changes which differed from each other but whose effects in most European countries were very similar: a demarcation of secondary from primary education; a growing distinction between differ-

ent educational routes in secondary schools and institutions of higher
education according to prestige, to access, and to subsequent employment opportunities; and increasing selectivity in the distribution of scholarships, in access to university education and to specialised forms of
higher education such as the French *grandes écoles* and the German
Referendarausbildung (post-university training programmes for the judiciary, administration, and secondary school teaching). These institutional
changes were alike in their detrimental effect on the social distribution of
educational opportunities, particularly in periods of stagnating relative
attendance at institutions of higher education. Slight improvements in the
distribution of opportunities, from which only certain social strata profited, came with the beginning of educational expansion in all the European countries for which we have information; they did not, except in
England, result from governmental egalitarian measures.

These similarities in educational opportunities appear surprisingly
large, chiefly because they have up to now been underestimated in
research (for example, in comparisons of France and Germany). Our
revised view of educational opportunities we owe, above all, to Fritz
Ringer's study. Viewed from the perspective of subsequent developments in the twentieth century, on the other hand, the differences become more noticeable. Differences in the magnitude of educational
opportunities increased steadily up to the First World War; they were
then considerably greater than in the post-1945 era. Differences in the
social distribution of educational opportunities were probably substantial,
though such judgements must still be made with extreme caution, since
we seldom possess even reasonably reliable data for an entire country
(Table 2.7). The distribution of educational opportunity according to sex
reveals no international similarities before 1914. The contrasts between
countries such as Switzerland, where female students represented 11 per
cent of the total, and the Netherlands (14 per cent) on the one hand, and
Germany (4 per cent) and Austria (8 per cent) on the other, were enormous and appear never to have been so great at any time after the First
World War[33] (Table 2.11). Finally, it appears that the role played by
higher education in a person's later career differed greatly from one
country to another. Lack of data precludes modern sociological methods
of career analysis, but studies of elite recruitment reveal considerable
differences.[34]

Yet even before 1914 a common European pattern is discernible, reflected — even more strongly than today — in the views of contemporary
social scientists, as when Max Weber writes of 'our continental, occidental
educational institutions'.[35] This overall European pattern of limited
educational opportunities is particularly evident by comparison with the
United States, where relative university attendance was far higher even
before 1914.[36] Indirect confirmation of its European character is derived

Table 2.7 *Social origins of university students in West European countries circa 1910*

Father's occupation	Denmark (Univ. of Copenhagen) 1913	Germany 1911–13	England 1900–29	France Ecole polytech. 1880–1913	France Ecole normale 1880–1909	Italy 1911	Austria (Univ. of Vienna) 1910–11	Sweden 1910
	(1)	(2)	(3)	(4)	(5)	(6)	(7)	(8)
Businessmen	14	10		25	6	2		10
Large land-owners	2	2	89	13[d]	3[f]	37[d]	28	2
Higher civil servants	20	16[b]		9	27[g]	13[k]		8
Professions	13	5		11	12	29		16
Artisans	} 12							
Shopkeepers		19		10	4	9		19
Farmers	12	9		—	—[f]	—		9
Lower civil servants	13[a]	24	(10)	20[e]	14[e]	—	52	29
White collar employees	7	3		—	11	—[k]		

Continued on page 68

Table 2.7 *continued*

Father's occupation	Denmark (Univ. of Copenhagen) 1913	Germany 1911–13	England 1900–29	France Ecole polytech. 1880–1913	France Ecole normale 1880–1909	Italy 1911	Austria (Univ. of Vienna) 1910–11	Sweden 1910
	(1)	(2)	(3)	(4)	(5)	(6)	(7)	(8)
Workers	4	3	(1)	11	6[h]	8[m]	4	5
Others	3	2	—	—	—	—	—	2
No answer	—						17	—
Total	100	100	100	100	100	100	100	100
No. of cases	2,692	39,984		2,717	1,268	8,859	?	1,285

a=incl. teachers at municipal and private schools; b=incl. lawyers; d='propertied, rentiers' (F) 'possidenti' (I); e='middle officials' and 'lower officials'; f=farmers, propertied, rentiers; g=teachers at high schools and universities: 18%; army officers: 5%; h=skilled workers: 5%; k=all 'impiegati', army officers; l=commercianti' only.

from the fact that differing political structures find only a slight reflection in differing educational opportunities, which were by no means always greater in democratic, liberal societies like France, England, the Netherlands and Switzerland, than in authoritarian societies such as Germany, Austria and Spain (Table 2.2). Compared with all European states, the four largest countries particularly resembled each other, despite their differing political systems.[37] The common European pattern and common European factors appear to have been powerful enough to assert themselves in the face of differing political systems.

The interwar period: the era of experimentation
In the interwar period, too, similarities between the European countries cannot be overlooked. In all cases, the chief point of resemblance was the contrast between the growing significance of equality of opportunity in educational policy, coupled with public debate on education, and the trivial improvements or even setbacks in the actual development of educational opportunities. The interwar period was a time of experimentation, when lessons were learned and the ground was being prepared for lasting political alliances in educational policy.

On the one hand, at least in those West European countries so far studied, the problem of equal or fair opportunity of access to secondary and higher education became a central issue in educational policy debates and decision-making, and also in social scientific research and discussion. The emergence of this aim in educational policy was closely connected with the changed power structure in Western Europe after 1918, which brought the labour movement a greater prospect of power and, in some countries, participation in government, while at the same time altering the political forces in other liberal and denominational parties. Thus for the first time the interests of the educationally disadvantaged social strata and classes were taken into account and allowed some chance of affecting educational policy. Parallels in political discussion are to be found, at least in the countries studied so far, right down to details of institutional

Note to table 2.7:

Col. 1: F. T. B. Friis, 'De studerende ven Københavns universitet', in *National Økonomisk Tidsskrift*, vol. 57 (1910), pp. 580ff.; col. 2: H. Kaelble, *Soziale Mobilität und Chancengleichheit im 19. und 20. Jahrhundert* (Vandenhoeck & Ruprecht, Göttingen, 1983), col. 3: approximation, calculated as described in note to table 2.9 from Ringer, *Education and Society*, p. 243 (class differentials of relative university attendance, age cohort 1900–1929, men only); col. 4 and 5: Ringer, *Education and Society*, p. 170, 175 (Ringer's table for the école technique from T. Shinn, 'The Dawning of a Bourgeois Élite: the école polytechnique and the Polytechnician Circle', unpubl. ms.); col. 6: M. Barbagli, *Disoccupazione intellectuale e sistema scholastico in Italia*, Il Mulino, Bologna 1974, p. 193; col. 7: *Yearbook of Education*, 1950, p. 596; col. 8: S. Moberg, *Vem blev Student och vad blev Studenten?*, Iduns, Malmö 1951, p. 33 (men only).

questions; for example, in the debates on comprehensive schools (*école unique, Einheitsschule*), the integration of primary with the first secondary school classes, the abolition of school fees and the educational opportunities of women.[38]

On the other hand, in almost all West European countries the actual development of educational opportunities lagged far behind the new priorities and expectations, a reality contradicting educational policy aims, both in the extent of opportunity and in class and sex distribution.

Firstly, the pace of improvement did not match new expectations. In most European countries, and in Western Europe as a whole, educational opportunities increased more slowly in the interwar years than during the last decades before the First World War (Table 2.2). Whilst before 1914 relative attendance in higher education had risen by 2.8 per cent per annum in Europe, the growth rate sank to about half this level between 1918 and 1939.[39] These rates must of course be interpreted with caution, since — especially between the wars — in many European countries unprecedented situations are being compared, such as the educational backlog caused by the First World War and the effects of the Depression on education, and because of widely varying trends in some European countries. Nevertheless, in the context of long-term educational expansion, the interwar period is clearly a time of slow growth (in a few cases even of reversals in educational opportunity), resulting partly from strains on public finance, partly from deceleration in the development rate of employment structures and in the demand for graduates, and partly from political factors, to which we shall return. This common European pattern is particularly obvious by comparison with the USA, where the growth rate of the magnitude of opportunities at institutions of higher education — that is, the enrolments in relation to age cohorts (4.3 per cent per annum, 1920-30; 3.4 per cent per annum, 1930-40) — was well above the European average. Despite all the variations within Europe, this rate was not even remotely approached by any West European country during the entire interwar period.[40]

Since educational opportunities had grown at about the same rate in different countries, similarities in their extent were more or less unchanged from the pre-1914 position. There were undoubtedly significant short-term fluctuations. Immediately after the war, relative differences in higher education attendance were greater than ever before (Table 2.2), in particular owing to unequal interruptions in the education of the groups of conscription age. Subsequently this short-term divergence evened out to prewar level. In the four largest European countries (France, Great Britain, Italy and Germany), in which the validity of statistics on higher education opportunities was less distorted by study abroad or by the presence of foreign students than in smaller countries, the similarity of educational opportunities remained particularly marked.[41] In comparison

Table 2.8 *Social origins of university students in West European countries in the 1930s*

Father's occupation	Germany 1931 (1)	England 1913–22 (2)	France 1939 (3)	Italy 1931–2 (4)	Netherlands 1936–7 (5)	Austria 1930–1 (6)	Switzerland 1935–6 (7)	Sweden 1930 (8)
Businessmen	12		16	5			20[e]	12
Large land-owners	1	38		11[a]				1
Higher civil servants	16		26[b]	24[b]	52	32		8
Professions	6		19	24			23	18
Artisans								
Shopkeepers	15		4[c]	22				13
Farmers	5		4	4			5	6
Lower civil service	31[d]	32			42	43	15	
White collar employees	6		13	4			15	28[d]

Continued on page 72

Table 2.8 continued

Father's occupation	Germany 1931	England 1913–22	France 1939	Italy 1931–2	Netherlands 1936–7	Austria 1930–1	Switzerland 1935–6	Sweden 1930
	(1)	(2)	(3)	(4)	(5)	(6)	(7)	(8)
Workers	2	29	2	2	2	4	5	7
Others	} 6		10	4	} 2	4	2	1
No answer			6			21		2
Total	100	100	100	100	100	100	100	100
Number of cases	124,072	32,125		39,053			7,204	1,344

a = 'proprietari'; b = all civil servants; c = artisans only; d = incl. lower civil servants and clerks; in table 2.9 included in category 'workers'; e = businessmen, independent artisans, shopkeepers

Source: as table 2.9

with the United States, the common European pattern of a slower growth of educational opportunities becomes still more striking. Whilst relative university attendance in the USA was roughly triple the European average in 1920, in 1930 and in 1940 it was roughly four times higher (Table 2.2).

Secondly, development of the social distribution of educational opportunities also disappointed rising expectations. Despite attempted reforms in educational policy in many countries, inequality in this field appears to have changed very little between the wars. For the 1930s, studies on students' social origins are available for about half the West European countries, including the four largest (Tables 2.8, 2.10). Almost everywhere, the basic pattern was the same as before 1914. The sons of the upper classes retained their privileged educational opportunities, sons of the petty bourgeoisie and of some civil servants continued to enjoy a reasonable chance of access to further education, while the sons of farmers or manual and white-collar workers were seldom, if at all, granted that privilege. This statement may be substantiated for the four largest European countries at least, since we know the distribution of opportunities in the educational sector for 1910 and for the 1930s, though admittedly only in outline. We shall return later to the fact that England and Sweden diverged from the common West European pattern in the interwar period.

Continued social inequality of educational opportunities between 1918 and 1939 partly arose from the fact that educational opportunities grew so slowly that there was no compulsion to break away from the previous social recruitment of students. A more important reason for the stable distribution of higher education opportunities was the failure of many educational reforms at this time: they were either totally ineffective or, at best, took effect only slowly. This was due in part to the inexperience of educational policy-makers, who inevitably had to learn by trial and error. The nature of educational reforms, too, played a part; for example, when educational barriers at school level were removed, the effect at university level was felt only after some ten to fifteen years. Thus in France it was the 1930s — during (and indeed before) the Blum government — which produced decisive educational reforms. School fees for secondary schools were abolished step by step, to disappear altogether by 1933. The gap between elementary and secondary schools was reduced; some secondary schools acquired the character of comprehensives. Of course, during the interwar period effects of these reforms were observable only in access to secondary schools. The results became evident at the universities only after the Second World War, and even then they do not appear to have altered the social distribution of educational opportunities (Table 2.9). In Germany, the early 1920s were the period offering the greatest opportunity for reforms, some of which were actually made at this time. For the first four school years, mixed classes were introduced which all pupils had to attend and the division between elementary school children (*Volksschüler*) and future secondary school pupils before the age of ten was gradually reduced. Opportunities for transfer from elementary to secondary schools at a later age were somewhat improved. A small government grant programme, the *Studienstiftung*, was set up, although this was chiefly orientated towards supporting gifted pupils and not towards a general alteration in the social distribution of educational opportunities. The effects of these reforms were slight or else they were nullified by Nazi educational policy, to which we shall return later. In Italy too, the early 1920s were the period of the most significant changes in the educational system — here, however, under the Fascist government. In an approach diametrically opposed to that of the democratic countries, the Fascist Minister of Education, Gentile, introduced numerous examinations in secondary schools and impeded access to the universities or denied it altogether to a substantial share of secondary school leavers. These policies drastically reduced relative attendance at institutions of higher education and greatly increased the inequality of educational opportunities between the sexes. Social distribution of educational opportunities appears to have changed only slightly as a result of this reverse educational policy (Tables 2.7, 2.8).[42]

Thirdly, the discrepancy between the aspirations of educational policy and actual development is not quite so extreme in the development of educational opportunities for women. In almost all European countries covered by recent statistical surveys, the proportion of female students and thus the educational opportunities of young women rose considerably in the long term. The main causes were the changed role of women within the family, the general expansion of education, the demands of the women's movement and, to some extent, the Second World War and subsequent government intervention specifically aimed at a more equal distribution of educational opportunities between the sexes. But the interwar educational opportunities of women were far lower than those of men and were still far from the improvements of the postwar period. The information available indicates that this development increased the similarity between European countries as regards sexual inequality of educational opportunities. At the same time, the contrast with the USA was enhanced.[43]

Besides these similarities, there existed obvious international differences which are quite distinct from the differences of the prewar period; these are for the most part closely connected with the experimental period of educational policy and with strongly–marked contrasts between political systems. Particularly striking are three new differences between countries which, however, were superimposed on rather than superseding prewar differences:

(1) The political divide between liberal democracies and fascist systems exerted a somewhat stronger influence on educational opportunities than had the differences between the pre-1914 political systems. This can be demonstrated by comparing educational opportunities in Germany and Spain with those in the rest of Europe. Generally speaking, educational opportunities in Germany were, until the 1930s, slightly better than the European average and, measured against the other large European countries, the German situation particularly resembled that in France. After the National Socialists had assumed power, educational opportunities declined abruptly; the decline was considerable in absolute terms and still greater in comparison with the rest of Europe. Germany became one of the most educationally backward countries in Europe (Table 2.2). This is connected in part with National Socialist ideological opposition to women's pursuit of a career; with the expulsion and later the murder of German Jewish students; with the diversion of potential students to become army officers or to build up Nazi organisations; and with the ease with which the Nazi regime could limit the number of university students. Compared with the rest of Europe, Germany and (after 1949) the Federal Republic of Germany recovered very slowly from the educational cutbacks of the Nazi regime.

In Spain the development of educational opportunities was similar to that in Germany. Here, too, educational opportunities during the Republic were very close to the European average. After the fascists' assumption of power, Spain fell further and further behind the European development; until 1970 she was one of the European countries with the lowest educational opportunities (Table 2.2). In Italy, the development is not so clear. In the early years of Fascist Italy, as a result of Gentile's educational policy during the 1920s, educational opportunities fell abruptly to below the European average — as they did in Germany and Spain ten years later. In the 1930s, however, university education in Italy seemed really to explode. In the European context, Italy rapidly became one of the countries with the highest relative university attendance (Table 2.2). This somewhat surprising expansion seems to have taken place contrary to rather than in accordance with the intentions of the fascist government: it may be explained by the educational backlog dating from the early years of fascism; the high birth rate; the escape offered by education from the unemployment of the Depression; narrowing opportunities for emigration; and the growing demand for education by women who, even during the educational expansion, accounted for a rapidly increasing proportion of students.[44]

An over-simplistic view of the effects of fascism in power on educational opportunities is to be avoided. There was no neat distinction between favourable educational opportunities in liberal democracies and unfavourable educational opportunities under fascism. Traditional educational differences between European countries were far too great; furthermore, the popular demand for education and the need for graduates did not necessarily reflect the ruling political ideology. Nevertheless, the danger of worsening educational opportunities at university level, of backwardness in comparison with the main trend of European development, is discernible in the fascist countries, even though it became a lasting reality only in Germany and Spain.

(2) A second important difference between West European countries in the interwar period is found in those political constellations and specific periods of time which proved favourable for educational reforms and improvement of educational opportunities. As has already been made clear, the 'reform' phase in Germany came during and immediately after the Revolution of 1918, while in France it was in the late 1920s and the 1930s. In Great Britain — the most reformist of the larger European countries — one can speak of periods of reform as early as the first decades of the twentieth century, then again between the end of the First World War and the Depression, and above all in the last years of the Second World War, a period which saw not only an important breakthrough for the welfare state in the proposals of the Beveridge Plan, but also marked a watershed in education with the Education Act of 1944.[45]

Despite surprisingly similar tendencies in debates on educational policy, the international differences of decision thus became greater in a period of transition such as that between the two World Wars. Since, however, it was only in a few countries that these policy decisions had any very considerable influence on opportunities for higher education, these differences were limited in significance.

(3) Finally, there was also in the interwar period a definite league table of educational opportunities among West European countries. Such a table admittedly depends to a large extent on how university education is defined. Regardless of the definition chosen, the leading group of countries with the most extensive educational opportunities consisted mainly of smaller countries or regions. In at least some of these, for example Austria, Switzerland and Scotland, the high influx of students from other European regions (for a variety of widely differing historical and linguistic reasons) must have played an important part in the high relative level of university attendance.[46] The great gap between these countries, with their comparatively favourable educational opportunities, and the rest of Western Europe was the main reason for the international differences during the interwar period. Educational opportunities in all the other West European countries, including the larger nations, were, even in a strictly statistical sense, very similar.[47]

The postwar period: the era of welfare opportunities

The postwar period was a time of unprecedented similarity in educational opportunities, behind which the divergencies recede without, however, becoming entirely irrelevant. This process of convergence in postwar Western Europe can be observed in the areas of the extent of the social distribution and of sexual equality in educational opportunities. Linked with all these is the actual relationship of educational to job opportunities.

The convergence of *educational opportunities* in Western Europe is undoubtedly most impressive in relative university attendance. Differences between countries became smaller than ever before. Since for the first time the coefficient of variation fell under 20 per cent (Table 2.2), it is also possible to speak in a strictly statistical sense of a growing similarity. At the same time America maintained her clear lead. It is true that the enormous margin in her favour — by about 1950 relative attendance at institutions of higher education was four times higher in the USA than in Europe — was somewhat reduced. Nevertheless, at the end of the 1970s a clear gap still existed. Even in those European countries with the highest relative university attendance, educational opportunities were well below those in the United States and conform to a West European pattern. This, too, was distinct from the development of educational opportunities in the communist countries of Eastern Europe where, immediately after the Second World War, participation in higher education was forced upward, partly for economic and partly for political reasons. The East–West contrast in Europe was reduced in the 1960s and 1970s. By the end of that period, however, educational opportunities in Eastern Europe were well below the average, both of Europe as a whole and also of the majority of most individual West European countries.[48]

In addition, educational opportunities in the postwar period were converging more than ever before. In almost all West European countries increases in university attendance had never, since the beginning of the secular educational expansion, been so great as in the postwar period. But, above all, educational opportunities had never before increased in *all* European countries. There were a number of reasons for this accelerated educational expansion.

Firstly, it was during this period that the Welfare State developed, which in turn led to a rapidly growing demand for university graduates to staff and administer the social services. Secondly, the nature of industrial enterprises altered significantly, resulting in an accelerated demand for university graduates, above all in applied research and the marketing field. Governments and administrative bodies also needed more university graduates than before, to take part in political decision-making and planning at various levels. Finally, the more rapid expansion of the educational sector led to a greater demand for teachers at secondary and tertiary level. In addition, there was a greater general demand for education. The historically unprecedented improvement in the standard of living, extremely rapid changes in occupational structures, above all the decline of agriculture and the petty bourgeoisie, as well as changes in family structure and the growing demand for occupations for qualified women, all increased the demand for education. Finally, governments pursued educational policies that were more effective than those of the interwar period and, in the more favourable conditions of a long economic boom, a long period of peace in which domestic policies had a clear priority and a broad consensus in educational policy, more was invested than at any previous time in educational institutions, personnel, grant programmes and support for education.[49]

All this, however, explains only the post-1945 growth of educational opportunities throughout Western Europe, not their great and historically unusual similarity. Four closely connected reasons appear to have been crucial to this development. Firstly, the postwar period was a time of increased economic similarity between West European countries, as can be observed in per capita income and in employment structures; this probably also led to greater similarity of demand for graduates by non-governmental institutions and organisations, and to a greater equality in parents' capacity to finance education out of the family budget.[50] Secondly, after widely differing beginnings and developments in the pre- and interwar periods, the Welfare State asserted itself with striking similarity in postwar West European countries.[51] We may assume that this meant a similarity in demands for graduates by both the state and the private service sector. Thirdly, the end of the political division between fascist and liberal democratic systems in Western Europe led to an unhampered mutual exchange of ideas on educational policy and to a greater similarity of those political constellations favouring a policy of equalisation of educational opportunities, though here there remained differences to which we shall return. Fourthly, the educational expansion of the postwar period eradicated the educational advantages hitherto enjoyed by Switzerland, Austria and Scotland, which had been an essential factor of inter-European divergencies; these countries now corresponded to the West European average. Finally, the question whether family structures, the changing role of women and women's demand for education converged in postwar Western Europe — providing a further explanation of the growing similarity of relative attendance in higher education — must remain unanswered until the history of the family in the twentieth century is as well researched as in previous centuries. The coming years will reveal either the extent to which the ending of the postwar boom and the crisis in the West European welfare states produced new and growing divergencies between West European countries — or the extent to which the similarities between them have been preserved to the 1970s and 1980s, albeit in a negative sense.[52]

Secondly, close parallels between West European countries may be observed in the development of the *social distribution of educational opportunities*. In all West European countries, the educational opportunities of children from the salaried middle class and also of working-class children improved considerably in the postwar period, although admittedly the proportion of students among working-class children everywhere remained well below the opportunity average for the respective country (Table 2.10, also 2.6). At the same time, the proportion of students from the wage-earning middle class and from the working class rose noticeably. The social distribution of educational opportunities in Western Europe was still extremely unequal; moreover, the changes achieved in the postwar period fell far short of expectations. Even so, the proportion of working-class children among West European students — if this is viewed as an index of the openness of higher education[53] — rose on a rough average from under 10 per cent to about 15 per cent. In many countries this was the first twentieth-century change, even though perhaps rather modest, in the social distribution of higher education (Table 2.9). There are several reasons for this slight improvement in social distribution. It is certainly connected with the rapid expansion of the educational sector and the growing demand for university graduates, which necessitated the recruitment of students from social strata of previously marginal representation in higher education. Moreover, the rapidly rising postwar standard of living made it easier for middle-class and to some extent also for working-class families to finance their children's education, a process which may have been encouraged by publicity for education in the mass media.

Finally, European governments' intervention in educational policy — favoured by economic growth and experience gained in the interwar period — became better aimed, more concerted and financially more -lavish than hitherto. Comprehensive high-cost grant programmes, the institutional integration of elementary and secondary schools, easier access to higher education and investment in better-sited secondary schools and higher education establishments, as well as in institutions for late starters and disadvantaged pupils: all this created the conditions for a somewhat more favourable distribution of educational opportunities.

Even this development, however, was a disappointment to the West European education world, since the changes in the distribution of opportunities fell far short of those originally hoped for from the far-reaching changes in the educational sector. On the one hand, the development of the conditions listed above for an equitable distribution of educational opportunities was uniquely favourable. Neither the first half of the present century nor the foreseeable future are comparable to the postwar period in the expansion of public and private expenditure on education, in that of the graduate labour market or in governmental

Table 2.9 *Social origin of students in West European countries, 1910–1970: fathers of working-class, lower-white-collar and professional status (%)*

		ca 1910 (1)	ca 1930 (2)	ca 1940 (3)	ca 1950 (4)	ca 1960 (5)	ca 1970 (6)
Sweden	Work.	11[r]	16[r]	12[r]	14[r]	16	23
	Empl.	14	17	21	21	12[a]	13[a]
	Prof.	19[b]	22[b]	23[b]	22[b]	21[b]	16[b]
Norway	Work.	–	–	–	–	24	18
	Empl.	–	–	–	–	11	16
	Prof.	–	–	–	–	34	41
England	Work.	(1)	(29)	(19)	(23)	23	–
	Empl.	(10)[h]	(32)[h]	(32)[h]	(23)[h]	12	–
	Prof.	(89)[i]	(38)[i]	(48)[i]	(54)[i]	(59)[l]	–
Finland	Work.	–	23	–	–	–	21
	Empl.	–	–	–	–	–	20
	Prof.	–	–	–	–	–	27
Denmark	Work.	3	2	–	7	9	16
	Empl.	8	18	–	41[c]	25	25
	Prof.	38[e]	28	–	26[b]	31	24[a]
Belgium	Work.	–	–	–	–	23	23
	Empl.	–	–	–	–	15	18
	Prof.	–	–	–	–	30	22
Italy	Work.	5	3	–	11	13	20
	Empl.	11[k]	24[k]	–	44[p]	44[p]	40[p]
	Prof.	25	26	–	19[i]	12[i]	9[i]
Greece	Work.	–	–	–	–	12	21
	Empl.	–	–	–	–	21	27
	Prof.	–	–	–	–	17	13
Switzer-	Work.	–	–	5	4	6	–
land	Empl.	–	–	15	13	28	–
	Prof.	–	–	15	16	24	–
France	Work.	–	–	3	4	6	13
	Empl.	–	–	13	13	31	29
	Prof.	–	–	19	16	34	37
Nether-	Work.	–	–	0	1	6	14
lands	Empl.	–	–	13	11[d]	24[h]	30[n]
	Prof.	–	–	18	14	46[i]	36[i]

		ca 1910 (1)	ca 1930 (2)	ca 1940 (3)	ca 1950 (4)	ca 1960 (5)	ca 1970 (6)
Austria	Work.	2	4	–	7	6	11
	Empl.	5	–	–	–	32	35
	Prof.	40^g	–	–	–	32	27^m
Germany	Work.	3	2	3	4	5	13
(W. Germany	Empl.	3	6	10	15	19	36
after 1945)	Prof.	5	9	9	9	10	26
Spain	Work.	–	–	–	4	7	11
	Empl.	–	–	–	39	38	29
	Prof.	–	–	–	36	36	32

Work.=workers; empl.=white collar employees; prof.=professionals
a=lower employees: b=all university graduates; c='*funktionarer*'; d=all civil servants; e=incl. civil servants; g=incl. higher civil servants, teachers; h=lower middle class, labour elite; i=incl. managers, top bureaucrats; k='*impiegati*'; l=higher professional and other professional and managerial; m=professionals, higher level employees; n=incl. primary school teachers; p=incl. higher level employees; q=incl. higher civil servants and higher level employees; r=lower class. From exact years, see Note.

efforts to reform education. On the other hand, the effects of this un-usually favourable situation on the social openness of higher education were very modest. Taking the proportion of students with working-class parents as one indicator among several possibilities, this has probably risen by no more than 10 per cent in the postwar period. Even in Sweden, perhaps the most socially open society, the proportion of working-class children who have become students is still well under one-tenth; in many other European countries it probably stays under 2 per cent (Table 2.10). Whilst the discrepancies between the educational opportunities of various social classes have undoubtedly diminished, they have never-theless remained considerable. The mountain of West European edu-cational systems has laboured mightily but seems, with hindsight, to have brought forth not much more than a mouse. Accordingly, most studies of the postwar history of education come to the pessimistic con-clusion that the classical tools of opportunity redistribution — expanding the number of students, higher investments in education, institutional

Note to table 2.9

The table contains only selected occupations of fathers since there is not enough room for all data. It must be taken into account that the definition of higher learning changed especially in the postwar period and differs from country to country. Nevertheless, conclusions on some basic tendencies and inner-European differences can be drawn from the table.
Sources: Sweden 1910, 1930, 1037, 1943: Moberg, *Vem blev Student*, p. 34, appendix tab. B (men only) 1962/63 and 1972/73: R. Premfors, *The Politics of Higher Education in a Comparative Perspective* (Gobob, Stockholm, 1980), p. 205; Norway: *Education, Inequality and Life Chances* (OECD, Paris, 1971), vol. 1, pp. 164ff.; England: except for 1961/2 men only; estimates thus in brackets from Ringer, *Education and Society*, p. 243 (20-year-olds 1900–1929); A. H. Halsey,

reforms — are blunt and rather ineffective, while a rigid policy of direct redistribution by limiting access, including a quota system for under-privileged groups, is politically either impracticable or would produce undesirable side-effects, so that its value as an instrument of long-term change is doubtful.[54]

Such a pessimistic conclusion does not by any means apply equally to all West European countries — least of all to countries such as England, Sweden and Norway who, with a proportion of some 20 to 25 per cent of working-class children among the total students in higher education, have achieved substantial changes without introducing quotas (Table 2.9). We shall return to this later. But the basically pessimistic view is re-inforced by the results of recent studies — including one on England — examining the central question in the history of this field, namely the effects of changing educational opportunities on the distribution of employment opportunities. Their conclusion is that no reduction in the inequality of job opportunity is discernible in the postwar period, despite the far-reaching changes in the educational sector and qualifi-cation structures.[55] In this negative respect too, the West European nations, or at least those researched, resemble each other. Postwar distribution of *educational opportunities between the sexes* in West Euro-pean countries developed along parallel lines. In all West European countries the proportion of women in higher education rose sharply in

Change in British Society (Oxford UP, Oxford 1978), p. 26 (labour force); 1930–1950: A. H. Halsey et al., *Origins and Destinations*, (Oxford UP, Oxford, 1980), pp. 20, 188; 1961/62: W. Schneider, 'Die soziale Bedingtheit der Ausbildungschancen' in F. Hess et al. (eds.), *Die Ungleichheit der Bildungschancen* (Walter, Olten, 1966), p. 18; Finland: 1935: C. A. Anderson, 'Access to Higher Education and Economic Development', A. H. Halsey et al. (eds.), *Education, Economy and Society* (Glencoe Free Press, New York, 1965), p. 265; 1959: OECD 1971; Denmark: 1913: F. T. B. Friis, 'De studerende ved Københavns universitet', pp. 580–1; 1934 (only University of Copenhagen) and 1959: *Conference on Policies for Educational Growth, Background Study No. 4: Group disparities in Educational Participation* (OECD, Paris, 1970), pp. 218–9; 1949: T. Geiger, *De danske studenters social oprindelse* (Gads, Copenhagen, 1950), appendix tab. II, V; 1964/65: OECD 1971; cf. also V. Skovgaard-Petersen, 'Towards an Educational Policy in Denmark', *Scandinavian Journal of History*, vol. 6 (1981), p. 62; Belgium (first term students): OECD 1971; Italy: 1911 and 1931: M. Barbagli, *Disoccupazione intelle-tuale*; pp. 193, 206 (other version 1931 in *Yearbook of Education 1950*, p. 622); 1953/54, 1960/61, 1967/68 (first term students): OECD 1971: Greece: OECD 1971; Switzerland: 1935/36: *Die Studierenden der schweizerischen Hochschulen, Sondererhebung 1936*, (Bern, 1938 — *Beiträge zur Schweizerischen Statistik*, part 7), p. 78; 1945/46: *Die Studierenden an Schweizerischen Hochschulen* (Bern, 1947 — *Beiträge zur Schweizerischen Statistik*, part 17), p. 66; 1959/60: Schneider, *Ausbildungschancen*, p. 18; Austria: 1909/10 (Univ. of Vienna only): K. Englis, 'Eine Erhebung über die Lebensverhältnisse der Wiener Studentenschaft', *Statistische Monatsschrift*, vol. 20 (1915), p. 282; 1930/31, 1953/54: *Yearbook of Education 1950*, p. 632; 1965/66 and 1970: OECD 1971; France: 1939, 1948: *Yearbook of Education 1950*, pp. 603–4 (also Ringer, *Education and Society*, p. 189); 1961, 1968: R. Premfors, *Higher Education*, p. 203; Netherlands: 1935/37: *Statistiek van hogere underwijs 1947/48*, pp. 49–56 (incl. higher education outside universities); 1947/48: *Yearbook of Education 1950*, p. 628; 1961/62 and 1970/71; Germany and after 1945 West Germany: 1910–1960: Kaelble, *Soziale Mobilität*, p. 130; 1970: Statist. Bundesamt, *Bevölkerung und Kultur V. Studenten an Hochschulen, Wintersemester 1970/71*; OECD 1971; Spain: OECD 1971.

Table 2.10 *Educational opportunities of working-class children in Western Europe, 1910–1970 (proportion of students among the 20- to 24-year-old descendants in %)*

	ca 1910	ca 1930	ca 1940	ca 1950	ca 1960	ca 1970
	(1)	(2)	(3)	(4)	(5)	(6)
Sweden	(2)	(2)	(2)	(4)	1.9	7.3
Norway	–	–	–	–	3.2	3.0
England	(0.2–0.6)	–	0.9	1.2	2.3	3.1
Denmark	–	–	–	0.6	1.3	2.7
Belgium	–	–	–	–	2.2	3.9
Italy	0.09	0.05	–	0.7	1.1	3.9
Greece	–	–	–	–	1.1	–
Switzerland	–	–	0.4	0.4	1.4	–
France	–	–	0.2	0.2	0.7	4.5
Netherlands	–	–	–	0.1	0.6	1.6
Austria	–	–	–	–	0.8	2.4
Germany (after 1945: West (Germany)	0.06	0.10	0.06	0.2	0.5	2.1
Spain	–	–	–	–	0.2	–

For the exact years, see Note on p.84.

the postwar period, almost to equality in a few countries such as Denmark, Finland, France and Portugal. The distribution of educational opportunities according to sex differed between European countries, especially before 1914, and also in the interwar period, but these variations now became much less marked. The figures for individual countries came ever nearer to the overall West European ratio of women students to all students. A West European pattern was established, although this was partly because most, if not all, of the countries involved clearly lagged behind both the United States and Eastern Europe in the distribution of educational opportunities according to sex (Table 2.11).

Such impressive similarities between West European countries do, however, conceal differences which should not be underestimated. Firstly, as before the Second World War, there was a leading group of countries with relatively favourable educational opportunities which admittedly, as we have said, did not approach the level of educational opportunities available in the United States, but which were clearly distinguishable from the majority of West European countries. Despite the many inescapable reservations towards such a method of classification, it appears that there was such a leading group, established in the 1950s, while in the 1960s and 1970s its outlines became more blurred (Diagram 2.2) as its composition changed considerably. Sweden and Holland were founding members; Belgium, France and Italy joined later — or rather, rejoined, since they had belonged to the group in the prewar or interwar periods. Austria left the leading group and has not rejoined it.

Reservations must be expressed about such a classification of educational opportunities, particularly in postwar Europe, since individual countries' definitions of what constitutes higher education differ widely. In most countries in the leading group, the proportion of trainee primary school teachers among students was particularly high (especially in the Netherlands, Belgium and Denmark). A narrower definition of higher education would thus produce a different result. Even so, Sweden, France, Italy and Denmark belong to the group of European countries offering the best educational opportunities. But reservations are still necessary, given unclear or incomplete definitions.[56]

Note to table 2.10:

The table expresses the percentage of working-class children enrolled at institutions of higher education in relation to all working-class children between the ages of 20–24. A similar calculation for other segments of the employed population does not seem worthwhile as occupations are not uniformly defined in the statistical material available. It is, therefore, impossible to make any exact quantitative statements concerning international differences in distribution of educational opportunities. One attempt, viewed very sceptically by the authors themselves, can be found in *Education, Inequality, and Life Chances* (OECD, Paris, 1975), vol. 1, p. 163.

With the exception of Sweden 1910–1950 (Moberg, *Vem blev Student*; men only: estimated and therefore in parentheses) and England, for which the data is taken from new surveys (for 1910; 20-year-olds from 1900–1929 as a rough estimation: *Robbins Report*, cited from Ringer, *Education and Society*, p. 243; the percentages of working-class students given separately for non-skilled and skilled workers including 'routine non–manual'; for 1940–1970: Halsey et al., *Origins and Destinations*, p. 188; col. 3 those born between 1913–22; col. 4 those born between 1923–32; col. 5 those born between 1933–42; col. 6 those born between 1943–52), all other entries are my own re-calculations. The percentages of students among working-class children were calculated according to a general formula also applicable to other professions:

$$h = \frac{\text{Number of students (N)} \times \begin{array}{l}\text{social origin of students}\\\text{according to profession}\\\text{of father (\%)}\end{array}}{\text{Size of student age cohorts (N)} \times \begin{array}{l}\text{proportional representation}\\\text{of fathers' professions}\\\text{among all employed (\%)}\end{array}}$$

or in simpler form:

h = relative attendance × association index

The age cohorts of the students have been standardised (if not taken over in a different form) as the age group between 20–24. For calculations according to the simple form, data taken from: Flora, *Quantitative Historical Sociology*, pp. 56f. (relative attendance) and *Education, Inequality and Life Chances*, p. 166. (The association index is here referred to as the 'selectivity ratio'.) The following calculations are based on these compilations: Sweden 1960,

This is why it is not easy to account for the divergencies within Western Europe. They are certainly not allied to varying levels of economic growth; countries with high economic growth rates are to be found not only in the leading group, but also among those with average educational opportunities. Neither does there seem to be a direct relation with the political persuasion of the government; in postwar France, the foremost new leader, a socialist government was rare before 1981, while Sweden, the other pace-setter, was governed by the Social Democratic Party during the entire period covered here. Finally, there is no simple correlation of relative numbers attending institutes of higher education with such direct factors as, for example, investments in education or demographic developments. Clearly, only a comparison of individual countries will take us further here and this method has been used in a large number of recent studies, all comparing the most important new leader, France, with various other West European nations. The results vary considerably. For example, Rune Premfors compared France and Sweden in the 1960s and

---

Denmark 1965, Norway 1970, Netherlands 1958/59 (OECD) and 1960 (Flora), 1970, Switzerland 1960, Austria 1965 and 1970, France 1959/60 (OECD) and 1960 (Flora), 1968/69 (OECD) and 1970 (Flora), Italy 1953/54 (OECD) and 1950 (Flora), 1960/61 (OECD) and 1960 (Flora), 1967/68 (OECD) and 1970 (Flora), Norway 1964/65 (OECD) and 1965 (Flora), 1970, Belgium 1962/63 (OECD) and 1960 (Flora), 1966/67 (OECD) and 1970 (Flora), Spain 1954/55 (OECD) and 1955 (Flora), 1958/59 (OECD) and 1960 (Flora), 1970/1960 and 1970; for Germany and the Federal Republic respectively the associations index taken over from Kaelble, *Soziale Mobilität*, Tables 2.3.2; the Belgian data were calculated according to the same simpler form using the figures from R. L. Geiger, *Two Paths to Mass Higher Education: Issues and Outcomes in Belgium and France* (Yale Higher Education Research Group, Working Paper, YHERG 34, Yale UP, New Haven, 1979), p. 31.

For all other periods the percentage of students among working-class children was calculated according to a complicated formula and the data were taken as follows: (1) for the percentage of students from working-class families in relation to the total number of students from table 2.9 (Switzerland: *Die Studierenden and den Schweizer Hochschulen* (1936), p. 23; (1946) p. 65); (2) for the percentage of workers in relation to all employed in Denmark: Geiger, *Sociale Oprindelse*, Tab. II, V; 1960: *Education, Inequality and Life Chances*, p. 165 (employment structure from 1960. Because the percentage of workers in relation to all employed was presumably lower in 1970, the percentage of students from working-class families in table 2.10 is probably too low as well); France: Toutain, *La population de la France*, tab. 66; Italy: P. Sylos Labini, *Saggio sulle classi sociali* (Laterza, Rome, 1978), pp. 156ff.; (3) for the number of students at institutions of higher education: Mitchell, *European Historical Statistics*, pp. 771ff.; (4) for the size of the age cohorts of student age, standardised as the age group between 20 and 24 years ibid., pp. 28ff.

When interpreting table 2.10, three possible inaccuracies should be considered. Firstly, the class-specific differences in the number of children of student age, as well as change in this factor over time, are not reflected in the table, because of the lack of adequate information. It may be assumed that this causes the figures for workers to be too high. Secondly, the international differences in the length of time spent studying are not taken into consideration, because of lack of information. In point of fact, it would be necessary to use different age groups accordingly. Thirdly, the definitions of institutions of higher education vary, as well as those of profession, so that on this point too, one is forced to make interpretations on the basis of very rough differences.

Table 2.11: *Educational opportunities of women in Western Europe, 1900–75 (proportion of female students in higher learning)*

Country	1900	1905	1910	1915	1920	1925	1930	1935	1940	1945	1950	1955	1960	1965	1970	1975
(a) Universities only																
Belgium	—	—	—	—	—	—	10	14	14	13	16	18	19	24	29	33
Denmark	—	—	—	12	—	14	16	20	—	20	19	21	26	30	30	36
West Germany[a]	—	—	4	9	9	12	18	16	14[b]	—	16	17	20	21	25	32
Finland	—	—	—	—	—	—	32	31	33	37	35	42	46	49	47	49
France	3	6	9	10[d]	13	20	26	27	34	33	34	36	41	42	45[e]	48
Greece	—	—	—	—	—	—	8	9	11	32	—	20	23	31	31	37
Great Britain	—	—	—	—	27	29	26	23	27	25	22	24	24	26	28	33[c]
Ireland	—	—	—	—	—	—	29	25	23	25	25	25	25	29	34	41
Italy	7	9	17[g]	18	20[h]	17	15	15	20	25	26	28	27	34	38	39
Netherlands	—	9	14	15	15	15	18	17	14	15	15	17	18	18	20	25
Norway	—	—	—	—	—	—	15	16	15	19	16	18	21	24	29	36
Austria	—	5	8	7[k]	14[l]	16	17	19	24	32	21	20	23	24	25	34
Portugal	—	—	—	—	—	—	—	12	20	22	26	30	31	40	46	46
Sweden	3	5	8	9	10	11	15	17	24	22	23	29	33	36	37	37
Switzerland	20	27	22	17	12	14	12	14	13	12	13	15	17	20	23	27
Spain	—	—	—	3[m]	4	7[o]	7[p]	—	12	12	14	16	18	21	26	34
Western Europe	(8)	(9)	(12)	(11)	14	15	18	17	20	22	21	25	25	29	32	37
Variation coefficient	(97)	(106)	(53)	(44)	49	39	43	40	37	39	32	31	31	29	26	17

(b) All institutions of higher education

Country	1900	1905	1910	1915	1920	1925	1930	1935	1940	1945	1950	1955	1960	1965	1970	1975
Belgium											16[q]	27	26	33	36	41
Denmark											24	28	35	38	36	44
West Germany											16	19	23	24	27	34
Finland											37	43	46	50	48	50
France											34[q]	36[q]	41[q]	42[q]	45[q]	48[q]
Greece											—	23	26	32	32	37
Great Britain											22[q]	24[q]	23	29	33	36[c]
Ireland											30	30	28	31	34	38
Italy											26[q]	28[q]	27	34	38	39
Netherlands											21	25	26	25	28	33
Norway											16[q]	18[q]	34	34	30	38
Austria											21[q]	20[q]	23	24	29	38
Portugal											26[q]	27	30	40	46	46
Sweden											23[q]	29[q]	36	41	42	40
Switzerland											13[q]	15[q]	17[q]	20[q]	24	30
Spain											14	16	24	23	27	36
Western Europe											22	25	29	32	34	39
Variation coefficient for Western Europe											31	27	26	25	21	13
Eastern Europe											34	32	33	36	42	48
USA											30	34	37	39	41	45
Japan											11[q]	18[q]	19[q]	25	28	32

a = before 1949, Germany, b = 1939, c = 1974, d = 1913, e = 1971, f = 1938, g = 1911, n = 1921, i = 1932, k = 1912, l = 1918, m = 1917, o = 1924, p = 1933,
q = Definition "Institution of Higher Education" identical with "University"

1970s with the United Kingdom, where relative attendance in higher education was no more than average. He explained the lead of France and Sweden as arising, on the one hand, from their greater economic prosperity and consequently better opportunities for financing education, although in the case of France educational investment was low if measured in terms of expenditure per student; and, on the other hand, from the greater consensus on the need for educational expansion and the stronger tradition of centralised planning in France and Sweden, which also favoured a rapid expansion of higher education. In France and Sweden there is a strong bureaucratic tradition and higher education has thus enjoyed great social prestige: to what extent the demand for education rose more sharply in such countries than in Britain is a question Premfors has left open. Roger Geiger chose to compare France with Belgium during the 1960s and 1970s. In this comparison, too, relative attendance in higher education in France still appears high. Geiger argues, however, that these favourable educational opportunities ought not to be viewed as exclusively positive, since educational expenditure in France did not keep up with the expansion of education, so that in general French universities were far less well equipped with libraries and teaching staff than their Belgian counterparts; moreover, social distribution of educational opportunities remained more unequal in France than in Belgium. In his comparison of France with Germany and England, Fritz Ringer reached similar conclusions. He explains France's considerable lead over Germany in the postwar period as resulting chiefly from the cuts in education made by the Nazis (to which reference has already been made and from which the Federal Republic of Germany only recovered slowly); however, he also sees it as a result of the traditionally less favourable educational opportunities of German women. In Ringer's view, the discrepancy between France and England, already obvious in

Note to table 2.11:

Sources in general: *World Survey of Education*, vol. 4 *Higher Education*, UNESCO, Paris, 1966; *Second Conference of Ministers of Education of European Member States* Bucharest 26 November–3 December 1973, UNESCO, Paris 1973, Final Report, Appendix: Statistical Tables, pp. 6ff.; *Statistical Yearbook 1977*, UNESCO, Paris, 1978, pp. 324ff.; Edding, *Internationale Tendenzen*, Appendix; for individual countries: Denmark 1915–1935: *Danmarks Statistik: Statistik Aarbog 1921*, pp. 158ff., 1928, pp. 135ff., 1932, p. 145 ff., 1957, p. 153 ff.; Germany (after 1945 West Germany; before 1938 universities only): 1974: *Stat. Jahrbuch f.d. Bundesrep. Deutschland*, p. 104 ff.; Italy: 1911–1930: *Annuario Statistico Italiano*, seconda serie vol. 4, 1913, pp. 87ff., vol. 7, 1917/18, pp. 104ff., vol. 9, 1923–25, pp. 89ff., terza serie vol. 1, 1927, pp. 78ff., vol. 6, 1932, pp. 108ff.; Netherlands from 1905 on incl. techn. colleges, from 1915 on incl. commercial colleges; Norway: 1920–1930 excl. universities; *Statistik Aarbok for Kongeriket Norge*, 42, 1922, p. 194 ff.; 45, 1925, p. 168 ff.; 50, 1931, p. 173; Austria (from 1905 on incl. technical colleges, 1905–1925: *Österr. Statistik* (vol. 36, part 2, p. 2ff.; N.F. vol. 11, part 2, p. 2f.; N.F. vol. 13, part 3, p. 2ff.); *Statist. Handbuch f.d. Republik Österreich*, 2, 1921, pp. 121ff.; 4, 1924, pp. 123ff., 8, 1927, pp. 164ff.; Sweden and Switzerland until 1925 universities only, Spain (until 1933 universities only): 1917–1924: *Anuario Estadistico de España*, 5, 1918, pp. 474ff., 8, 1921/22, pp.

the second half of the nineteenth century, is mainly the result of the general nature of higher education in England, which was not orientated towards specialised job training and therefore of less direct career relevance; but he sees it also as resulting from the less favourable educational opportunities of women in England. However, in his comparison of France with England (though not with Germany) Ringer, like Geiger, does not arrive at a purely positive judgement on France since, while educational opportunities there were more extensive, their social distribution was also more uneven.[57] We shall return to this point shortly.

A second important difference between West European countries generally was the extent and date of improvements in the social distribution of educational opportunities. Both factors vary considerably, although a slight tendency towards a socially more balanced distribution may be observed in almost all the countries under discussion. As far as we can judge on the basis of the research results available, the pioneer countries, where the social distribution of opportunities in higher education improved especially early, were England and Sweden. In England — for which it is only possible to make very rough estimates — the proportion of working-class children in higher education initially increased to over 20 per cent of total students during the interwar period; it then fell somewhat as a result of the Depression and growing competition from middle-class children, before rising again to its former level (Table 2.9).[58]

The reasons for the unusual social openness of the English higher education system (which, however, was not attended by a very large proportion of the population) are not yet very clear. Some important causes appear to have been the educational reform of 1902 and the rapid rise in the number of free places at state secondary schools thereafter; the development of a scholarship system at institutions of higher education; the fact that in England comparatively less political pressure was exerted

---

366ff., 12 1925/26, p. 576, *Annuaire international de l'Éducation et de l'Enseignement*, Geneva, Bureau international d'éducation, 1935, p. 168.

Numbers for West Europe (i.e. Europe without communist East Europe) are not averages of all countries, but the total of West European women students in relation to all West European students. Before 1920 these numbers are put in brackets, because information is not complete for all European countries or because women had not yet achieved access to universities in all West European countries. The variation coefficient has been calculated on the basis of this West European share of women students. It was computed from five year averages as I am interested in tendencies rather than in short-term fluctuations. The proportion of women students at all institutions of higher learning was given only from 1950 on since the differences in practice between all higher education institutes and universities had previously been small and in most cases nonexistent. After 1950, the international comparison of the proportion of women students at *all* institutions is difficult because the definition of what is higher learning varies from country to country and also over time. Nevertheless, one cannot omit this category, because women often had better chances of access to higher learning outside the universities in the strict sense. Data collection and calculations were made by Rüdiger Hohls.

by the academic élites; and the greater degree of institutional flexibility in an educational system only very loosely connected with employment and careers.[59] In Sweden, too, the proportion of working-class children among students was also comparatively high in the interwar period, then fell as in England, presumably as a result of the Depression of the 1930s, rising again in the 1950s (Table 2.9). Unfortunately no detailed research has as yet dealt with the reasons for the relatively high percentage of working-class children.[60]

Decades after the lead set by these pioneering nations (who may have included other Scandinavian countries, although hardly any research appears to be available in this field),[61] the 1950s saw a definite shift in the social origin of students, at least in Denmark, Belgium and Italy, and higher education in these follower countries became more socially open. In addition to this lag, although the proportion of working-class children in the total student body rose rapidly, reaching the 20 per cent level of the pioneer countries, the percentage of students among working-class children remained far lower. In England more than 3 per cent of working-class children were obtaining higher education in 1970, while in Sweden the percentage was far higher; the corresponding figures for Belgium and Italy were only 1 to 2 per cent (Table 2.10). Unfortunately, very few comparative studies have been directed to the causes of this shift in student social origins within this group of early follower countries; thus the reasons for it are still not clear.

Finally, in the 1960s, educational opportunities underwent changes within a group of latecomers — the Netherlands, Austria, Switzerland, France, Spain and the Federal Republic of Germany (FRG). Here, not only was there a time lag in the shift in student social origins; until 1970 the change also stopped short at a lower level than elsewhere — only a little over 10 per cent of working-class children (Table 2.9). Thus in the latecomers higher education has remained noticeably more closed than in both the pioneer and the follower countries. Moreover, effects on the educational opportunities of working-class children have differed greatly from one country to another, even taking into account the fact that in all West European countries only a tiny minority of working-class children have received higher education. In some latecomer countries, this minority was somewhat larger than in others since the educational system as a whole expanded rapidly. Thus, by 1970 the percentage of working-class children in higher education in France had risen above the level in pioneering England; in the Netherlands, Austria and probably also in Switzerland it rose above the level in the follower nations of Belgium and Italy. In other latecomer countries, however, the proportion of working-class children in higher education remained well under the European average as late as 1970. Especially in the Federal Republic of Germany and in Spain, the effects of a socially comparatively closed higher education system were not counteracted, as in other late-comer countries, by a rapid expansion of the university system.

In the case of the latecomers too, little historical research has been carried out on the causes of the shift in social origins of students in higher education, or why this shift was later and less extensive than in other countries. Furthermore, these issues have seldom been discussed in a comparative context. The most detailed studies so far have been on France. Research here highlights the earlier change in social origins of secondary-school pupils, which shifted in the 1930s towards the lower-middle class and the working class. This is seen as a result of the abolition of school fees in the late 1920s, the greater degree of integration between primary and secondary schools in the 1930s and, finally, the considerable expansion of relative attendance at school and in higher education.[62] Yet why a shift in the social composition of secondary school pupils in the 1930s should not be reflected in the social structure of students until the 1960s is not clear; indeed, it is paradoxical, since we are dealing here with completely different generations of school pupils and students. Evidently, an answer can be found only by detailed analysis of the pupil intakes. We know that in Germany, in contrast to France, social inequality of access to secondary schools had not lessened by 1960, and had probably even increased slightly, partly as a result of Nazi educational policy, partly because educational reforms were not carried out immediately after the Second World War.[63] But there has so far been a lack of research into why the social origins of secondary school pupils and students had shifted by 1970, and the roles played in this process by institutional changes in the educational system, abolition of school fees and introduction of a widespread grant programme, changes in the admission rules of universities, the rising standard of living and improved opportunities for the private financing of education.

Nor are detailed historical analyses of the shift in educational opportunities during the postwar period found in relation to other countries. It is conceivable that, apart from factors specific to individual nations, changes in social distribution of educational opportunities were delayed by a later lowering of the barriers separating primary and secondary schools, or a longer gap before the introduction of financial means of reducing inequality of opportunity (abolition of school fees, development of student and pupil grants). Possibly the considerable significance of higher education degrees for later careers, and the resulting upper- and middle-class pressure on available education, also had a detrimental effect on the social distribution of opportunities.[64] However, at present this can only be speculation.

To summarise: in this section we have traced the development of educational opportunities in twentieth-century Western Europe. Two related aspects have been examined: firstly, whether educational opportunities improved during the present century, to what extent the supply of educational opportunities in higher education increased and how far inequality of educational opportunity was reduced; secondly, whether differences between West European countries in the field of educational opportunity — a central aspect of the modern social and welfare state — were reduced during the course of the twentieth century and whether there emerged a common West European pattern in the supply and distribution of educational opportunities in higher education.

The most important conclusion is that, viewed from both these aspects, the end of the Second World War was a decisive historical dividing line for Western Europe as a whole. Although a common European pattern of educational opportunities was already recognisable before 1945, at the same time there were clear divergences; among the European countries — and on the European scale, which was clearly at a lower level than in the USA — there were considerable differences in higher education opportunities. This situation did not change fundamentally before 1945; the gap between the general European trend in educational opportunities even increased in the Fascist countries — in Spain and Germany permanently, in Italy temporarily. There were also considerable differences in the social distribution of educational opportunities, and these differences increased somewhat in the interwar period, above all because of the isolated reduction of inequality of opportunity which took place in England and Sweden. The only aspect of which one might conceivably say that there was a slight tendency towards convergence is the inequality of educational opportunities between the sexes.

In the postwar period, however, it is the similarities that have predominated; at the same time there has been a substantial improvement in educational opportunities, even if public expectations were not met and the amendment may well have been limited to the period between the 1950s and the 1970s: the supply of education and the extent of educational opportunities in higher education increased with extraordinary rapidity. This explosive growth was common to all West European countries; differences between them diminished so considerably that for the first time it was possible to speak of a similarity of educational opportunity in Western Europe. The social inequality of educational opportunities decreased slightly in all the West European countries for which we possess data, a trend which also slightly raised the percentage of working-class children among students, not merely benefiting sections of the middle class, as in the first half of the century. Finally, in all these countries there was a considerable reduction of inequality of educational opportunities between the sexes, which led to a greater convergence, though not to complete similarity, of opportunities in higher education for men and women.

Of course, the divergences which continued to exist in postwar Europe cannot be overlooked. In the 1970s a slight tendency towards greater differences in relative attendance at institutions of higher education reappeared. Though these differences were not as great as in the first half of the century, it remains to be seen in the next few years whether they may increase still further in the course of the present education crisis. Moreover, the slight improvement in the social distribution of educational opportunities not only took place at very different times in various European countries, but also varied considerably in extent. In a small group of pioneer countries, to which England, Sweden and possibly other countries belonged, the social distribution of educational opportunities had already improved in the interwar period as a result of early educational reforms, so that the proportion of working-class students to students as a whole rose to about 20 per cent. In a group of follower countries, to which Belgium and Italy certainly belonged, the social distribution of educational chances improved in the 1950s. The proportion of working-class students rose to about the same level as in the pioneer countries, but this improvement had a more limited effect, since educational opportunities in general did not increase so rapidly. Finally, in a group of latecomer countries — France, the Federal Republic of Germany, the Netherlands, Austria, Switzerland and Spain — social distribution of educational opportunities did not improve until the 1970s and the improvements were less substantial than elsewhere: the percentage of working-class students to the student total remained at a lower level than in the pioneer and follower countries. Only in a few of these latecomers — above all in France — did a greater expansion of the educational system make up for the delay. The coming years will show whether these or other divergences have increased in the economic and educational crisis of the 1970s and 1980s or whether new convergences, even though in themselves negative, are to appear. In the latter case, the cut-off point of 1945 would be even more marked.

3 Social Mobility and the Business Élite

A third major aspect of the history of social mobility is the history of the rich and powerful, spectacular success and Buddenbrook-like decay. We look at it today with many more reservations than the historians of twenty years ago, before the computer opened up new perspectives on the social mobility of ordinary people. We know now that a simple history of the self-made man is misleading in its one-sided impression of social history. However, there is no doubt that the history of the average individual is only one part of the general study of social mobility. Though the spectacular successes and the dramatic failures are very rare, and so statistically marginal, compared to the innumerable life-stories of the mass population, they should not be totally disregarded. They are, at worst, symbols of social mobility or rigidity and thus affect the minds of those who can never hope for such careers. Moreover, they are important for the history of the middle class, demonstrating its openness or exclusiveness, with many consequences for the relationship between the middle and other classes of a society.

This chapter is confined to a single section of the rich and powerful, the business élite, for two reasons. Firstly, in any study of middle-class social mobility the business élite is a central topic. To omit it would mean to ignore the core of the rising bourgeoisie, one of the driving forces of economic development, and one of the most dramatic changes in the class structures of modern societies. Moreover, the social mobility of the business élite is better explored by far than all other sections of the upper and middle classes during the nineteenth and twentieth centuries. We know much less about the social origins of the landed élites, politicians, top administrators, bishops, high-ranking military, senior judges, the very rich, distinguished academics, the most successful professionals. It is possible to find good single studies of these social groups for individual countries. But there is as yet no basis for an international comparison of long-term development. Only the comparative study of the business élite can cover the larger European countries, such as France, Britain, and Germany, as well as the United States — mostly from the industrial revolution on.

The questions asked in the previous chapters will be put once again.

Long-term changes in social mobility will form one topic: was access to the business élite, the ascent from the lower or lower-middle classes to becoming a wealthy businessman, more frequent during the social upheaval of the industrial revolution than in the large bureaucratised enterprises of the twentieth century, as suggested by some historians? Is the career of the modern manager, based as it is on education rather than on capital, more open than were the careers of nineteenth-century capitalists and owners of family firms, as others suggest? In other words, we ask whether the long-term change in social origins of the business élite parallels or in some respects runs counter to the change from restricted competitive educational opportunities to the era of more open welfare opportunities. Beyond that, what were the differences between various countries? Again, an attempt will be made to determine whether the American business élite really was more open to social ascent, so that American society gave more promise and provided more examples of spectacular individual successes, as suggested by many contemporary observers and popular terms like 'self-made man'. Conversely, we shall try to find out whether the European business élite was more exclusive, more confined to an economic oligarchy of a few rich families and closer to the implications of such common European expressions as 'from clogs to clogs'. It will be interesting to see whether this contrast was as limited as shown in Chapter 1 or as apparently clear as in Chapter 2. Putting such questions in a historical context means asking about change: we shall also investigate whether variances between America and Europe were perhaps most distinct in the nineteenth century and were gradually eroded in the twentieth century, or whether the contrast still survives in some measure. Finally, we shall look specifically at Germany, asking whether the social origins of the German business élite are consonant with the more general idea of a closed, rigidly stratified, immobile German society or whether Germany's notoriously rapid industrialisation led to more accessible business careers and the creation of numerous self-made men.

Postwar historical research on the recruitment of business élites has abandoned the old, somewhat nostalgic idea of spectacular economic opportunities during the industrial revolution, contrasted with growing exclusiveness of the business élite in the period of corporate capitalism. Symbols of this myth, such as Carnegie, Wilkinson or Borsig, have turned out to be exceptions when modern quantitative methods were applied to this field of research. It became clear that the entrepreneur of the industrial revolution came mostly from the upper or upper-middle class; in the majority of cases he started from the favourable background of a business family, often belonging to that tiny section of society with a public school or university education. It has also been demonstrated that no dramatic changes occurred after the industrial revolution: access to the business élite during the rise of corporate capitalism was rather similar to that shown by classic capitalist society during the industrial revolution.

This argument was established about twenty years ago by research carried out or stimulated by Reinhard Bendix and William Miller.[1] Since that time the debate has focused almost entirely on the United States.[2] However, the argument leaves open several questions requiring further research, only partly dealt with by subsequent studies:

(1) Bendix's argument was based almost exclusively on American evidence. As economic opportunity in the United States is considered generally to have been different from that in Europe, at least in the nineteenth century, it is possible that the American trend of recruitment to the business élite could also be unique. When Bendix and Miller were working on the recruitment of the American business élite, corresponding quantitative research on Europe was very poor. Recently, however, several quantitative historical studies have been published on the British business élite and also — concealed by the language barrier — on the French, Swedish and German business élites of the nineteenth and twentieth centuries. None of these studies were carried out for the purpose of comparison, so that each is distinctive in its method and approach. Nevertheless, careful comparisons may yield some ideas as to the differences and similarities in patterns and trends of recruitment.

(2) The wider influences on the pattern of and change in the recruitment of businessmen during the nineteenth and twentieth centuries were discussed by Bendix and Miller from a mainly American perspective. Since their pioneering work, a broad and lively debate has opened on the American as well as on the European history of business structure and personnel. The debate covers four major topics, all strongly related to the social origins of the business élite: the rise of big business and modern business structures; the decline of the family enterprise and the emergence of the modern manager; the rise of formal university training among businessmen; the sharp changes in the class position from the early industrial middle class to the twentieth-century bourgeois élite, in terms of wealth, power, social relations, life styles and social values. Most of the contributions in this debate are not comparative. They do not cover the most important countries in the same way, but ask different questions and use divergent methods. Nevertheless, we now know much more about the comparable wider factors and conditions relating to social mobility of the business élite.

(3) Research has concentrated mostly on the business élite. The entrepreneur at the head of the middle-sized and small firm has remained a somewhat obscure figure in social history. It is not impossible that studies on these strata of businessmen might reveal quite different trends and contrasts among industrial areas and countries.

(4) Research has mostly been limited to the social *origins* of businessmen. Investigation of the social *destiny* of the second and third gener-

ation of descendants is rare. The historical stability or fluctuation of business dynasties, the persistent control of economies by a few families or the continuous replacement of business élites — at least in the most important economic positions — was not a major concern. From that perspective, the social mobility of businessmen might well have developed differently.

This chapter deals with some of these questions. Firstly it looks at the similarities and contrasts of recruitment patterns among the American, British, French, Swedish and German business élites during the industrial revolution. Thereafter, we shall focus on the rise of a new entrepreneur during the transition from the classic capitalist society to managerial capitalism. In this section the author treats of those economic, social, and political changes which may affect recruitment of business leaders, presented in the form of a set of hypothetical assessments which might be useful for further research in a larger number of countries. Finally, the hypothetical assessments are applied to long-term trends in business élite recruitment in Germany compared with those in Britain, France, Sweden and the United States during the nineteenth and twentieth centuries. For other aspects of the rise of the managerial society, it might be useful to concentrate on a shorter period. The development of the recruitment of the business élite should be investigated over a longer period, partly because the available statistics do not allow the discussion of small changes, partly because it was only in the long run, if at all, that the rise of managerial capitalism had clear consequences for ease or otherwise of access to the business élite.

The Recruitment of Business Élites During the Industrial Revolution

Studies of business élite recruitment during the industrial revolution are not abundant. The national level has been investigated only for the United States and, more recently, for Germany. For Britain, Sweden and France, historical investigations reach only as far back as the 1880s and 1900. Thus on this level Britain and, particularly, France can be included in a comparison only in a limited way. Apart from this, studies for more than one country relating to any particular branch of industry are few indeed. Research on steel manufacturers is the most advanced. British business leaders of this sector are explored, in an excellent study, from the 1850s until the middle of the twentieth century. Their American counterparts have been investigated twice, from the 1870s on, the German counterparts once for the same period. Comparisons on textile manufacturers are sketchier. This group has been investigated for the United States in the 1870s, for one section of the British counterpart, the hosiery industry, from the 1850s to the 1950s and, in a rather incomplete way, for three industrial areas in Germany (Thuringia, Hessen, Berlin) in the nineteenth century. All other economic branches have been explored either for one country only or for one area, or with non-quantitative methods. In these situations comparative conclusions are impossible.[3]

During the industrial revolution the recruitment of the American, British, French, Swedish and German business élites resembled each other in various respects. The first and most important similarity is the high proportion of businessmen coming from business families (Table 3.5). It was the largest single group with a common background. This is not only true for the business élite as a whole but also for manufacturers in the textile and steel industries. Secondly, in all three countries a vast majority of the business élite was brought up in families in which the father was economically independent, usually a businessman, but frequently also a large landowner, a farmer, an artisan or a shopkeeper. In the United States and Germany, about 80 per cent, in Great Britain shortly before the turn of the century about 90 per cent, in France and Sweden around 1900 about 60 per cent of the business élite came from this typical nineteenth-century background (Tables 3.1–3.4). This is also a common characteristic of the British, American and German manufacturers in the steel and textile industries during the industrial revolution in so far as these have been explored.[4] Thirdly, in none of the five countries does the family background of the business élite indicate widespread upward social mobility. The business career seems to have been only very rarely a rise from rags to riches. Very few members of the business élite show a working-class background; only a minority came from the lower-middle class, usually from families of farmers or artisans.[5] Though we do not know very much about the role of the family in business careers, few members of the business élite seem to have been self-made men with social positions vastly higher than those of their fathers. Hence, few of them seem to have succeeded without any direct or indirect help from their family. There are some exceptions to this pattern, the most spectacular being the machine-building manufacturers. As has been shown in a case study of American manufacturers in this sector, the majority started in blue-collar positions, which seems to illustrate the theme of the 'self-made man' of the industrial revolution. The German counterparts also came from the families of farmers and artisans to a much greater extent than did the average businessman.[6] But this pattern is uncommon. Studies of manufacturers in the textile, steel, and other industrial sectors demonstrate that upward social mobility into the business élite was low during the industrial revolution. Fourthly, in all five countries the business élite was much better educated than the average citizen; the majority of them had attended secondary schools. In a period in which rarely more than 2 per cent of the population reached higher education, a large minority of the business leaders — 33 per cent in Great Britain in the 1880s, up to 27 per cent in the United States during the nineteenth century, almost half in France and Sweden around 1900 and up to 26 per cent in Germany during the nineteenth century — had university training. Though these numbers are not really comparable, they serve to give an impression of the privileged level of education of the business élite.[7]

Unfortunately the initial positions and occupational careers of these men have been studied, if at all, in such diverse ways that comparisons are impossible. Some scholars who have explored only the occupational careers, disregarding family and educational background, considered those businessmen who initially and temporarily held blue-collar jobs as self-made men. But as the data demonstrate, the family and educational background, which played an important role during the industrial revolution, is at variance with this conclusion. Thus, research limited to the occupational career tends to overrate upward social mobility. In sum, studies of Britain, France, Sweden and Germany support the argument of Bendix that the business élite of the industrial revolution was recruited in an exclusive way, that it came mostly from economically privileged families, had a distinctly better than average education, and started in a very limited number of occupations. As industrialisation in Europe and the United States had many characteristics in common, it affected business élite recruitment in a basically similar way.

However, the differences in the recruitment patterns are as important as the similarities. At the present state of research no single study has been planned for comparative purposes. Therefore only very pronounced differences can be discussed here, since minor differences which seem to emerge from the available studies are too laden with technical problems and doubts. The major differences are linked predominantly to remnants or consequences of pre-industrial features of these societies rather than to variations in the process of industrialisation.

(1) The German business élite stemmed from large landowners much less frequently than did the American and the British (Tables 3.1, 3.2).[8] This is related to the tenacious anti-industrial value system of the large Prussian landowners, even non-aristocrats, who regarded the business élite as socially inferior and who considered most entrepreneurial activity outside or even within agriculture as non-aristocratic. Hence these landowners avoided industrial investments much more than their British and American counterparts and encouraged their sons more vigorously to enter careers in the army, state bureaucracy or agriculture rather than in business.[9]

(2) The German business élite much more rarely came from families of middle-sized and small farmers than their American counterparts (Tables 3.1, 3.2). The economic situation as well as the dominant value system of the

Table 3.1 *Percentage distribution of the American business élite born in specified years, by father's occupation*

| Father's occupation | Year of birth | | | | |
	1771–1800	1801–1830	1831–1860	1861–1890	1891–1920
Businessmen	40	52	66	70	69
Gentry farmers	25	11	3	3	5
Master craftsmen and small entrepreneurs	9	4	3	1	
Professionals	3	12	11	12	11
Government officials[a]	4	7	3	3	3
White-collar workers (includes foremen)	7	2	2	3	6
Farmers	12	11	10	6	4
Manual workers		2	1	2	3
Total[b]	100	100	100	100	100
Number of subjects	125	89	360	380	143
Data on father's occupation available	91	56	225	281	106
Data on father's occupation not available	34	33	135	99	37
Percentage for whom information was not available	27	37	37	26	26

[a] Includes a few school officials and army officers
[b] Details do not always add to totals because of rounding
Source: Bendix/Howton, 'American Business Elite', p.122

German peasantry seems to have influenced the recruitment pattern of the business élite. Technological progress in German agriculture during the early nineteenth century was more backward than in Britain and America. Productivity (and probably also profits) were lower. Hence in Germany agricultural background did not include access to capital to the same degree as in the other countries.[10] In addition the American farming family, at least, adopted economic attitudes which were more favourable to entrepreneurial activity than were the attitudes of the German peasant family.

(3) German business leaders came very rarely from families of professionals. The proportion of American, French and perhaps also Swedish business leaders with this background was much higher. Once again this seems to be closely related to remnants of pre-industrial society in Germany. Mediated by the apathy or hostility of large sections of the highly prestigious German academic community towards the rise of industrial society, the value system of German professionals seems to have remained more anti-industrial than that of their American counterparts, at least. Sons of professionals were therefore discouraged from

Table 3.2: *Social origin of the business elite in Germany 1800–1970*

Father's position or occupation	1800–70 (NDB)	1871–1914 (NDB)	1918–33 All higher executives (NDB)	1918–33 Owners (NDB)	1918–33 Salaried executives (NDB)	1922 All higher executives (Wer ist's)	1922 Owners (Wer ist's)	1922 Salaried exec. (Wer ist's)	1964 West Germ.	1965 West Germ.	1969 West Germ.	1970 West Germ.
	(1)	(2)	(3)	(4)	(5)	(6)	(7)	(8)	(9)	(10)	(11)	(12)
Higher civil servant	9	9	7	2	13	13	8	23	15	8	8	1
Businessman	54	53	53	63	40	51	63	30	36	21	18	32
Large landowner	2	2	4	3	4	4	3	4	–	–	1	–
Army officer	1	–	–	–	–	2	1	2	–	2	–	–
Professional	1	3	3	2	4	5	5	10	18	7	7	2
Master craftsman, retail dealer	24	20	16	13	17	9	6	14	5	15	10	12
Farmer	2	4	4	5	4	2	2	2	2	3	3	8
Lower civil servant	5	7	5	5	5	6	5	6	17	24	24	9
White collar	1	2	7	5	9	1	–	2	3	13	16	13
Worker	0	0	1	2	1	2	2	1	5	5	7	18
Other occupation or no answer	0	0	1	–	3	7	4	8	–	5	4	6
Total	100	100	100	100	100	100	100	100	100	100	100	100
No. of cases	235	297	232	130	102	670	412	258	118	537	1,528	2,474
Employers	85	82	80	86	69	71	79	60	61	46	39	54
Wage earners	6	9	13	12	15	9	7	6	25	42	48	40

entering business careers.[11]

(4) On the other hand, the proportion of business leaders from families of higher civil servants was far higher in Germany than in America (Tables 3.1, 3.2) and much closer to the French and possibly the Swedish pattern. This difference vis-à-vis the United States is linked to the rise of the Prussian and French bureaucracies before the industrial revolution, involving larger numbers of higher civil servants than developed in America. Even if the propensity of young men from this social group to enter business careers had been the same in the four countries, the actual number was more substantial in France and Germany. On top of that, because of the relative economic backwardness of Germany, the public administration became involved more directly in industrialisation. Some departments of public administration were thus closely linked with entrepreneurial activity; in a limited number of cases civil servants entered directly entrepreneurial positions. For the same reason, even at the end of the nineteenth century German public administration was a model for the operation of business firms. So individuals from the families of higher civil servants might well have had an advantage in business careers.[12]

(5) General differences in upward social mobility into the business élites cannot be explored at present. The available studies are too diverse for comparative conclusions on the question of whether the American business élite was more open than its European counterpart during the nineteenth century. However, there are some indications that upward

Note to table 3.2:

Col. 1 to 5: Based on a postwar biographical dictionary, *Neue Deutsche Biographie*. The sample includes businessmen covered by a whole article and active in Germany within the borders of 1871. There are no clearly defined selection criteria in the dictionary. As far as businessmen are concerned, the bulk of the entries are members of the business elite, but a good many of the entries are small businessmen who became known as inventors, patrons and sportsmen. Col. 6–8: *Sozialer Auf- und Abstieg im deutschen Volke. Beiträge zur Statistik Bayerns*, vol. 117 (T. Lindauersche Univ.–Buchhandlung, Munich, 1930), pp. 136f. (based on a contemporary biographical dictionary *Wer ist's*, 8th ed., 1922). Col. 9: W. Zapf, 'Die deutschen Manager' in idem (ed.), *Beiträge zur Analyse der deutschen Oberschicht* (Piper, Munich, 1965), p. 139 (chairmen of the fifty largest industrial corporations in West Germany); col. 10: H. Pross and K. W. Boetticher, *Manager des Kapitalismus* (Suhrkamp, Frankfurt, 1971), pp. 33, 43 (chief executives in thirteen large corporations in West Germany); col. 11: M. Kruk, *Die großen Unternehmer* (Societäts Verlag, Frankfurt, 1972), p. 44, appendix table 12 (chairmen, directors and owners of the 200 largest industrial corporations, of banks with more than 2 mill. Deutschmark business, insurance companies with more than 150 mill. premium returns and leading corporations of the tertiary sector); vol. 12: H. Hofbauer and H. Kraft, 'Materialien zur Statusmobilität bei männlichen Erwerbspersonen in der Bundesrepublik Deutschland', *Mitteilungen der Berufs- und Arbeitsmarktforschung*, 5 (1972), p. 214f (owners of enterprises only. All businessmen from a microcensus of about 0.5 million inhabitants of West Germany). None of the postwar investigations is exactly comparable to the data on the German business elite before 1945. Hence this paper only discusses those trends which are corroborated by all postwar studies. Unfortunately the recruitment of the business elite during the late Nazi era and during the twenty years immediately after the Second World War has not so far been explored.

Table 3.3 *Social origin of the French business elite, 1912–73*

Father's position or occupation	1912	1919	1929	1939	1959	1973
Businessmen	40.3	48.8	51.9	54.2	36.3	38.0
Higher civil servants	10.4	13.8	13.6	8.5	8.8	6.0
Professions	16.4	9.9	13.6	23.2	29.7	27.0
Higher white-collar employees	7.5	11.3	11.1	7.3	15.4	17.0
Small business	11.9	8.7	2.5	4.9	6.6	7.0
Artisan, shopkeeper	4.5	1.2	1.2	–	–	1.0
Workers	3.0	2.5	2.5	1.2	–	3.0
White-collar employees	6.0	2.5	2.5	–	2.2	1.0
Labourers	–	1.3	1.2	–	1.1	–
Total	100.0	100.0	100.0	100.0	100.0	100.0
No. of cases	67	81	81	82	91	100

Source: M. Lévy-Leboyer, 'Le patronat francais, 1912–1973' in idem, (ed.), *Le patronat de la seconde industrialisation* (Editions Ouvrières, Paris, 1979), p. 142. The sample of the study contains 588 French business leaders over the whole period from 103 leading French industrial business leaders (ibid., p. 140). Some of the categories cannot be translated exactly into English. Hence, the French terms ought to be given. Businessmen stands for *dirigeants*; higher civil servants for the more exclusive *functionnaires supérieurs*, higher white-collar employees for *cadres moyens*, small business for *entreprise moyenne*, skilled workers for *ouvrier*, white-collar employees for *employés*, and labourers for *manoeuvres*.

social mobility into the top positions, at least in Germany, was less frequent than in the United States during the latter part of the century. American manufacturers in the steel industry more frequently had a working-class background than their British and German counterparts.* American and British manufacturers in the textile industry stemmed from working-class families less rarely than the German industrialists in this branch.† Once again the diversity of the studies does not allow more than this limited observation.[13] It still cannot be ruled out that the rate of upward social mobility into the business élite as a whole did not differ very much in the United States, Britain, France and Germany during the industrial revolution.

*USA: 11 per cent (Gregory/New); 7–20 per cent (Ingham).
Britain: 4 per cent in 1865 and 3 per cent in 1875–95 (Erickson).
Germany: nil (Pierenkemper). Unfortunately other possible kinds of upward social mobility, e.g., from the petty bourgeoisie, into the steel business élite cannot be traced as the

Changing Preconditions Since the Industrial Revolution

The transition from the classic capitalism of the industrial revolution to corporate capitalism transformed the conditions of business élite recruitment in various respects. These transformations are first listed in the form of hypothetical assessments. The factual effect of the transformations on the recruitment will be assessed in the next section of this chapter.

First of all, *the rise of the large corporations* and the changing structure of private enterprise transformed the recruitment of the business élite in at least three respects.

The shift from the small or middle-sized, relatively simply structured, paternalistic firm owned by the entrepreneur, often together with other members of his family, gave way partially and gradually to the large corporation with a much more complicated structure. The main consequence of this shift in size and differentiation was the emergence of the 'bureaucratic career', as Bendix calls it. With this career an individual did not start in the position of an heir-presumptive or of a founder but as an employee, usually at the supervisory level, who eventually reached the top position of the same or another large corporation. To a growing degree, a career did not terminate in a position as a single dominant entrepreneur, but in a group consisting of leading specialists in various fields of business. Therefore the occupational experience of these bureaucratic entrepreneurs was different from that of the typical career during the industrial revolution.

As a consequence, the access to business careers was based on knowledge, experience and achievements rather than on the family connections of an heir or on the foundation of a successful enterprise. Thus the educational level became more important for occupational selection. A growing share of the business élite was educated at a college, vocational school or university, depending on the educational system of the country. For the same reason, an increasing proportion came from families of professionals, as the children of these families were most likely to continue to higher education.

Another consequence of the rise of the large corporation and its financing techniques was the separation of ownership and decision-making. To an increasing degree business leaders did not possess substantial shares of the capital of the firm which they headed. This also transformed the

---

categories in the available studies are too diverse.
†USA: 15 per cent (Gregory/New). Britain, for hosiery only: 8 per cent in 1844; 16 per cent in 1871 (Erickson). Thuringia: 5 per cent (Huschke).
Berlin: nil from 1830–70 (according to the author).

Table 3.4 *Social origin of the Swedish business élite, 1900–57*

Father's occupation	1900	1924	1944	1957
Businessmen	60%	51%	57%	47%
Professionals and white-collar employees	33%	52%	35%	40%
Farmers	3%	11%	7%	10%
Artisans, workers	3%	6%	1%	3%
Total	100%	100%	100%	100%
No. of cases	60	101	180	245
Unknown cases	27	21	20	–

pattern of recruitment. As capital was less a precondition of the business career than during the industrial revolution, a social origin in business families or, more generally, in rich families became less important, in terms both of inheritance and of more general access to family capital.

The decline of the business family was another crucial change. Three aspects are important here.

The family firm, in the strict sense in which a family owned and, hence, controlled an enterprise, declined in big business and gave way to the anonymous organisation in which managers controlled rather than owned big firms. This transition might have occurred either directly or via an intermediate stage in which the family made the basic strategic decisions whereas the routine decisions had already been transferred to the managers. To be sure, there is no consensus among economic historians as to the reasons for the decline of the family firm. The limited financial resources of family groups and their inability to finance rapid business expansion, the careful investment strategies of the business families and their unwillingness to compete with anonymous organisations in risky rapid business growth, the limited efficiency of traditional family businesses, the Buddenbrook effect, that is, the declining entrepreneurial qualities of the second and third generations, inappropriate appointments, in which family relationships were of prime importance, are all

Note to Table 3.4

R. Torstendahl, 'Les chefs d'entreprise en Suède de 1880 à 1950: Selection et milieu social' in M. Lévy-Leboyer (ed.), *Le patronat française de la seconde industrialisation* (Éd. Ouvrières, Paris, 1979), p. 46. The table contains enterprises with a labour force of 500 and more. The comparison with the other tables given in this chapter often has to be tentative as the occupation of fathers in the Swedish study was arranged in a few groupings only.

reasons which have been discussed. There is, however consensus about the demise of family firms, at least in big business, in the late nineteenth and early twentieth centuries which led to a decline in businesses handed down from father to son and an increase of other social origins in the business élite.

More subtly, the influence of business families decreased in the careers of those businessmen who did not inherit firms directly but took business leadership as brothers, cousins or sons-in-law of entrepreneurs.[14] These careers became rarer. Loyalties of kinship were needed less than qualifications based on education and achievement. To be sure, business families adapted to these tendencies. Descendants of businessmen more and more often trained in the sciences, in engineering and in economics, so limiting the loss of influence by business families. Nevertheless, the rising need of educational qualifications in specific fields reduced the impact of the business family on social mobility.

Finally, there are demographic reasons for the decline of the business family. Nineteenth-century business families were large. Various top positions in an enterprise could be easily filled by family members. The strategy of loyalty by kinship could count on the existence of large families. By the early twentieth century, business families were probably among the harbingers of the reduction of the number of children; they became modern and small. Traditional business strategies could no longer be based on families with two or three descendants and, hence, were weakened by the change in demographic patterns.

Occupational change related to the transition from classical capitalist society to corporate society also greatly influenced social origins of the business élite. With the declining proportion of small employers in agriculture and industry, relatively fewer of the business élite came from that background; while, as white-collar occupations increased, a higher ratio of business leaders originated in that sector. Although more apparent in a later stage of economic development, this was a period when professional occupations expanded and businessmen with this background also became more common. These shifts do not, however, indicate any change in the accessibility of the top economic positions. They merely represent adaptation to the change in the occupational structure.

The long-term expansion of secondary and higher education was also important for recruitment of the business élite. This expansion started in Europe and the United States in the late nineteenth century and was related — as far as the direction of growth rather than the level is concerned — to a rising propensity to attend higher educational institutions as well as to a growing demand for graduates from these institutions because of more developed marketing techniques and production control, more research on products and production processes and the expansion of public administration. Therefore the shift in the educational background of business leaders in favor of post-primary education does not necessarily indicate a more exclusive access to business careers. On the contrary, it might even be based in part on the general expansion of post-primary education.

A further important condition for the change in recruitment patterns was the *intensification of industrialism*, which changed the motivation of social groups outside the business community to enter business careers. The classic capitalistic society of the industrial revolution never existed in a pure form, but was always merged with pre-industrial agrarian sectors and always coexisted with churches, universities, secondary schools, professions, local administrations and 'home towns' not yet touched by industrialisation. Accordingly, members of numerous sections of society during the industrial revolution were not eager to enter business careers. The rise of corporate capitalism, at least in Europe and America, coincided with the gradual extension of the impact of industrialism, the reduction of pre-industrial value systems and greater esteem for business careers. Thus large landowners, craftsmen, peasants and professionals gradually became more interested in entering business or in stimulating their sons to do so. In addition, the wide contrasts between countries and regions, with respect to the strength of pre-industrial sectors and attitudes, were reduced in the course of progressive industrialisation. So differences which existed among German, British, French, Swedish and American professionals, aristocrats and large landowners, peasants and farmers, were diminished though not eliminated. Business careers in Europe and America became more similar.[15]

The change of the social status of the business élite had a similar consequence. During the industrial revolution the business community was considered usually only on the local level, in individual industrial areas, to be part of the upper class in terms of income, wealth, social prestige and power. Generally the richest, most prestigious and powerful groups on the national level were the large landowners, the aristocracy and the bureaucratic, military and ecclesiastical élites. The rise of managerial capitalism coincided with and partly comprised a basic change of social stratification on the national level. Because of its growing economic importance, the business élite increasingly became a dominant factor in political decision-making, a more prestigious class and part of the élite of wealth; we know, for example, that in England and Germany on the eve of the First World War about half of the very rich were businessmen.[16] This increased the attractiveness of business careers relative to the civil service, the army, the professions and large-scale agriculture. Once again pre-industrial contrasts of social stratification in these societies were reduced, though with well-marked time-lags. This is another reason why business careers became more similar in Europe and the United States.

The impact of politics on business careers generally became somewhat stronger in indirect ways.

As higher education became more common among businessmen, the effects of educational policies became more important for the recruitment of the business élite, as for other positions in the upper and upper-middle class, with access depending more on access to secondary and higher education. Exclusion from post-primary education was more likely to coincide with exclusion from business careers. In some industrial sectors in which the positions of business leaders had been particularly open during the Industrial Revolution, the rising educational level led to an increasing exclusiveness in the business career. However, in most sectors the rising proportion of educated business leaders diversified the social recruitment, at least among those social classes which had easy access to post-primary education. Moreover, differences of educational opportunities between America and Europe and also between individual European countries did not disappear during the first half of the twentieth century, as has been shown in Chapter 2. This might also have had consequences for differences in access to the business élite up to the present.[17]

As mixed careers which combined experience in public administration and business became more common, the appointment strategies of the state bureaucracy became more important, at least for those business careers which started in public administration. A similar situation existed in countries such as Germany where the forms and appointment strategies of the civil service were partly taken over in private business. Once again, this indirect influence of government decision-making did not lead to a change of recruitment patterns in a single general direction. Rather, it might have enlarged the differences between countries, since the method of selecting higher civil servants in America, France, Great Britain and Germany were not the same in the late nineteenth and early twentieth centuries.[18]

On the other hand, direct government involvement in appointment of incumbents of the top economic positions was still rare and was linked much more to the emergence of mixed economies in postwar Western Europe; only then could access to top economic positions be changed by direct interference of the government.

In general, it must be stressed that all these economic, social and political alterations proceeded slowly. The social origin of business leaders was affected at an even slower rate, since there is a time lag between occupational change among the fathers of entrepreneurs, and alterations

Table 3.5 *American, British, French, Swedish, and German business leaders coming from business families*

1. USA (Mills)	1760–1789* 53.3%	1790–1819* 29.3%	1820–1849* 35.5%	1850–1879* 47.7%					
2. USA (Bendix/Howton)		1771–1800* 40%	1801–1830* 52%	1831–1860* 66%	1861–1890* 70%	1891–1920* 69%			
3. USA (Newcomer)				1900 75.4%	1925 69.8%	1950 63.1%			
4. USA (Warner/Abegglen)					1928 31%	1952 24%			
5. Britain (Perkin)				1880–1899 62.5%	1900–1919 59.6%	1920–1939 54.6%	1940–1959 51.5%	1960–1970 46.3%	
6. Britain (Clements)				1925–1929** 22%	1930–1934** 18%	1935–1939** 18%	1940–1944** 10%	1945–1949** 16%	1950–1955** 17%
7. Britain (steel) (Erickson)			1865 60%	1875–1895 54%	1905–1925 55%	1935–1947 42%			1953 34%
8. Britain (hosiery) (Erickson)			1844 50%	1871 44%	1905 54%	1932 39%			1952 47%
9. France (Lévy-Leboyer)				1912 43.3%	1919 48.8%	1929 51.9%	1939 54.2%	1959 36.3%	1972 38.0%

Continued on page 110

Table 3.5 Continued

	1800–1870	1871–1914	1900	1918–1933	1924	1944	1957	1964–1969
10. Sweden (Torstendahl)			60%		51%	57%	47%	18%–36%
11. Germany (Kaelble/Zapf/Pross/Kruk)	54%	53%		53%				

*year or period of birth
**time of appointment

Note to table 3.5:

Mills, C. W., 'The American Business Elite: A Collective Portrait', *Journal of Economic History*, vol. 5 (1945), supplement, p. 32; Bendix and Howton, 'Social Mobility', p. 122; M. Newcomer, The Big Business Executive/1964: A Study of his Social and Educational Background' (unpubl. paper, 1965), p. 59 (industry only: the percentage numbers include 'independent businessmen' and 'head of the same corporation as son'); W. L. Warner and J. C. Abegglen, *Occupational Mobility in American Business and Industry, 1928–1952* (Univ. of Minnesota Press, Minneapolis, 1955), p. 45; H. Perkin, 'The Recruitment of Elites in British Society since 1880' (unpubl. paper, 1976), table 5; Clements, R. V., *Managers: A Study of their Careers in Industry* (Allen & Unwin, London, 1958); C. Erickson, *British Industrialists, Steel and Hosiery 1850–1950* (Cambridge Univ. Press, Cambridge, 1959), pp. 12, 93; M. Lévy-Leboyer (ed.), *Le Patronat dans la seconde Industrialisation* (Ed. Ouvrières, Paris, 1979); Torstendahl, 'Les chefs d'entreprise', p. 46, table 1; W. Zapf, 'Die deutschen Manager' in idem (ed.), *Beiträge zur Analyse der deutschen Oberschicht* (Piper, Munich, 1965), p. 139; Pross and Boetticher, *Manager des Kapitalismus*, p. 33; Kruk, *Die großen Unternehmer*.

of the educational system and even of the initial steps of business careers, on the one hand, and the origins of the business élite, on the other. Hence a short-term perspective of twenty or thirty years would conceal rather than reveal the effects of the rise of managerial society on the recruitment of the business leaders.

Changing Recruitment of the Business Élite after the Industrial Revolution

The transition from industrial revolution to corporate capitalism affected various aspects of the recruitment of the business élite in very different ways: family background, education, occupational career and upward social mobility did not change to the same degree. In all these respects, the transition led to a common trend of recruitment as well as to a change in the differences which had existed during the Industrial Revolution and which have been discussed above.

Once again, most historical research has been done on the American business élite, in several studies utilising different methods. The bulk of the investigation was done in the 1950s. In recent years, British and French research has caught up with the American work in sociological and historical investigations. In Germany, interest has also shifted from the industrial revolution to the late nineteenth and early twentieth centuries. In contrast to the other countries, development after the Second World War in Germany is still almost totally neglected.[19]

(1) The transformation of the *family background* of American, French, British, Swedish and German business leaders exhibits various common trends. The most important common change — shown by most, though not all, available studies — is the long-term reduction in the proportion of business leaders coming from business families. However, the qualification should be made that this long-term change proceeded during the twentieth century rather than during the initial rise of large corporations in the late nineteenth century. In Britain the proportion of business leaders with business family background dropped nationally, as well as in individual industries such as textiles and steel. In the United States, studies of the chief executives of the largest American corporations and of some 1,000 top executives, partners and owners of business demonstrate that the proportion of those coming from business families declined somewhat during the twentieth century. In France, a study on the business leaders in the thirty top enterprises shows that the proportion of self-recruitment dropped from about a half, in the first part of the century, to almost a third after the Second World War, rising again during the last decades. In Sweden, a study of the business leaders in enterprises with a labour force of 500 and over shows a slight reduction in self-

recruitment and a more pronounced decline in business inheritance. In Germany, where the research is much less abundant, one can at least judge that among post-1945 business leaders the proportion of those from business families was lower than among the members of the Imperial business élite (Table 3.2).[20] The main reason for this common trend seems to be the rise of large corporations and the separation of ownership and decision-making, which reduced the advantage of the sons of businessmen in a business career. Hence managers came from business families less frequently than did owners of firms; in the present state of research this can be demonstrated for France and Germany, at least, during the early twentieth century.[21]

A second common change, and a clearer one, is the reduction of the proportion of business leaders who had been brought up in families of economically independent employers, or at least the self-employed, which had been the typical family background of businessmen during the industrial revolution. In four out of the five countries this background declined or started to decline.[22]* Apart from the loss of the sons of businessmen among business leaders, occupational changes have been a major reason for this transformation. The decline of independent farmers and small businessmen led to a loss of business leaders from this background after about one generation. Moreover, for sons of small business owners the bureaucratic business career characteristic of corporate capitalism might have become to some extent a psychic barrier. In addition, the rise of large corporations cut down the business career advantage of sons of the wealthy classes in general. Access to capital did not open up business careers to the same degree as it had during the industrial revolution. Hence, for example, sons of large landowners became less common among British and American business leaders, where their share had previously been considerable. Parallel to the reduced proportion of businessmen stemming from families of employers (in a broad sense), the share of business leaders from wage-earning families increased. Occupational change and the rise of the large corporation and the bureaucratic career are again the main reasons.

Finally, common limitations in the change of the family background are apparent. The numbers of sons of white-collar employees increased but they remained disproportionately rare. Sons of workers did not rise at all. The business leaders from business families remained the largest single group. Inequality of opportunity in secondary and higher education was

---

*American chief executives, from 62 per cent (1900) to 50 per cent (1950);
British business élite, from 88 per cent (1880–99) to 72 per cent (1940–59);
British steel manufacturers, from 90 per cent (1865) to ca. 65 per cent (1953);
French business élite, from 58 per cent (1919) to 45 per cent (1972);
German (West German) business élite, from ca. 80 per cent (1870–1914) to ca. 60 per cent (post-1945).

one reason for this. In addition, the role of the family in the business career was only gradually eroded and remained comparatively strong, as Bendix has shown. Even among managers, inheritance of top business positions did not fully disappear.[23]

Conclusions about the *different trends* in the family background among the various countries are more risky, once again because of the diversity of the available studies. It seems that what most different trends have in common is a reduction in the contrast of recruitment patterns that prevailed during the industrial revolution. The loss of business leaders from large landowning families was stronger in the United States and Britain than in Germany. Since this family background had been more common during the industrial revolution in these countries than in Germany, this increased the similarity in patterns of recruitment. The decline in the share of business leaders from families of farmers was more pronounced in the United States than in Germany; once again contrasts in recruitment patterns were reduced in this way. The large share of American business leaders coming from a professional background remained comparatively stable whereas the relatively low proportion of German business leaders with this background increased, reflecting the reduction of anti-industrial value systems among German professionals and also leading to more similar recruitment patterns.

The trend of the *educational experience* of the business élite was also similar in most of the five countries, in at least one major respect: the increase of secondary and higher education. In most studies this trend is more distinct in higher than in secondary education. One could even argue that it is higher education which marks the difference between this period and that of the industrial revolution, when the majority of the business élite had some secondary education but thereafter entered directly into business careers or obtained vocational training and apprenticeships rather than going to universities. During the rise of the managerial economy, college and/or university training increased among business leaders, though only in the course of the twentieth century was a majority educated on this level (Table 3.6). On the one hand this change is closely related to the rise of large corporations and bureaucratic careers in which the importance of knowledge and therefore of the educational background expanded. Hence managers had higher education much more frequently than owners of firms.[24] In addition, the secular expansion of higher education influenced the recruitment of the business leaders. Even among owners of firms, higher education became more common. There were several reasons for this: family entrepreneurs needed to 'catch up' with the more highly-trained managers; the social standing of university training increased in the business community; certain academic disciplines became more appropriate economically; and that section of society from which the business élite was mainly recruited was more likely to have received higher education. In at least four out of the five countries, the rising proportion of academic graduates among business leaders did not indicate a process of growing exclusiveness, but ran parallel to the substantial expansion of higher education. Hence, access to business positions for university graduates probably did not become more privileged.

Once again it is very difficult to say anything about the observable differences in the trend of educational recruitment. Methodologies of the available enquiries as well as the educational systems themselves are too diverse. The field of higher education, which may well have been different among business leaders of the various countries, has not been explored sufficiently. Nevertheless, the bulk of the available studies yields two impressions: firstly, the proportion of business leaders with higher education seems to have increased more rapidly in America than in the European countries. If this is so, it would be closely linked to the more rapid and more substantial expansion of secondary and higher education in the United States, perhaps also to the more rapid augmentation of the bureaucratic business career. Secondly, higher education among business leaders seems to have been more frequent in four of the European countries than in the United States of the late nineteenth century. If these impressions should be corroborated by further studies, then educational recruitment would also appear to have become more similar.

It is even more difficult to assess the trend of *upward social mobility* into the business élite. As mentioned before, the main obstacle is that the occupational careers of the American, British, French, Swedish and German business leaders have been investigated either in a rather diverse way or else simply neglected. So comparison has to be limited to family background and education. In addition, this question is so laden with problems of social stratification that one can only compare the trends without saying very much about their strength and effects. The available studies indicate that any *change* was very limited. It might be suggested that the common rise of salaried business leaders opened up business careers for persons without capital in the five countries and so generally increased upward social mobility into the business élite. But a more sceptical judgment is supported by most of the published research. Nevertheless, the available studies give the impression that the trend of upward social mobility into top economic positions may have differed as between the United States and Europe. Studies on the European business élites covered here often come to somewhat more optimistic conclusions than studies on the American business leaders. Scholars dealing with the latter either argue that upward social mobility remained stable or that the access to the American business élite became more exclusive during the period from the industrial revolution to corporate capitalism. Scholars exploring the long-term trend among European business leaders either

Table 3.6: *College or university attendance of British, American, French, Swedish and German business leaders (graduates only, if specified)*

1. USA (Mills)	1760–1789* 10.9%	1790–1819* 13.8%	1820–1849* 20.0%	1850–1979* 27.4%		
2. USA (Bendix/Howton)	1771–1800* 22%	1801–1830* 8%	1831–1860* 15%	1861–1890* 39%	1891–1920* 67%	
3. USA (Newcomer)			1900 28%	1925 40%	1950 62%	
4. USA (Warner/Abegglen)			1928 32%	1952 57%		
5. Britain, Steel (Erickson)	1865 13%	1875–1895 15%	1905–1925 19%	1935–1947 31%		
6. Britain (Perkin)	1880–1899 37.5%	1900–1919 37.6%	1920–1939 37.3%	1940–1959 41.0%	1960–1970 55.9%	
7. Britain (Clements)		before 1925** 25%	1935–1939** 28%	1950–1955** 34%		
8. France (Lévy-Leboyer)	1912 75.3%	1919 81.6%	1929 95.7%	1939 93.3%	1959 93.5%	1973 96.9%
9. Sweden (Torstendahl)	1900 46%	1924 45%	1944 22%	1957 44%		

Continued on page 116

Table 3.6 *Continued*

	1800–1870	1871–1914	1918–1933	18th and 19th centuries*
10. Germany (Kaelble I/Stahl)				
Owners of firms	13%	25%	30%	25%
Salaried business leaders	(50%)+	(60%)+	60%	62%
Total	14%	26%	44%	34%
11. Germany (Kaelble II)	1907	1914	1929	1935
Owners of firms	31.9%	41.2%	47.3%	51.5%
Salaried business leaders	77.4%	77.1%	74.3%	71.4%
Total	49.3%	54.2%	62.5%	62.8%
	(42.5%)+ +	(53.0%)+ +	(64.5%)+ +	(65.7%)+ +

*year or period of birth.   **time of appointment.   + very small numbers of cases.   + +in brackets: industrialists only.

Sources: USA: Mills, 'American Business Elite', p. 33; Bendix/Howton, 'American Business Elite', p. 126: Newcomer, *Big Business Executives*, p. 68 ('younger' ones and 'older' ones added up); Warner/Abegglen, 'Occupational Mobility', p. 108. Britain: Perkin, *Elites*, table 5; Clements, *Managers*, p. 187 (in table 3.6 only a selection of the data from Clements, which on the whole do not show such a clear trend, probably because of the impact of the Great Depression and the war). France: calculated from Lévy-Leboyer, *Patronat*, table 5. Sweden: Torstendahl, 'Chefs d'entreprise', p. 48. Germany: Stahl, 'Kreislauf', pp. 229, 232, 235 (18th and 19th century): Kaelble I (1800–1933): unpublished data from a survey described in the footnotes to table 3.2; Kaelble II (1907–1935): unpublished data from a study based on the editions of 1907, 1914, 1929, 1935 of another German biographical dictionary; *Wer ist's*, which covers more exclusively the top business positions and a large and slightly rising population of managers who were not owners of the corporation (1907: 47.4%; 1935: 53.6%). Since in *Wer ist's* the proportion of business leaders engaged in industries increases substantially, higher education has been shown relating to the whole business elite as well as for the industrialists. Further checks of the data which are preliminary may lead to minor changes. Higher education includes technical universities (*Technische Hochschulen*).

have demonstrated that there is no clear evolution or have come to the conclusion (especially when including the late nineteenth century) that access to the business élite became somewhat more open. Two studies on the British business élite have put forward this argument, as has one study on the French; my impression from the available data on Germany is similar.[25] However, I would make the qualification that the change in Germany has been more limited than in Britain and has been confined to one social group, the lower government officials whose opportunities in business careers improved parallel to their greater opportunities in higher education. In sum, the available research does not exclude the possibility that the trend in the United States and the European countries was different, with only the European business élite becoming somewhat more open. Once again my impression is that this different trend reduced variations which existed during the Industrial Revolution and hence led to less pronounced dissimilarities among the countries rather than to a more clear-cut individuality of any of them.

Summary

This chapter has offered three major conclusions about the long-term trend in business élite recruitment. Firstly, despite similar patterns of recruitment during the industrial revolution, pre-industrial contrasts among British, American, French, Swedish and German societies did influence family background very clearly and probably also the education of business élites. In particular, the proportion of business leaders who came from the families of large landowners, farmers, professionals and from the lower-middle classes in Germany was different from that in France, Britain, Sweden (probably) and the United States. Pre-industrial value systems and economic backwardness in Germany are the main causes for these differences. Secondly, the change in the recruitment pattern from the industrial revolution to the corporate economy seems to have proceeded in a rather similar way in four of the countries, somewhat reducing the share of businessmen from employer backgrounds, especially from families of large businessmen, somewhat enlarging the proportion of business leaders from wage-earning families and increasing the number of business leaders who graduated from colleges or universities. Only in Sweden is the position unclear. Limitations to this change seem to have been common to all five countries, leaving untouched the disproportionately high number of business leaders from business families and the disproportionately low number from families of white- and blue-collar workers. Thirdly, if there were differences in the trend of recruitment, the result in almost all respects was a convergence of recruitment patterns in the five countries. Remnants of pre-industrial societies

were reduced by the rise of the corporate economy and on-going industrialisation; hence they did not affect recruitment patterns to the same
degree as during the industrial revolution. American, British, French,
Swedish and German business leaders in the twentieth century had more
social characteristics in common than during the industrial revolution.

4 Eras of Social Mobility

In the previous chapters we have dealt with specific aspects of the history of social mobility: the chances of ordinary individuals for social advancement; opportunities for higher education; and the social origins of the business élite, that core group of the rising bourgeoisie. Here we shall take a broader view and trace the general development of social mobility in nineteenth- and twentieth-century Atlantic societies.

With this in mind, it is possible to detect two quite separate histories of social mobility. Firstly, there is the historian's history, in which contrasts prevail. Distinct changes and clear differences are revealed between rural and urban, proto-industrial and industrial, manufacturing and commercial, European and American communities. Usually this version of the history of social mobility covers only a few decades. Its cliometrics are simple and can be understood by everybody. The sources are archival: census returns, urban directories, marriage registers, augmented by other local documents. The main debates centre on the impact of urbanisation, migration, local guild and property regulations, the local mentality of individual social classes or groups and changes in family structure. Secondly, there is the sociologist's history, which is a long-term history of entire countries during the twentieth century. Stability and similarities predominate. Changes during this century as well as differences between industrial societies are seen as very limited. Advanced techniques of measuring and analysing the trend of social mobility are applied; only experts can fully understand them. The debates concentrate on occupational change, educational opportunities and achievement motivation as the major factors influencing social mobility. The main sources are recent surveys and the past is reconstructed by tracing social mobility from the younger to older respondents.

These two theatres of the history of social mobility have none of their actors and very few of their spectators in common. Sociologists mostly do not know the historical studies since they often regard them as too limited, too crude in their statistical methods, too narrow-minded in their analytical approach, too far removed from the long-term view of present trends. Historians usually take little interest in sociological studies since they are regarded as not taking account of social history in its entirety, as being too difficult to interpret because of the quantitative techniques employed, as remaining too general and vague in their conclusions.

119

Historians are often mistrustful of attempts to reconstruct the past from recent surveys. There is no doubt that historical and sociological studies deal with different periods. They are, however, often interested in the same basic questions, so that it is a pity that there is no bridge, no debate, no division of labour.

This chapter tries to start the building of a bridge, from the historian's side. It has four purposes. First of all, it discusses the very long-term changes in social mobility during the nineteenth century, the century of the historians, as well as during the twentieth, the century of the sociologists. Since we have no country-wide and very few local time series of social mobility in nineteenth-century communities, we cannot here undertake a strictly quantitative sociological study of the long-term trend. Building upon bits and pieces from historical studies of the preconditions of social mobility, we will try to assess what was the probable overall tendency of social mobility. Thus it is an interpretative rather than a statistical analysis. Secondly, in dealing with the long-term trend, we shall try to avoid two different approaches, the one often found in historical works, the other characteristic of sociological studies. On the one hand, we shall seek to extend the short-term perspective of the historical studies which, for good reasons, often cover only a few decades. On the other hand, we shall attempt to disprove the assumption made by some sociologists that the transition from pre-industrial to industrial society was accompanied by a definite increase in social mobility, which is seen either as having risen gradually or, alternatively, through an abrupt and unique upheaval during the industrial revolution. It is argued here, and in more general terms than in Chapter 1, that there have been different eras of social mobility from the industrial revolution until the present, and that the idea of a sustained growth in social mobility during the industrialisation is a popular assumption rather than a well-founded conclusion. The history of social mobility since the industrial revolution should be seen as a crisis and a subsequent response rather than as a steady development. At least three eras should be distinguished: the industrial revolution, the period of organised capitalism and post-industrial society. Each of these eras comprises a peculiar set of conditions conducive or detrimental to social mobility. Thirdly, a central assessment is that the historical development of social mobility did not result from any single factor such as structural change or new ideologies and values; rather, a multitude of factors affected the level it reached. As we hope to show in the following pages, occupational change, the rise of capitalism, changes in family structures, the demographic transition, types of migration, the ways in which individuals coped with life-crises, altered mentalities and government intervention were all factors which influenced the level of social mobility and all must be considered in any study of its history; the impact of each of these factors during the three eras will be dealt with. Finally, we shall endeavour to integrate two concepts which recur in every debate on long-term changes in the quality of life and in historical studies. According to one view, the history of social mobility is to be seen as the *overall* increase or stagnation of social opportunities generally, while the other aproach is concerned with the increase or decrease in *inequality* of opportunities, especially between classes. Here we try to show that the two approaches depend on each other, in fact, and that the historian cannot totally understand the past if he restricts his attention to only one of the two aspects. Judgements on the social inequality of opportunity depend very much on whether social opportunities generally increase or decrease; judgments on the rise of social opportunities depend equally on whether inequality of opportunity is reinforced or diminishing. Hence, both aspects will be dealt with in some detail for each of the periods under discussion.

The Industrial Revolution

Assessments of the impact of the industrial revolution on social mobility are often based upon sweeping assumptions about the pre-industrial society, where social mobility is generally considered to have been low, impeded by rigid barriers between social classes and by a lack of achievement orientation, a failure to appreciate the advantages to be gained from social ascent. Conversely, pre-industrial society is sometimes regarded as a golden age of social opportunities in which the modern bureaucratic or capitalist barriers to mobility had not yet come into being.

Grave doubts are cast on both views by three pieces of evidence. Firstly, comparisons with even such remote societies as the Roman Empire yield no clear or straightforward evidence that the incidence of social mobility was any lower in pre-industrial societies. To be sure, these comparisons are both difficult and ambiguous. But since historians of the Roman Empire have started to use modern approaches, their studies have shown substantial social mobility, especially into élite positions and into the Roman upper class. It proves difficult to establish that the upper class of an industrialising society such as Wilhelmine Germany was distinctly more open towards social climbers than the Roman Empire (overall rates of social mobility being excluded from the comparison for lack of sources on the Roman past).[1] Secondly, studies — especially on early modern Europe — do not support the view of a rigid pre-industrial society with low and stable rates of social mobility. Various studies of the long-term changes in social mobility in early modern Europe have clearly demonstrated that it did not by any means remain constant. Hence, the assumption of higher rates of social mobility in modern societies depends very much upon which industrial or industrialising society is compared with which pre-industrial period and society.[2] Finally, the debate on proto-industrialisation has questioned our view of the industrial revolution as having led to higher rates of social mobility. Franklin Mendels argues that proto-industrialisation had a strong impact on social mobility, above all in reinforcing downward mobility. If this view is corroborated by empirical studies of proto-industrial communities, then low social mobility rates, above all low rates of upward mobility in these pre-industrial communities run counter to the common assumption, since rates are low because of the earlier beginnings of industrialisation rather than because it is lacking. In this case, low rates of social mobility cannot be interpreted simply as pre-industrial.[3]

These arguments against the simplistic view of social mobility *before* the industrial revolution proper are the more important as our view of the increase in social mobility *during* the industrial revolution has also been modified by the results of recent research. This period now seems to be characterised by a restriction of rather than by any spectacular increase in the rate of mobility. Some of the main factors mentioned above led only, if at all, to a limited increase in social mobility, whereas others worked against or even counterbalanced the modest improvements. This is true for both of the two perspectives discussed here, that is, for the overall development of social mobility as well as for class inequality of opportunity.

A first crucial factor in the overall development of social mobility is occupational change. The industrial revolution is usually regarded as a period of occupational upheaval, as a sudden or at least rapid transition from a predominantly agricultural to a predominantly industrial society. As we have already seen in Chapter 1, the idea of occupational upheaval may make some sense for certain types of industrialising communities — though we know of surprisingly low rates of social mobility in nineteenth-century industrial cities. On a national scale, however, occupational change during the industrial revolution was neither very rapid nor dramatic. For example, the proportion of industrial workers rose in Belgium between 1846 and 1910 from 23 per cent to 33 per cent, in France between 1866 and 1921 from 16 per cent to 22 per cent and in Italy between 1881 and 1921 from 13 per cent to only 20 per cent. In Prussia, a notoriously rapid industrialiser, the proportion of factory workers proper rose between 1821 and 1861 from 3 per cent to a mere 7 per cent.[4] The decline in the proportion of farmers, master artisans and agricultural workers was correspondingly slow. The moderate extent of occupational change during the industrial revolution led to moderate rates of social mobility. Moreover, viewed from the perspective of the twentieth century, in many countries the industrial revolution was by no means outstanding for intensity of occupational change. Even in industrial cities and regions, occupational change was just as significant after the industrial revolution and this is even more true if we look at developments on the national scale. Generally speaking, it was in the postwar period that occupational structures changed most dramatically. Thus, agricultural employment shrank in Sweden, Belgium, Italy, Germany and the United States by around only 1 per cent per annum during the industrial revolution, compared to 4–5 per cent per annum in the postwar era. The industrial sector also changed much more dramatically after the Second World War: in most European countries, it shrank more rapidly during the 1970s than it had grown before 1914.[5] Hence, the industrial revolution should be seen as the gradual beginning of a long-term and irreversible process of industrialisation, with rates of social mobility that rose only slowly or stagnated, rather than as a sudden leap from agrarian to industrial society accompanied by extraordinarily high rates of social molbility caused by spectacular occupational change.

The demographic transition which, in some countries, partly coincided with the industrial revolution, also reduced rather than reinforced social mobility in two respects. Life expectancy increased during the demographic transition not only for children but also, though to a lesser extent, for adults. Because rates of adult mortality during the active life cycle fell,[6] fewer occupational positions were open to those entering the labour market; hence chances of mobility decreased. Furthermore, the rapid population growth during the demographic transition led to a rising demand for jobs, especially on the part of the younger generation starting work. The available jobs on the labour market had to be shared among an increasing number of people and this also tended to reduce the chances of social mobility. The extent to which these potential reductions in social mobility during the demographic transition actually took effect depended very much upon the speed of population growth and life extension on the one hand, and on the expansion of the domestic and overseas labour markets on the other. In any case, the demographic transition was clearly not a factor that increased rates of social mobility during the industrial revolution.

Geographic mobility was also a factor whose influence on social mobility during the industrial revolution was, to say the least, ambivalent. To be sure, the liberation of the individual from feudal restrictions on migration, together with the improvement of transportation, opened up new educational and occupational opportunities and therefore increased the chances of social ascent. If, however, we analyse actual geographic mobility during the Industrial Revolution, we can see that a good deal of migration led to dead ends rather than to social ascent since early industrial society was generally not able to offer all migrants adequate housing, education, medical treatment, a healthy environment, social networks, social security or help in adjusting to an unknown and industrialising society. What studies of geographical mobility during the Industrial Revolution often reveal is insecurity, fluctuation and vicious circles of poverty rather than purposeful migration to better economic opportunities. Industrial cities came into being at a time when there was a large surplus of migration and when the quality of urban life was undergoing a crisis; thus the conditions for individual social ascent were often unfavourable. So far, it is difficult to say whether migration to better opportunities or desperate unsteadiness prevailed during this period. But the simple fact that geographical migration was far higher during the industrial revolution than in the interwar and post-1945 periods indicates a substantial level of restlessness which would have lessened rather than increased the chances of social mobility.[7]

Moreover, the rise of meritocratic mentalities and social values, and the opening of the lower-middle and middle classes to all talents was far less pronounced than is often assumed. It need come as no surprise that the habit of transmitting land and property within the family remained strong or was even reinforced in the agricultural sector, and that farms and landed estates were virtually closed to upward social mobility.[8] Similarly, we are not surprised to find that artisan workshops were very frequently passed on from father to son. What is more important, however, is the fact that in the modern strata of industrialising society, such as businessmen and skilled workers, the industrial revolution did not pave the way to full meritocracy. From various recent studies of the early industrial business élite, discussed in Chapter 3, we know that the family played a very important role — either directly through inheritance of the family enterprise or more indirectly through help with capital formation and education — in the recruitment of management.[9] Moreover, recent studies on skilled workers have shown that in early industrial factories even positions on this level were often handed down from father to son and were not open to all talents. In particular, the labour aristocracy was a social stratum with high self-recruitment, so that it also cannot be regarded as a major example of a break with traditional notions of social immobility during the industrial revolution.[10] White-collar workers, who were often more openly recruited, were still rare in the factories of this era. Hence, the persistence of a non-meritocratic mentality restricted mobility chances during the industrial revolution.

This sceptical view of social mobility during the period under discussion is corroborated if the factors influencing the *distribution* of social opportunities are examined. Most of them reinforced rather than diminished the inequality of mobility chances. A first important factor was access to capital in an economic era in which direct ownership prevailed even in large enterprises and in which capital intensity was already substantial, at least in such economic sectors as textiles, mining, the iron and steel industries, shipbuilding and banking. Business careers in these sectors very much depended upon the ownership of capital, hence businessmen were mostly recruited from among the rich and the middle class. True, one should not overrate this factor since the overall rate of social mobility was not greatly influenced by the degree of openness of this relatively small number of positions and since, moreover, in some other branches such as the engineering industry, capital intensity was still low and a successful business career depended on technical knowledge rather than on capital ownership. Nevertheless, as shown in Chapter 3, in this early industrial period business careers were clearly not open to talents from a wider range of social classes than in the twentieth century.

Demographic factors seem to have worked in the same direction. Everything we know about social differentials of life expectancy and family size suggests that, during the industrial revolution, the higher an individual's position in the social hierarchy, the greater was his life expectancy and the larger was his family. Therefore whoever aspired to a better position in society had to face the fact that the competitors who stemmed from the social stratum he wanted to reach were numerous and that greater life expectancy in the higher strata restricted the number of openings. There is no evidence that these socio-biological barriers to social ascent diminished during the industrial revolution; what little information we have leads us to assume that social differentials of life expectancy and family size increased rather than decreased in this economic era.[11]

Geographical mobility seems to have reinforced these effects of capital and demographic differentials on class inequality of opportunities. The few studies we have on the social history of geographical mobility during the industrial revolution indicate that the differences between social classes were distinct. In general, unskilled workers were more mobile than skilled workers, who in their turn were more mobile still than white-collar workers. Moreover, it seems that enforced restlessness was especially strong among unskilled workers, whereas a larger degree of geographical mobility among skilled workers is explained by a wider labour market and a purposeful use of occupational chances.[12] Hence, it seems that enforced migration prevented unskilled workers from using educational or occupational opportunities more often than skilled workers. Inequality of social opportunities was intensified by migration.

The ability to cope with critical life situations was also an important factor affecting class inequality of social mobility, since childbirth, disease, disability, unemployment or the death of the family breadwinner could all have a marked impact on the use of educational and occupational chances. On the one hand, the traditional ways of coping with critical life situations, with support being given by the family, the social network of neighbours, the community or the feudal lord, weakened; on the other hand, self-help organisations and welfare institutions emerged only gradually. Therefore, the industrial revolution was a particularly difficult period for coping with individual life crises. It is important for the inequality of opportunities that the ability to cope with critical life situations differed so clearly between social classes. Such situations were especially difficult for highly mobile unskilled workers with loosened family ties, little inclination to organise self-help, large families, high infant mortality, few savings and for whom employers made little provision. It was less hard for many skilled workers, with their greater readiness to organise self-help, smaller families and substantial savings, and for whom employers made better provision, and easier still for the middle class.

All in all, therefore, the industrial revolution was not an era of dramatic rise in social mobility and of exceptional opportunities for newcomers from all social classes, as is often assumed. This examination of factors influencing social mobility indicates that the expansion of social mobility must have been modest, since occupational change was undramatic; since population growth led to a strong demand for the available opportunities; since extensive geographical mobility often impeded rather than improved the use of occupational chances; and since the non-meritocratic mentality, that is the habit of handing down occupational positions within the family, was still largely unbroken. Moreover, the inequality of opportunities was exacerbated by the fact that, for business careers, access to capital played an important role; that there were distinct sociobiological barriers to social ascent; that enforced migration had negative consequences for social ascent; and that material and mental preconditions for coping with critical life situations clearly differed between social classes. This does not mean that the industrial revolution in general offered fewer social opportunities than non-industrial societies. However, it seems more appropriate to regard it as a period of crisis for important strata of society rather than as a golden age of high social mobility with opportunities open to all talents.

The Era of Organised Capitalism

'Organised capitalism' is regarded here not in a clear-cut temporal sense, but as a set of crucial historical developments. It is true that social scientists do not agree on the theoretical implications, the timing, or even on the detailed content of this or similar terms. They largely agree, however, that the rise of the large enterprises in the Atlantic societies and the emergence of the interventionist state in Europe were major historical turning points. In many countries, these developments coincided with the demographic transition, or at least with its later stage. Lacking space for a detailed discussion of organised capitalism, we have taken these major changes as a starting-point. They had a strong impact on social mobility and made the development as well as the distribution of social opportunities during the period of organised capitalism clearly different from what they were during the industrial revolution. To show this in more detail, we shall look once again at the factors of social mobility discussed above in connection with the industrial revolution, and try to assess how they affected mobility in the era of organised capitalism.

Various occupational changes were a first important consequence of the developments which are usually comprised under the terms 'organised capitalism' or 'second industrialisation'. Above all, the number of white-collar workers expanded rapidly in most European countries and in North America where, due mainly to the expansion of large enterprises and/or the growth of public administrations, they became a substantial part of the workforce. The rise in white-collar positions led to new and substantial opportunities for workers as well as for small artisans and farmers. This was the most important respect in which occupational change in the period of organised capitalism differed from that of the industrial revolution. It led to a distinct increase in rates of social mobility and social ascent — an increase which has been established in various studies of long-term changes in social mobility in the late nineteenth and early twentieth centuries.[13] Moreover, the number of managers who ran enterprises but did not necessarily own them increased in this period; they became a substantial part of the social class of businessmen. Since a managerial career did not depend upon capital ownership, as had the careers of most early industrial business leaders, new social opportunities were opened. This occupational change also depended to a large degree on the rise of large corporations and the parallel demise of the family enterprise in big business. True, the rise of the managers barely influenced the overall rates of social mobility since managers remained only a tiny proportion of the workforce as a whole; it had an important impact, however, upon élite mobility, a point which we discussed in Chapter 3 and to which we shall return.

Moreover, social stratification changed in various important respects with clear consequences for social mobility. The social differentials between unskilled workers and the artisan élite tended to become smaller. Various studies, especially those on European countries, have demonstrated that the demarcation line between these two groups was strictly maintained during the industrial revolution and that this rendered it difficult for unskilled workers to advance within the working class. After the industrial revolution proper, the reduction of social differentials of income, autonomy at work, education, unemployment and adjustment to industrial society made social ascent easier, even if they depreciated its value somewhat. Furthermore, the social differentials between workers and lower grades of white-collar employees also tended to become smaller, if only to a slight extent. The advantages which white-collar employees enjoyed with regard to income, autonomy at work and preferential treatment by the employer became less distinct. This, too, led to workers gaining access to such positions more easily and, again, the process was accompanied by a certain devaluation of upward mobility.[14] Furthermore, the period of organised capitalism coincided in a number of European countries and in North America with the rise of the professions — physicians, lawyers, pharmacists, chemists, engineers, teachers and civil servants. Professionalisation created a new stratum which was prestigious, highly qualified and generally well-to-do, and this gave rise to new, if highly formalised, opportunities for social ascent, although the effect on overall rates of social mobility was still very limited in this period. Finally, the emergence of the large enterprise led to a rise in the social status of the business élite. In general, the business élite of the industrial revolution had headed only medium-sized enterprises, those with at most a few thousand employees. Its members did not belong to their country's upper class in terms of wealth, prestige or social contacts. In politics it was not generally powerful, except for its influence in industrial cities and regions. The business élite in the period of organised capitalism was much more powerful economically, with enterprise workforces reaching tens of thousands. It rose to become part of the upper class and played an important role in political decision-making processes on a national level. Hence, in the period of organised capitalism it was a much greater step to rise to the ranks of the business élite than it had been during the industrial revolution. All these changes in social stratification cannot be seen simply as direct consequences of the crucial developments which took place during the period under discussion. They were, however, influenced by these developments or at any rate coincided with them.

A further, less obvious factor leading to increased overall social mobility was the strengthening of the meritocracy. Admittedly, we do not know a great deal about this aspect of the history of social mobility, an aspect which is concerned with the development of social values and mentalities. It seems clear, however, that the emergence of new social groups such as white-collar workers, civil servants, the professions and managers led to a rising number of occupations where access depended less on direct inheritance and ownership and more on qualification and competition, although at the same time other, if less effective, ways of placing family members were found. It might well be that the more meritocratic occupations also had a wider impact on society and led to a change in the accessibility of the more traditional spheres. Family enterprises were forced to change their methods of training presumptive heirs under the pressure of the more successful managerial economy; this may also have been partly true for small business and for agriculture.

The rise of various social services should also be considered as a factor increasing the chances of social mobility and social ascent. For an unprecedented number of people, the spread of literacy which, at least in some European countries and in North America was only completed during this period, opened up a range of jobs that required elementary education. This was true especially of routine white-collar work, which was becoming increasingly important. The development of inner urban transportation networks in the early twentieth century widened the labour market and increased occupational opportunities for those commuters who were now able to rely on transport and were no longer restricted to workplaces within walking distance. The gradual, if incomplete, rise of the welfare state in Europe helped in coping with critical life situations and made it easier to take advantage of educational and occupational opportunities.

True, there were also powerful factors which impeded social mobility during the period of organised capitalism. The demand for occupational chances increased, or at least remained high, mainly because its early stages coincided in many parts of Europe with the later stages of the demographic transition, that is, rates of population growth were still high and there was a large demand for jobs for young people. Moreover, geographical mobility remained high during the early part of this era, at least in some countries. It still consisted to a substantial degree of enforced restlessness and hence impeded rather than improved the use of occupational chances. Compared to the industrial revolution, however, it seems that the factors which impeded overall social mobility did not noticeably strengthen. Hence one can conclude that, on balance, the period of organised capitalism in general offered more occupational chances than had the period of industrial revolution.

Changes in the class distribution of occupational chances are not so clear during this period. Some slight changes should be noted, however. Firstly, at least two reasons led to the unequal access to capital becoming somewhat less significant for occupational mobility and social ascent. On the one hand, small-scale business became less dominating as a channel of social ascent to the lower-middle class and was in this respect partly replaced by the positions of white-collar workers and lower civil servants. This does not necessarily mean that social ascent became easier; however, access to capital lost its crucial role. On the other hand, as mentioned above, some business élite careers also became disconnected from capital ownership, since access to capital was not a direct precondition of access to managerial positions. Once again, different barriers depending on other factors replaced the capital barrier, often leading to new forms of unequal distribution.[15]

Secondly, social differentials in family size seem to have changed. Once again, for lack of extensive research, our information on this topic is far from clear. It seems, however, that the significant differentials in family size of the industrial revolution were reduced in the late nineteenth century owing to a more equal distribution of life expectancy (itself due to a general improvement in sanitary conditions, medical treatment and nutrition) and also to the expansion of middle-class values of family and natality. Hence, the differences in family size between classes seem not to have been so great as in the preceding period. Upper- and middle-class families may have become comparatively smaller. Thus the pressure exerted by the transmission of positions within upper- and middle-class families became relatively less strong; opportunities of social ascent improved somewhat.[16]

Thirdly, at least after the First World War, the strong social differentials in the rate and type of geographical mobility seem to have been reduced with the overall increase in rootedness. Hence the social cleavage between those who were forced to migrate and people who chose to better themselves by migration became less distinct, especially among wage earners.[17]

Fourthly, the class inequality of critical life situations was gradually and slightly reduced by the rise in the standard of living and in life expectancy, the declining size of the family, improvements in housing, increasing job security, the development — especially in Europe — of public social insurance systems covering health, disability and unemployment, and by the gradual reduction of social differentials among wage earners. Hence the chances of planning vocational training and occupational careers over longer time spans became somewhat less unequal. However, these developments should not be overestimated since we do not yet know enough about their intensity and since the effects on the distribution of occupational chances were probably small.

In various aspects, government activity was ambiguous during the era of organised capitalism. On the one hand, this was a period of transition to a decision-making process in which the bureaucracy, big business and organised labour were the most influential factors. It was especially with the rise of the latter as a major political force that equality of opportunities became increasingly a political issue, either because of direct pressure from labour, or through anticipation of such pressure. On the other hand, the process by which equality of opportunities became a goal of government policy was not homogeneous and gradual, but was marked by spurts of progress and reversal and by the emergence of striking differences between countries. Contrasting political systems, with fascism versus liberal democracy as the predominant Atlantic conflict, led to differing evaluations of equality of opportunities as a goal of government policy and, even more so, to great differences in the actual effects of government intervention.

To sum up: the era of organised capitalism was a period of rising overall opportunities owing to far-reaching alterations in occupational structure and social stratification, the more competitive access to occupations and, in the later part of the era, the increase in geographical immobility and decrease in job demand that followed the demographic transition. Changes in the distribution of occupational chances between classes are much less clear. Rising opportunities may have been somewhat less unequally distributed, partly because capital became rather less influential as a factor affecting social mobility, partly because social differentials of family size, geographical mobility and the material and mental aspects of critical life situations diminished somewhat. It must be pointed out, however, that in the era of organised capitalism, very forceful short-term events such as the two World Wars, the Great Depression and politically enforced mass migrations had a marked impact on social mobility and in many respects overshadowed those long-term changes in which we are primarily interested.

Post-Industrial Society

Like the era of organised capitalism, the post-industrial society is also regarded here as a set of developments rather than as a specific period of time. However, in most European countries and in North America it coincides largely with the postwar period. Once again, the term has many meanings and there is little agreement among social scientists about this era.[18] Recent debates on the long-term changes in modern societies have focused upon three main tendencies which most social scientists would regard as important, even if they prefer to label them with different terms. All these are developments which have had a significant effect on the development of social mobility. Firstly, the service sector is considered to be the most dynamic sector in modern Atlantic societies. True, the result of this dynamism has not been the same all over Europe and the United States. In some countries the service sector has remained somewhat smaller than the industrial sector; in others, by far the greater part of the working population is employed in services. Moreover, not all branches of the service sector have expanded; domestic services have even declined. Social and economic services were the core of the dynamic expansion.[19] In general, however, there is no doubt that post-industrial society differs clearly from its predecessors in this respect. Secondly, the expansion of a highly-qualified group in the working population, the professions, is regarded as a characteristic of modern Atlantic societies. To be sure, the rise of highly-qualified professions had already started in many countries in the late nineteenth or early twentieth centuries, at least in education. However, the expansion has been much more rapid in the postwar period and has given rise to a substantial proportion of highly qualified professionals in the working population, whereas they formerly represented only a small percentage. Some social scientists even believe that this change in the work-force has brought with it a change in the power structure and has made the professions the new ruling class. Thirdly, the postwar period is characterised by the definite establishment of a new power structure: the emergence of a tripartite system in which big business, the bureaucrats and organised labour are the most influential groups. The integration of organised labour, in particular, has made the power structure of modern Atlantic societies different from that of previous periods. The tripartite system is not completely new; but it remained highly unstable, especially in Europe in the period between the wars, above all because of the threat of fascism.

These basic tendencies of the era have all influenced social mobility. Again, these consequences will be shown, first for the overall development of social mobility and thereafter for the social distribution of chances.

As in previous periods, the most obvious factor influencing the overall development of social mobility is occupational change. The two basic characteristics of post-industrial society, the rise of the professions and the dynamics of the service sector, have brought about a situation that is completely different from that of previous periods. Owing to their rapid expansion, the professions made up a substantial proportion of the work-force and the growth of this sector had an impact on the overall rates of social mobility. Since access to the professions is highly formalised, the increase in rates of social mobility has been largely restricted to mobility between generations, whereas in the period of organised capitalism career mobility probably also accounted for at least part of the rise in social mobility. Unfortunately, since there is very little quantitative research on the expansion of the professions, we have no exact information on the growth of this occupational group except in a few countries. None the less, this is the most important and most widely-mentioned factor of the increase in mobility rates that has taken place in postwar Europe, and became ever more true as the white-collar sector continued to expand. Hence the new occupational chances represented by the rise of the professions were added to the factors which had enlarged occupational chances during the period of organised capitalism. Furthermore, the dynamics of the service sector enhanced occupational chances and stimulated occupational mobility from the agricultural as well as from the industrial sector. For Europe as a whole, it has been estimated that during the period from 1960 to 1980 the service sector rose from 37 per cent to 50 per cent, although this varied slightly from country to country.[20] In the United States, in the same period, it rose from 56 per cent to 66 per cent. What is important is the speed at which employment sectors changed, which was much more rapid in the post-war period than at any previous time. This is true not only of the above mentioned rates of shrinkage in the agricultural sector, which after all had already declined and made little impact on overall rates of social mobility; it was true also of the service sector, which often expanded much more quickly than its counterpart, the industrial sector, had done in previous periods. Hence, rapid sectoral change of employment is to be considered as a second major reason why rates of occupational mobility are particularly high in post-industrial society.

A further factor leading to high rates of social mobility in post-industrial society is the change in social stratification. Once again, the rise of the professions is the most important new development. Since it has led to the substantial growth of a prestigious, well-paid, highly-qualified stratum, chances of upward social mobility have increased. No doubt the expansion of the professions has led also to a certain social depreciation of this group but, on the whole, the chances of social ascent have been enlarged. This is also the argument which is most widely used to explain the historical increase in upward social mobility revealed by recent surveys.[21] Its effect was the greater as factors which reinforced upward social mobility during the era of organised capitalism did not at the same time disappear: as we have seen, the number of white-collar employees continued to expand and the chances of upward social mobility for workers remained high.

A third, less obvious factor influencing social mobility was the rise of the welfare state, whose institutions were already starting to emerge in the prewar and interwar periods. It was not until after 1945, however, that its actual payments and non-monetary services became really effective in most European countries and in the United States. Payment in case of sickness and/or unemployment, scholarships for students and old age pensions increased to such an extent that many critical life situations which previously had inhibited the use of educational and occupational chances, became less significant. Hence indirectly and to an extent which is still not fully clear the rise of the welfare state led to increased rates of occupational mobility.[22]

With one possible exception, which will be discussed below, these factors reinforcing occupational and social mobility were not counterbalanced by developments which worked in the opposite direction. There has been a long-term decline in population growth and in the demand for jobs from the young, although in the short term contrary developments overshadow this long-term trend. Meritocratic values may have gained an even stronger hold than in the period of organised capitalism, though we have no clear information on this point. Government intervention, if weak in its positive influence on social mobility, at least has not impeded it. All in all, the overall development of social mobility seems to have led to higher rates than in earlier periods.

Changes in the class distribution of mobility chances are less spectacular. Nevertheless, various factors in favour of a less unequal distribution have emerged in this era. First of all, the rise of the professions as a substantial group in the work force is again important. The expansion has been so rapid that recruitment to the professions has had to be opened to other social classes. Members of the lower-middle and even the working classes clearly had better chances of entering this stratum and rising in the social hierarchy. This does not mean that members of the middle class were forced to step back; their chances seem to have improved as well. The higher ranks of society became more open for all.[23]

Moreover, the definite establishment of the welfare state not only helped to improve the use of occupational and educational opportunities, but also reduced inequalities in coping with critical life situations. The calculability of life increased for the average citizen. Individual planning of the life course, a major precondition of better educational opportunities, was facilitated or even initiated by the welfare bureaucracies. Unequal insecurity in the individual life situation became less characteristic. Hence a major factor influencing inequality of chances became of less importance.[24]

Finally, with the firm establishment of the tripartite power system, equality of opportunities became a central issue in politics. In spite of variations in specific goals, a broad consensus among Labour, Liberal and Conservative politicians emerged in this respect in postwar Europe. This issue became increasingly important in such political areas as education, the family and appointments to the public administration. To be sure, equality of opportunity as a political goal was not totally new; in many respects it had been important in the interwar period. However, it did not emerge in its present significance until after the Second World War. This does not necessarily mean that the political goal of equality of opportunity effectively changed the distribution of chances since it is difficult to ascertain the workings of such policies and since they can only take effect in the long run. Nevertheless, a historical analysis of social mobility must take this factor into consideration.[25]

At least one further factor influencing the distribution of chances may have worked partly in the opposite direction. From scattered and still very inconsistent pieces of information, we have the impression that social differentials of family size changed. An A-shaped pattern in which families decreased with higher standing in the social hierarchy seems to have been replaced by an X-shaped pattern in which it was the upper and working classes who had relatively large families while the lower-middle classes had a restricted number of children.[26] Under conditions of low population growth, the latter pattern was favourable to social ascent into the lower-middle class, since those who aspired to that level met relatively few competitors from its ranks. It was unfavourable to social ascent into the upper-middle classes, since the ambitious were confronted by a substantial number of competitors from that class. However, this must still be regarded as speculation, since exact information on long-term changes in social differentials of family size is scarce.

To sum up: in this chapter we have tried to present a series of arguments and hypotheses for empirical research rather than a historical theory of social mobility. These arguments are examined in the context of three historical eras which are seen as changes in long-term developments rather than as clear-cut periods of time. The chapter attempts to draw conclusions from the available evidence rather than to present a strictly quantitative analysis of the long-term trend of social mobility on which, in any case, we do not have precise data for the period before the First World War. We have tried to show how the factors of social mobility — occupational change, alterations in the economic structure and in social stratification, demographic developments, changes in the family, alterations in ways of coping with individual life crises, mass migration, mental attitudes, government intervention — had an impact on the overall development as well as on the distribution of mobility chances. It is argued that the idea of a steady and continuous increase in social mobility rates from the industrial revolution on, as well as the converse idea of a sudden rupture of occupational structure during that period, accompanied by extremely high rates of social mobility, does not really square with what we know about factors and rates of social mobility. It seems more plausible that the increase in overall social mobility during the industrial revolution was small, or even that there was an actual decline in the rates, depending upon whether the reinforcing or impeding factors became stronger in a particular country and that the distribution of mobility chances did not become less unequal. We can conclude from what we know about factors of social mobility that only thereafter, in the era of organised capitalism, did strong forces favouring an increase in overall social mobility come into effect. Even then, the factors which tended to equalise the social distribution of opportunities had only a modest effect which was largely counterbalanced by reverse developments. In the post-industrial society, the tendency for rates of social mobility to rise has become even stronger, owing to new developments in occupational and social change. Factors which equalised the distribution of mobility chances, if ambiguous, did become more influential, though the actual effects are still unclear. In one sentence: the continuous rise in social mobility rates started after rather than during the industrial revolution; the trend towards greater chances for social ascent was not accompanied by a powerful momentum for redistribution of occupational and social opportunities. It should be stressed that these are arguments drawn from a review of the history of the *factors* of social mobility; much more research needs to be done, before we shall know exactly *how* these factors worked and what effects they had in Europe and the United States.

Conclusion

This book is not a comprehensive history of social mobility. Rather, it deals primarily with the rates and structures of long-term change and the comparison between Atlantic societies; mainly for lack of available research it does not look at the impact of major short-term events such as wars, economic crises, revolutions and counter-revolutions. It is concerned primarily with mobility between social classes. Again for lack of research, it has not been possible to deal as intensively as the author would have wished with the chances of women, who are included only in the chapter on education, and with the chances of minority groups and migrants; neither does it explore the change in the ideas of the average individual on social ascent and descent, since this seems to be an extremely difficult area. Moreover, the book is not to be seen as a handbook of our historical knowledge of social mobility over the last 100 years, since it centres upon specific problems.

In the Introduction, we asked four closely interrelated questions: firstly, whether the industrial revolution does in fact, as many social scientists believe, play a crucial role in the history of social mobility as a watershed from limited pre-industrial rates to unprecedented modern rates of upwards and downwards social mobility, or whether the history of social mobility has other landmarks. Secondly, we asked whether the comparison of social mobility in America and Europe during the nineteenth and twentieth centuries does in fact support the influential de Tocquevillian tradition of regarding the United States as the country which provides her average citizen with much more promising chances of social mobility than do the West European countries, or whether industrialisation and modernisation led to the same level of social mobility in America and Europe and dissipated the pre-industrial differences which de Tocqueville had observed. Thirdly, we asked whether a thorough comparative investigation of social mobility in Germany corroborates our view of a society which was more traditional, more immobile and more rigidly stratified than other West European countries and/or America and which, as a half-modernised contradictory society, was therefore more receptive to fascist influences, or whether, at least as far as social mobility is concerned, she followed the normal and unspectacular process of industrialisation. Finally, we asked what, after twenty years of intensive historical research on social mobility, can be considered as the major factors of historical change and what, apart from economic development, are the primary concerns for historians in this field. All these questions are obviously linked to one central topic and focus on the problem as to whether the history of social mobility can, in the end, be considered as a mere appendix to the history of economic development and changing employment, whether it takes its own course as a consequence of the additional impact of change in the family, the population, mental attitudes, the basic economic structure and government policies. While there are no straightforward or final answers to these somewhat simplified questions, there are some conclusions which might prove useful for the debate on social mobility, a debate which will very probably continue even after having lasted among social scientists and the wider public for 150 years.

The industrial revolution seems to have been much less of a watershed in the history of social mobility than has usually been considered. To be sure, research on the long-term changes in social mobility during the nineteenth century is neither abundant nor easy to interpret. As far as we know, neither direct nor circumstantial evidence provides definite proof that it was the industrial revolution that was the crucial period. Direct evidence of a striking change in social mobility is more limited than one might suppose. A distinctive increase in rates of social mobility is shown only in a few studies of rural areas which industrialised or developed under the indirect impact of industrialisation. In contrast, cities which have been investigated for the local industrialisation experience did not show any long-term rise of social mobility rates. Industrial cities do not exhibit more social mobility during the nineteenth century than non-industrialised cities. Hence a few studies in direct recent research lead us to expect slight but definite increases in social mobility in rural areas and no clear changes in industrialising cities. Indirect evidence reinforces this impression. The development of major factors of social mobility during the industrial revolution might have led to stagnation or decline rather than to an increase in social mobility. At least at national level, occupational change during the industrial revolution was not more and was often less dramatic than during the twentieth century. The rapid growth of population enlarged the demand for jobs rather than the supply of chances. Migration was often enforced and led to volatility and unsteadiness rather than to an improvement in the informations of the labour market and to more rational choices between jobs. Even in the most newly developed sections of the societies, that is, among businessmen and skilled workers, the prevailing mentality was orientated towards the inheritance of jobs rather than towards competition. Chances of social mobility were not only more unequally distributed than is often believed of the period 'open to all talents'; neither did they increase very rapidly, at least if observed from the wider perspective of the last two centuries.

This impression is corroborated by research on what could be called the 'other end' of the industrial revolution, that is, the transition to later stages of economic development during which rates of social mobility are expected to level off or even to decline. To be sure, massive evidence exists for such a change. Important studies have demonstrated a decline of social mobility rates during the first half of this century. However, there is a strong recent consensus among social scientists that this change is connected with events such as the Depression or the World Wars rather than with the end of the industrialisation process. Indirect evidence from the development of the major factors of social mobility also does not support the interpretation of a fall in social mobility rates after the industrial revolution. Occupational change and, especially, the increase in white-collar employees, the end of the demographic transition and the slowing down in the intense demand for jobs from large birth cohorts, business changes and the rise of business careers no longer linked to the ownership of capital, the decline of the role of the family and the rise of competitive mentalities led to an increase rather than to a fall in rates of social mobility and of social ascent. It is the postwar period rather than the industrial revolution that has emerged as the decisive watershed for social mobility. Studies of the most important Atlantic countries show that there is an unquestionable increase in the rates of social mobility following the Second World War. It is still too early to assess whether this will prove to have been the most marked period of change in the last two centuries. Very long-term studies of social mobility during more than one century are still rare. But there is no doubt that the postwar period has been an era of dramatic changes in social mobility. What is still unclear are the reasons. Superficially, the main momentum came from changes in the labour force, but whether what lay behind these changes was merely the economic development of other factors such as migration, change of population structure, modernisation of attitudes and/or government policies is still under debate.

Our second question was concerned with whether American society has proved to be more promising for the chances of the average citizen. Two contrasting views have been put forward by social scientists. One follows in the tradition of Alexis de Tocqueville who believed, in the 1830s, that American society offered more chances of social ascent than the European societies. The other and more recent view was first put forward by Seymour M. Lipset and Reinhard Bendix, who made the assessment that all societies have similar rates of social mobility as soon as they reach a certain level of industrialisation. Originally the two views were not opposed to each other, since de Tocqueville was dealing with a pre-industrial society whereas Lipset and Bendix referred only to industrial societies. In fact, however, the two views as they were expounded after the Second World War were clearly opposed.

In certain respects American society was more promising than her European counterparts. Firstly, the available studies on pre-1914 cities in America and Europe show that unskilled workers were more successful in America than in Europe and more often became white-collar employees or independent shopkeepers and artisans than they would have done in Europe. For this lowest strata of industrialising societies de Tocqueville was right; whether this difference has endured until the present and whether, therefore, the argument by Lipset and Bendix has to be substantially modified is not yet clear, since postwar studies have not yet compared career mobility internationally. Secondly, the study of educational opportunities in higher learning demonstrates that from the late nineteenth century on many more Americans attended universities than did Europeans. The lead given by America in educational opportunities has remained constant during the twentieth century up to the present. This is true not only for the overall student ratio, but also for the access to universities for women and for the lower classes. No doubt the standards of American universities in the late nineteenth and early twentieth centuries was often lower than in the European universities. In the context of this book, however, what counts are the mobility chances opened up by education rather than the actual quality of that education. To be sure, we do not yet have a comparative investigation of the social origins of the professions. It might well be that the more open access to American higher learning led to a more open access to the higher white-collar strata in America. This aspect of social mobility is the more important since higher education during the twentieth century became more and more the major switchboard of mobility chances in America as well as in Europe. Finally there are some indications that the American business élite was more open to social ascent during the nineteenth century than the European one. We cannot ignore the fact (though it may need qualifying) that the sons of farmers, workers and migrants made a successful business career more often in America than in Europe. It might be surprising that the statistical evidence for a massive American lead in the numbers of self-made men is not clear-cut; but one should not forget that all our conclusions are based on studies which were never intended to be comparative. Thus only very spectacular differences can be traced.

However it does seem that America and Europe were much more similar than social scientists often believe. More important perhaps than the better career chances available to American unskilled workers is the lack of other clear differences between European and American cities in the nineteenth century. Neither overall rates of mobility between fathers and sons show any distinct lead in America or any particular backwardness in Europe. Even among skilled workers there are no noticeable differences. The striking differences are those between American and European *cities*, rather than between the two shores of the Atlantic

Ocean. De Tocqueville's assessment, which had been made for the whole of American society and not just for the unskilled sector, has to be strongly modified by the comparison of nineteenth-century 'modern' (industrial) and traditional cities. This is the more important as it was during the nineteenth century that America was more promising than Europe. After almost thirty years of controversy among sociologists, nobody would now expect to find rates of upward mobility in twentieth-century America to be greatly superior to those in the industrial societies of Europe. Moreover, in the long-term view, America and Europe appear to have converged in those aspects of social mobility in which the American society was previously more promising than its European counterparts. The social origins of the business élites, which are symbols rather than indicators of the social mobility of the average citizen, were more similar in the post-1945 era than during the nineteenth century. The gap in educational opportunities has persisted, but it has become less great in the recent past than it was at the beginning of the present century. At the beginning of the 1980s the magnitude of educational opportunities, that is, enrolments related to age cohorts, in higher education was only twenty years behind America compared to a forty-year gap around 1910. Access to higher learning for West European women differed only by some percentage points from the United States; indeed, in such European societies as France or Scandinavia it was the same. The gap had been much larger in the interwar period. The social distribution of educational opportunities changed in Europe and approached the American pattern. In all these respects the structures support the de Tocquevillian view; the tendencies corroborate those of Lipset and Bendix.

Is there a specifically German pattern of social mobility? Was Germany as backward in this respect as she was in the establishment of a stable democracy, supported by the élites and the electorate? The answer is not a simple yes or no. In two important respects we could not find clear and reliable evidence for a German way that differed from America as well as from Western Europe. This is true especially for social mobility in nineteenth-century cities. There is no proof yet that upward social mobility was definitely less frequent and social descent definitely more likely in German societies as compared to American and other West European communities. To be sure, in certain ways the chances of social mobility were better not only in the United States but also in the Netherlands and Sweden. But for there to have been a distinctively German pattern there would need to have been clearly superior chances in France and England also, and this we cannot establish at this stage. This does not mean that a 'German way' can be definitely ruled out, although the number of local studies on European communities are by no means sufficient for any conclusive statement and the handful of relevant studies that are available do not reveal any specifically German pattern. One also has to take into account that Germany was not behind in the major factors affecting overall social mobility such as the demographic transition, the structure of the labour force and of enterprises, migration and urbanisation. Another (though less strong) qualification of the German pattern was in the educational opportunities available. The social distribution of educational opportunities in secondary and higher learning does not appear to have been more unequal in nineteenth-century Germany than in nineteenth-century France or England. The magnitude of opportunities in higher learning, that is, enrolments per age cohorts, was also not lower at German universities than elsewhere in Europe. There seem to be common European patterns throughout. Nevertheless, Germany does appear to differ in certain important aspects. What Fritz Ringer referred to as segmentations, that is, differences between streams of secondary and higher education in social access, social prestige and mobility chances, were greater in Germany than in France, England or America and made German education more rigidly stratified. Access for women to universities came later in Germany than in America and Western Europe, especially in Prussian universities. Educational opportunities for women in Germany generally remained below European standards until the postwar period. Finally, after displaying a normal pattern of development of educational opportunities up to the end of the First World War and during the Weimar Republic, student ratios in Germany dropped below their European counterparts during the Nazi period, recovering only slowly thereafter. No doubt German education was not simply backward; it contains many modern and sometimes even pioneering elements. However such backwardness as it did evince should not be overlooked.

A distinctively German pattern can also be traced in the career of the business élites. The strong traditional pre-capitalist and pre- and anti-industrial values among German landed aristocrats, professionals, academics and small farmers led to a rarity of these sectors as family backgrounds in the nineteenth-century German business élite in comparison with England, France and the United States. On the other hand, the strong bureaucratic traditions led to a relatively large number of German businessmen stemming from families of higher civil servants. Once again, common Atlantic patterns in the social origins of the business élite, such as the predominance of the sons of businessmen and the marginality of the sons of workers, farmers and lower-white-collar employees are important and should not be omitted. But certain 'German' elements existed even though they did not have a great major impact on the performance of German businessmen or on their social ascent.

On the whole, social mobility has both modern and traditional elements in Germany. It is as modern as anywhere else in Western Europe and America wherever economic development, the history of employment, demography and migration have the strongest impact on social mobility. This is true for the chances of most average citizens. Social mobility in Germany has been more traditional in those societies where politics and upper-class values and mentalities counted. This is true for certain traditional elements in higher education and for certain aspects of the social origins of the business élite. If more studies on the traditional elements of the upper classes become available, meaningful comparison will become a possibility.

What, then, were the predominating influences on social mobility during the period under discussion? General economic development and changes in the labour force played a vital role in establishing the occupational structure of the developing societies of Western Europe and the United States. Of lesser importance, perhaps, but also not to be left out are such factors as social stratification, the family, attitudes, migration, demography and government policies.

But is this the whole story? Is the historian of social mobility rather the historian of occupations and employment? The first, rather paradoxical answer is that this is more true than is often believed. The impact of employment structures and occupations on social mobility has been often underestimated by historians, more perhaps, than by other social scientists. For example, the accepted view that American society was both more mobile and more open to social ascent appears to be based on the assumption that this was the result of American attitudes and orientation towards striving for upward mobility as well as a matter of the more traditional European commitment to the occupation or class of one's social origin. What was under-estimated here was the fact that the structure of the American labour force was more favourable for social ascent and, hence, that the better chances of unskilled workers in nineteenth-century American cities can be explained more easily by reference to employment structures than to attitudes. I have tried to deal with this problem more thoroughly in a current project on the employment structure in Europe and America during the twentieth century. My first conclusions may be found in Kaelble, 'Prometheus'.

Speaking more generally, we have tried to show that national differences of social mobility can be and often are based on different paths of economic development and employment structures rather than on attitudes and political developed. With this taken for granted, we have then tried to demonstrate that the historian of social mobility does not of necessity end as a historian of occupations and employment.

In Chapter 4 we have tried to show that other factors (demographic change, changes in the basic structure of capitalistic enterprises, alteration in migration, change in the role of the family and in individual life crises, the rise of the competitive mentality and the change in government policies towards greater egalitarianism) were also important. But above all we have sought to establish that these factors were important because of the way they have *changed* during the last two hundred years and have therefore led to *changes* in social mobility in specific societies in Europe and America. Thus our argument is linked to specific periods and areas rather than to social mobility in general. To be sure, the weight of each of these factors is not susceptible to checking by the historian with the advanced quantitative methods we know from sociological studies. For lack of appropriate data the historian can refer only in a less strict way to empirical findings. From all that we know so far, however, we can say that the history of social mobility is as much a history of the family, of the structures of enterprises, of migration, of individual life crises, of the rise of the welfare state and of government policies, as it is a history of occupations and the labour force.

Notes

Notes to the Introduction

1. Cf. Ringer, *Education and Society*; Kocka et. al., *Familie und soziale Plazierung*; Kocka, 'Family and Class Formation'; R. Erikson, J. Goldthorpe and L. Portocarero, 'Intergenerational Class Mobility and the Convergence Thesis', *British Journal of Sociology*, vol. 34 (1983).
2. I should mention, however, that my own interest in the comparative history of social mobility started when I did a primary local study on the nineteenth century business élite in Berlin. See H. Kaelble, *Berliner Unternehmer während der frühen Industrialisierung* (de Gruyter, Berlin, 1972).
3. I am grateful for permission to publish revised versions of my 'Social Mobility in America and Europe. A Comparison of 19th-century Cities', in *Urban History Yearbook 1981*; 'Educational Opportunities and Government Policies in Europe in the Period of Industrialization' in P. Flora and A. Heidenheimer (eds.), *The Development of the Welfare States in Europe* (Transaction Books, New Brunswick, 1981); 'Long–term Changes in the Recruitment of the Business Elite: Germany Compared to the US, Britain, and France since the Industrial Revolution', *Journal of Social History*, vol. 13 (1979/80); for my studies of Germany, cf. 'Social Mobility in Germany 1900-1960', *Journal of Modern History*, vol. 50, with *Soziale Mobilität und Chancengleichheit*. The longer German version includes material not found in the English version: three detailed chapters on Germany and a short comparison of Germany with France. The present English version contains the original English articles in a greatly revised form. Only the second part of Chapter 2 was translated from German into English. Moreover, the Introduction, the second part of Chapter 1, and the Conclusion were written after the publication of the German version. Several other recent publications have been also integrated into the English version.

Notes to Chapter 1

1. A. de Tocqueville, *Democracy in America* (1840; repr. Knopf, New York, 1945), II, pp. 180f.
2. Thernstrom, *The Other Bostonians*, pp. 259ff.; Sewell, 'Social Mobility'; Crew, 'Definitions of Modernity', pp. 66f.; idem, *Town in the Ruhr*.
3. S. M. Lipset and R. Bendix, *Social Mobility in Industrial Society* (Univ. of Cal. Press, Berkeley, 1967), p. 13.
4. P. M. Blau and O. D. Duncan, *The American Occupational Structure* (John Wiley & Sons, New York, 1967); R. M. Hauser et al., 'Structural Changes in Occupational Mobility among Men in the United States', *American Sociological Review*, vol. 40 (1975); A. Darbel, 'L'évolution récente de la mobilité

sociale', in *Économie et statistique*, vol. 71 (1975), pp. 18ff.; G. Carlsson, *Social Mobility and Class Structure* (Gleerup, Lund, 1958), pp. 94ff.; J. H. Goldthorpe, C. Llewellyn, C. Payne, *Social Mobility and Class Structure in Modern Britain* (Clarendon Press, Oxford, 1980), pp. 68ff.; J. J. M. van Tulder, *De beroepsmobiliteit in Nederland van 1919 tot 1954* (Stenfert Kroese, Leiden, 1962), pp. 94ff.; G. Kleining, 'Struktur– und Berufsmobilität in der Bundesrepublik Deutschland', *Kölner Zeitschrift für Soziologie*, vol. 23 (1971); A. Heath, *Social Mobility* (Fontana, London, 1981), Chap. 3; K. R. Allerbeck and H. R. Stock, 'Soziale Mobilität in Deutschland 1833–1970', *Kölner Zeitschrift für Soziologie und Sozialpsychologie*. vol. 32 (1980), pp. 93ff.; Erikson, Goldthorpe and Portocarero, 'Intergenerational Class Mobility'.

5. For the comparison of access to the business élite and to higher education, see Chapters 2 and 3.

6. An important effort to overcome the shortcomings of this definition of social classes was made by Kocka and the other members of the Bielefeld family history group. See J. Kocka, 'The Study of Social Mobility and the Formation of the Working Class in the Nineteenth Century', *Le mouvement social*, vol 111 (1980); Kocka et al., *Familie und soziale Plazierung*.

7. Comparisons that include mothers and daughters, or more than two generations, are not yet possible owing to the almost total lack of any research. Ruth Federspiel's work (in progress) on twentieth-century Berlin is a rare example of an historical study of the social mobility of women.

8. It is not fully clear what sort of downward mobility, that is, mobility between which social classes, made the difference, since the social class schemes used in studies of American cities are much too wide. From some European research we know that mobility between small independent masters and shopkeepers and the working class was by far the most important part of downward mobility. Undoubtedly the 'downward' character of this mobility is often ambiguous and unclear. Hence one has to be careful with the argument that there is a clear difference between America and Europe in this respect.

9. Career mobility downward into the working class was 9 per cent on the average in American as well as in European cities (based on Table 4, calculated from the averages for each city).

10. However, unskilled workers did not become skilled any more often in America than in Europe. It is interesting that in spite of the peculiar continuity or even reactivation of artisan guilds in nineteenth-century central Europe, skilled work was not more open for unskilled workers in the USA. The proportion of unskilled workers who became skilled was 7 per cent in Bochum (Germany) and 11 per cent in Graz (Austria), against 7 per cent in Boston, 4 per cent in Atlanta, 9 per cent in New Orleans, 11 per cent in Newburyport, 11 per cent in Poughkeepsie and 12 per cent in Warren (for sources, see note to Table 1.3). American skilled workers seem to have used other techniques to keep the unskilled out of their trade.

11. Moreover, it is unclear what a detailed comparison of upward career mobility would tell us — a comparison which showed between which exact occupational groups upward mobility took place. If mobility from the working class into the class of small masters and shopkeepers makes the difference between America and Europe, the 'upward' character of mobility would often be ambiguous and the argument of superior American rates even more unconvincing. Available studies usually do not allow us to check this aspect.

12. The following remarks as well as table 1.5 compare the USA with *industrial-*

ising Western Europe since the comparative discussion of the findings of social mobility was based upon cities in *industrialising* West European countries, too. No doubt the definition of 'industrialising West Europe' in table 1.5 by countries rather than by regions is not very satisfactory. However, statistical information for a regional approach does not yet exist. Calculations which include all West European countries show basically the same difference between Europe and America though to a lesser degree. Only in the twentieth century when industrialisation became more widespread in Europe, was the peculiar course of European occupational development statistically clear for the whole of West Europe. (Cf. P. Bairoch and J. M. Limbor, 'Changes in the Industrial Distribution of the World Labour Force by Region, 1880–1960', *International Labour Review*, vol. 98 (1968), pp. 326f; H. Kaelble, 'Was Prometheus Most Unbound in Europe? Labour Force in Europe during the Late 19th and 20th Centuries', *Journal of European Economic History*, vol. 14 (1985); J. Singelmann, *From Agriculture to Services. The Transformation of Industrial Employment* (Sage, London, 1978) pp. 109ff.

13. It would take too much space to print the data for all West European countries. Behind the overall numbers substantial variations exist. Some European countries come close to the American structure. However, one should take into account that the high proportion of the active population in commerce or transportation in some European countries such as Denmark, the Netherlands and Norway reflects a European division of labour. Hence, a single European country cannot be compared to the whole of the USA.

14. Roughly comparable statistical information exists at least for white-collar employees. It seems that at least at the end of the nineteenth century, the proportion of white-collar employees in the total active population was somewhat higher in the USA (1900:12 per cent, 1910: 15 per cent) than in most European countries such as Belgium (1900: 8 per cent, 1910: 9 per cent), France (1911: 12 per cent). Germany (1895: 11 per cent, 1907: 13 per cent), Britain (1891: 6 per cent, 1911: 7 per cent), Italy (1900: 2 per cent). See for the USA and Germany: J. Kocka, *Angestellte zwischen Faschismus und Demokratie* (Vandenhoeck & Ruprecht, Göttingen, 1977), p. 43; for Belgium: Bairoch (ed.) *The Working Population*, p. 149; for France: Toutain, *La population de la France*, Table 66; for Britain: G. Crossick (ed.), *The Lower–Middle Class in Britain 1870–1914* (Croom Helm, London, 1977), p. 19; for Italy: Sylos Labini, *Saggio sulle classe sociali* p. 157. Because of diverging definitions comparable data for the petty bourgeoisie could not be found.

15. It should be stressed that these data are not to be considered as representative for the USA and Europe.

16. For European backwardness in mechanisation, see R. Samuel, 'The Workshop of the World: Steam Power and Hand Technology in Mid-Victorian Britain', *History Workshop*, vol. 3 (1977), pp. 48f.; S. B. Saul (ed.), *Technological Change, the United States and Britain in the Nineteenth Century* (Methuen, London, 1970; H. J. Habakkuk, *American and British Technology in the Nineteenth Century* (Cambridge UP, Cambridge, 1962); A. Maddison, *Phases of Capitalist Development* (Oxford UP, Oxford, 1982), pp. 56f., 102ff.; for the social implications of the rise of modern unskilled work cf. P. N. Stearns, 'The Unskilled and Industrialization. A Transformation of Consciousness', *Archiv für Sozialgeschichte*, vol. 16 (1976); for the comparison of specific industrial branches I. Yellowitz, *Industrialization and the American Labor Movement, 1850–1900* (Kennikat Press, Port Washington, NY, 1977), pp. 27f., 69f., 76ff.; I. Yellowitz, 'Skilled Workers and Mechanization: The Lasters in the 1800s', *Labor History*, vol. 8, (1977); W. H. Schröder, *Ar-*

beitergeschichte und Arbeiterbewegung (Campus Verlag, Frankfurt, 1978); J. Vidalenc, *La société francaise de 1815 à 1848* (2 vols., Ed. M. Rivière, Paris, 1970, 1973).

17. For non-retirement in the USA: H. P. Chudacoff and T. K. Hareven, 'Family Transitions into Old Age', in T. K. Hareven (ed.), *Transitions, Family and the Life Course in Historical Perspective* (Academic Press, New York, 1978); idem, 'From Empty Nest to Family Dissolution: Life Course and Transition into Old Age', *Journal of Family History*, vol. 1 (1979); for retirement in Europe: cf. J. Albers, 'Die Entstehung der westeuropäischen Sozialversicherungssysteme im Kontext von Industrialisierung und Demokratisierung', unpubl. art., (1980), pp. 46f.; P. N. Stearns, *Old Age in European Society* (Croom Helm, London, 1977), pp. 54ff., 142f.; *Statistik des Deutschen Reiches*, vol 103 (Berlin, 1897), pp. 3, 121 (almost 90 per cent of the retired people, being heads of households, lived on their property or on pensions). Age-specific upward and downward mobility: Griffen, *Natives and Newcomers*, pp. 59ff.; Gitelman, *Workingmen of Waltham*, pp. 67, 100f. (also property of the old); Katz, *The People of Hamilton*, pp. 16ff. (also property of the old). For the debate on old-age poverty in the USA: T. K. Hareven, 'The Last Stage of Adulthood and Old Age', in *Daedalus*, vol. 60 (1976); downward mobility and the lower–middle class: Kocka, *Angestellte*, pp. 134ff., 299f.; G. Crossick, 'The Emergence of the Lower Middle Class in Britain: a Discussion', in Crossick (ed.), *The Lower Middle Class*, pp. 30ff.; J. Ehmer, 'Zur Stellung alter Menschen in Haushalt und Familie', in H. Konrad (ed.), *Der alte Mensch in der Geschichte* (Verlag für Gesellschaftskritik, Vienna, 1982).

18. Among the urban studies of intergenerational mobility in America only the study of Indianapolis, being based solely on marriage licence files, shows high rates of downward mobility (cf. Table 1.2).

19. For the more open attitudes of the American middle class towards social ascent cf. S. M. Lipset, *The First New Nation*, (Basic Books, New York, 1963); Kocka, *Angestellte*, p. 308.

20. Cf. Kaelble, 'Social Mobility in Germany', pp. 115ff.; see also Chapters 2 and 3 above.

21. C. Erickson, *Invisible Immigrants* (Weidenfeld & Nicolson, London 1972); M. Walker, *Germany and the Emigration 1816–1885* (Harvard UP, Cambridge, Mass., 1964); G. Moltmann (ed.), *Deutsche Amerikaauswanderung im 19. Jahrhundert* (Metzler, Stuttgart, 1976); H. Runblom and H. Norman (eds.), *From Sweden to America* (University of Minnesota Press, Minneapolis, 1976). See also the comparison of the standard of living in a European city (Birmingham) and an American city (Pittsburgh) in the nineteenth century by P. R. Shergold, *Working Class Life. The 'American Standard' in Comparative Perspective 1899–1913* (University of Pittsburgh Press, Pittsburgh, 1982).

22. See, for the strong contrast between rural Europe and rural 'frontier' America: I. Eriksson and J. Rogers, *Rural Labor and Population Change. Social and Demographic Developments in East-Central Sweden during the 19th Century* (Almqvist & Wiksell, Uppsala, 1978); J. Kocka et. al., *Familie und soziale Plazierung*; M. Curti, *The Making of an American Community. A Case Study of Democracy in a Frontier Community* (Stanford UP, Stanford, 1959); W. von Hippel, 'Industrieller Wandel im Ländlichen Raum', in *Archiv für Sozialgeschichte*, vol. 14 (1979); R. Hubscher, *L'agriculture et la société rurale dans le Pas–de–Calais* (2 vols., Commission départment de monuments historiques du Pas–de–Calais, Arras, 1980), vol. 2, pp. 791–824; J. Söderberg, *Agrar fattigdom i Sydswerige under 1800-talet* (Almqvist & Wiksell, Stockholm, 1978, with an English summary); van Dijk, Visser, Wolst, 'Regional Differences in

Social Mobility Patterns'.

23. W. L. Warner and J. O. Low, *The Social System of the Modern Factory* (Greenwood Press, Westport, 1976), p. 182.

24. For a good brief summary, very much to the point: D. B. Grusky and R. M. Hauser, 'Comparative Social Mobility Revisited: Models of Convergence and Divergence in 16 Countries', *American Sociological Review*, vol. 49 (1984), pp. 19ff.

25. A major project on the documentation of long-term time series of social mobility between generations in nineteenth- and twentieth-century German cities and villages was started recently by a research group; Ruth Federspiel, William H. Hubbard, Jürgen Kocka, Reinhard Schüren, Sylvia Schraut and the author are participating.

26. See Kocka, 'Family and Class Formation'; R. Schüren, 'Familie und soziale Plazierung in einer durch Landwirtschaft, Heimgewerbe und Industrialisierung geprägten Gemeinde am Beispiel des Kirchspiels Borghorst im 19. Jahrhundert', in Kocka et al., 'Familie und soziale Plazierung', pp. 214ff., 226ff.; van Dijk, Visser and Wolst, 'Regional Differences in Social Mobility Patterns'.

27. All rates are calculated from Table 1.3.

28. A similar pattern of stable mobility between generations and rising career mobility can be found in Rotterdam between 1830 and 1880 (Tables 1.2 and 1.4). Though Rotterdam did not become an industrial city proper during that period, it profited as a seaport from the industrialisation of the Ruhr Valley. Industrialisation might have indirectly affected social mobility in this way.

29. See Kocka, 'Family'; K. Ditt, 'Familie und soziale Plazierung in den Bielefelder Unterschichten im 19. Jahrhundert', in Kocka, et. al., *Familie*, pp. 289ff., 302ff. Long-term studies of social mobility exist for three Dutch villages, with interesting conclusions. In all these cases, however, the impact of the industrial revolution was much more indirect and complicated than in Borghorst. So they do not give a clear answer to our specific question. See van Dijk et. al., 'Regional Differences'.

30. See, for low rates of upward social mobility in villages besides rural Borghorst in 1830, mentioned above: Kocka et. al., *Familie*; von Hippel, 'Ländlichen Raum',; Söderberg, *Agrar fattigdom*; van Dijk, Visser, Wolst, 'Regional Differences'; Hubscher, *Agriculture*.

31. G. Kleining, 'Soziale Mobilität in der Bundesrepublik Deutschland', *Kölner Zeitschrift für Soziologie*, vol. 27 (1975), pp. 115 (the explanation), 286 (the rates of upward social mobility. They rose only from the age cohorts of the 1860s on, not from earlier age cohorts).

32. For a more detailed presentation of these studies by Theodor Geiger, Tom Rishoy, Stephen Thernstrom, Guy Pourcher and David Glass, see H. Kaelble, *Historical Research on Social Mobility* (Croom Helm, London, 1981), pp. 22ff.; for the German case, cf. K. U. Mayer, 'Gesellschaftlicher Wandel und soziale Struktur des Lebenslaufs' in G. Matthes (ed.),*Lebenswelt und soziale Probleme* (Campus Verlag, Frankfurt, 1981).

33. See Kaelble, *Social Mobility*, pp. 22ff.

34. See Mayer, 'Lebenslauf', pp.

35. For studies which show no clear change, see Kaelble, *Social Mobility*, pp. 22ff.

36. See Hauser et al., 'Structural Changes'; Kleining, 'Soziale Mobilität'; Erikson, Goldthorpe and Protocarero, 'Intergenerational Class Mobility'; the latter includes references to earlier research.

Notes to Chapter 2

1. Comparative studies of the nineteenth and twentieth centuries: Ringer, *Education and Society*; A. J. Heidenheimer, 'Education and Social Security Entitlements in Europe and America' in P. Flora and A. J. Heidenheimer (eds.), *The Development of the Welfare State* (Transaction Books, New Brunswick, 1981); J. E. Craig, 'Higher Education and Social Mobility in Germany' in K. H. Jarausch (ed.), *The Transformation of Higher Learning 1860–1930* (Klett-Cotta, Stuttgart, 1983); K. H. Jarausch, 'Higher Education and Social Change: Some Comparative Perspectives' in idem, op. cit.; L. O'Boyle, 'A Possible Model for the Study of 19th Century Secondary Education in Europe', *Journal of Social History*, vol. 12 (1978); J. C. Albisetti, 'French Secondary School Reform in German Perspective, 1850–1914' in D. K. Müller, F. K. Ringer and B. Simon (eds.), *The Rise of the Modern Educational System. Structural Change and Social Reproduction, 1820–1920* (1985); P. Flora, 'Die Bildungsentwicklung. Eine vergleichende Analyse' in P. C. Ludz (ed.), *Soziologie und Sozialgeschichte* (Westdeutscher Verlag, Opladen, 1973); J. Kocka, 'Bildung, soziale Schichtung und soziale Mobilität im Deutschen Kaiserreich am Beispiel der gewerblich–technischen Ausbildung' in B. J. Wendt, D. Stegmann and P. C. Witt (eds.), *Industrielle Gesellschaft und politisches System* (Neue Gesellschaft, Bonn, 1978), pp. 297–314; for the postwar period, note 32 (Chap. 2). For an important effort to bring some current projects into relation with each other, see L. Stone (ed.), *The University in Society*, vol. 2 (Princeton UP, Princeton, 1974) and idem, *Schooling and Society* (Johns Hopkins UP, Baltimore, 1976). For a summary of the studies on educational opportunities in Western Europe during the nineteenth and twentieth centuries, see H. Kaelble, *Historical Research on Social Mobility. Western Europe and the USA in the 19th and 20th Centuries* (Croom Helm, London, 1981) pp. 58–80. For the beginning of a comparative discussion on early modern times, see R. Chartier and J. Revel, 'Université et société dans l'Europe nouvelle', in *Revue d'histoire moderne et contemporaine*, vol. 25 (1978).

2. Sections of secondary education that did not lead to university studies have been largely omitted in this essay since a comparison turned out to be very difficult. Secondary education has been included only as a substitute if information on the sections linked to higher education was lacking.

3. See, for a summary of the research on the inequality of education in France, England and Germany, H. Kaelble, *Industrialisierung und soziale Ungleichheit. Europa im 19. Jahrhundert* (Vandenhoek & Ruprecht, Göttingen, 1983), Chap. 4 (transl. as *Industrialisation and Social Inequality in 19th-Century Europe*, Berg Publishers, Leamington Spa, 1986).

4. Two structural components are very often omitted in historical investigations of educational opportunities: on the one hand, enrolment figures are frequently not related to the respective age cohorts and so might lead to mistaken conclusions about the historical changes or differences between countries; on the other hand, the social origin of students is usually not related to the social structure of a society; so changes of social origin that might be mere consequences of changes of the social structure can be considered erroneously as alterations of educational opportunities. The definition put forward above avoids these shortcomings. It has been introduced by sociologists dealing with current education such as Bourdieu,

Westergaard, Bühl, Anderson (see: P. Bourdieu and J-C. Passeron, *Les Héritiers* (Ed. de Minuit, Paris, 1964), pp. 136ff.; A. Little and J. Westergaard, 'The Trend of Class Differentials in Educational Opportunity in England and Wales', *British Journal of Sociology*, vol. 15 (1964), pp. 301–16; W. L. Bühl, *Schule und gesellschaftlicher Wandel* (Klett–Cotta, Stuttgart, 1968); Anderson, 'Access to Higher Education, p. 253). For an elegant presentation of the various aspects of educational opportunities, see F. Ringer, 'On Segmentation in Modern European Educational Systems' in Müller et. al. (eds.), *The Rise of the Modern Educational System*.

5. Furthermore, the social origin of the students is given separately in the following tables, in order to make it easier to follow up separately the two main components of the social distribution of educational opportunities. Unfortunately, an important demographic component of the definition, the social or occupational differential of family size, cannot be dealt with for lack of any data covering the nineteenth century. This component could be neglected if the differential of family size had remained constant during the nineteenth century; this was probably not the case, however. Hence I would see here a greatly neglected and so far incalculable aspect that limits the conclusion of the essay. For an interesting approximative answer to this problem, see Craig, 'Higher Education'.

6. Apart from the special studies, to which reference is made later on, the general works most stimulating for the following conception of areas of educational opportunities were: Ringer, *Education and Society*; J. Kocka, 'Organisierter Kapitalismus oder Staatsmonopolistischer Kapitalismus' in H. A. Winkler (ed.), *Organisierter Kapitalismus* (Vandenhoeck & Ruprecht, Göttingen, 1974), pp. 19–35; H.–U. Wehler, 'Der Aufstieg des Organisierten Kapitalismus und Interventionstaates in Deutschland' in Winkler (ed.), *Organisierter Kapitalismus*, pp. 36–57; C. S. Maier, *Recasting Bourgeois Europe: Stabilization in France, Germany, and Italy in the Decade after World War I* (Princeton UP, Princeton, 1975); Heidenheimer, 'Education and Social Security'; H. Heclo, 'Toward a New Welfare State' in P. Flora and A. J. Heidenheimer (eds.), *The Development of the Welfare State* (Transaction Books, New Brunswick, 1981). For a discussion of the differences between eras of educational opportunities and eras of social mobility, see Chap. 4, note 1.

7. See Ringer, *Education and Society*.

8. For the previous period information on enrolments and on the population size broken down by age cohorts is lacking.

9. England: Stone (ed.), *The University in Society*, pp. 6f., 65ff. Germany: Ringer, *Education and Society*; K. H. Jarausch, 'The Social Transformation of the University. The Case of Prussia 1865–1914', in *Journal of Social History*, vol. 12, (1979), pp. 609–30; P. Lundgreen, 'Educational Expansion and Economic Growth in Nineteenth-Century Germany: a Quantitative Study' in Stone (ed.), *Schooling in Society*, pp. 27ff.; Müller, *Sozialstruktur und Schulsystem*, pp. 441ff. (case study of secondary education in Berlin). France: Ringer, *Education and Society*; M-R. Mouton, 'L'enseignement supérieur en France de 1890 à nos jours' in P. Chevallier (ed.), *La scolarisation en France depuis un siècle* (Mouton, Paris, 1974), pp. 176ff. (also covering the period before 1890); J. Maillet, 'L'évolution des effectifs', pp. 129ff. (stressing the small rates of growth before 1914 rather than dealing with the take-off of growth); Toutain, *La population de la France*, pp. 231ff.; Flora, 'Die Bildungssentwicklung', pp. 305ff.

10. For a higher magnitude of educational opportunities in the USA since 1860,

see also Jarausch, 'Higher education', pp. 12ff. (esp. Table 3); C. B. Burke, 'The Expansion of American Higher Education' in K. H. Jarausch (ed.), *The Transformation of Higher Education 1860–1936* (Klett–Cotta, Stuttgart, 1983).
11. T. W. Bamford, 'Public Schools and Social Class', pp. 229ff.; C. A. Anderson, 'Secondary Education in Mid–Nineteenth Century France: Some Social Aspects', *Past and Present*, vol. 50 (1971); T. Zeldin, *France 1848–1945*, vol. 2 (Clarendon Press, Oxford, 1977), pp. 294ff.; M. Kraul, 'Untersuchungen zur sozialen Struktur der Schülerschaft des preußischen Gymnasiums im Vormärz', in *Bildung und Erziehung*, vol. 29 (1976), pp. 509–19; idem, *Gymnasium und Gesellschaft*; Müller, *Sozialstruktur und Schulsystem*, pp. 430ff., 517ff.; for early modern Europe cf. Chartier and Revel, 'Université et société', pp. 357ff.; for a similar though less straightforward interpretation of French secondary schools in the south up to the Third Republic: R. Gildea, 'Education and the Classes Moyennes in the 19th Century' in D. N. Baker and P. J. Harrigan (eds.), *The Making of Frenchmen: Current Directions in the History of Education in France, 1679–1979* (Historical Reflections Press, Waterloo, 1980); for the rural population and the reforms of the 1880s and 1890s: P. J. Harrigan, *Mobility, Elites and Education in Second Empire France* (Laurier, Waterloo, 1980), pp. 147f., 159f.
12. See also G. Weisz, *The Emergence of Modern Universities in France, 1863–1914* (Princeton UP, Princeton, 1983), pp. 24f.
13. Stone, *University in Society*, pp. 37ff., 93; C. A. Anderson and M. Schnaper, *School and Society in England: Social Background of Oxford and Cambridge Students* (Public Affairs Press, Washington, DC, 1952); C. E. McClelland, 'The Aristocracy and University Reform in Eighteenth-Century Germany' in Stone (ed.), *Schooling and Society*, pp. 146–73; W. Zorn, 'Hochschule und höhere Schule in der deutschen Sozialgeschichte der Neuzeit', in K. Repgen and Skalweit (eds.), *Spiegel der Geschichte*, Festgabe Braubach (Aschendorff, Münster, 1964).
14. W. M Mathew, 'The Origins and Occupations of Glasgow Students, 1740–1839', *Past and Present*, vol. 33 (1966), pp. 74–94; Lévy-Leboyer, 'Innovation and Business Strategies', pp. 108ff.; C. R. Day, 'Making Men and Training Technicians; Boarding Schools of the Écoles des Arts et Métiers during the 19th Century' in Baker and Harrigan (eds.), *The Making of Frenchmen*.
15. Jarausch, 'Higher Education and Social Change', pp. 23ff.
16. R. D. Anderson, *Education and Opportunity in Victorian Scotland* (Clarendon Press, Oxford, 1983), pp. 103ff., 202ff., 320f.
17. See R. Angelo, 'The Social Transformation of American Higher Education', in Jarausch (ed.), *The Transformation of Higher Learning*, pp. 273ff.; C. Jenks and D. Riesman, *The Academic Revolution*, (Garden City, 1968), pp. 10ff.; P. A. Sorokin, *Social and Cultural Mobility* (Harper, 1927; repr. Free Press of Glencoe, London, 1964), pp. 429ff.; for a perspective on recent American studies, see J. McLachlan, 'The American College in the 19th Century. Toward a Reappraisal', *Teachers College Record*, vol. 80 (1978); C. B. Burke, *American Collegiate Populations* (New York UP, New York, 1982), p. 114 (for lack of studies of social origins of students of the first half of the nineteenth century); M. G. Synnot, *The Half–Opened Door. Discrimination and Admission at Harvard, Yale and Princeton, 1900–1970* (Greenwood Press, Westport, 1979); H. S. Wechsler, *The Qualified Student. A History of Selective College Admission in America* (Wiley, New York, 1977).
18. For very considerable differences see England: M. Sanderson, *The Universities and British Industry 1850–1870* (Routledge & Kegan Paul, London, 1972),

p. 97; T. J. Bishop and R. Wilkinson, *Winchester and the Public School Elite. A Statistical Analysis* (Faber, London, 1967), pp. 110f.; France: Gildea, 'Education and the Classes Moyennes'; Germany: note to Table 3.4 above.

19. See Table 2.11 above

20. See Heidenheimer, 'Education and Social Security'; F. K. Ringer, 'Higher Education in Germany in the 19th Century', in *Journal of Contemporary History*, vol. 2 (1967), pp. 123–38; idem, 'The Education of Elites in Modern Europe', *History of Education Quarterly* (Summer 1978), pp. 159–72; J. Kocka, 'Bildung, soziale Schichtung' pp. 297–314; K. H. Jarausch, 'The Sources of German Student Unrest 1815–1848' in Stone (ed.), *The University in Society*, vol. 2, pp. 206–35; idem, 'Die neuhumanistische Universtität und die bürgerliche Gesellschaft, 1800–1870' in C. Probst (ed.), *Darstellungen und Quellen zur Geschichte der deutschen Einheitsbewegung im 19. und 20. Jahrhundert* (Winter, Heidelberg, 1978); J. A. Armstrong, *The European Administrative Elite* (Princeton UP, Princeton, 1973), pp. 73ff.; Kaelble, *Historical Research on Social Mobility*; Ringer, *Education and Society*; idem, 'Bildung, Wirtschaft und Gesellschaft in Deutschland, 1800–1960', in *Geschichte und Gesellschaft*, vol. 6 (1980), pp. 5–35; V. Karady, 'Normaliens et autres enseignants à la belle époque', *Revue Française de sociologie*, vol. 13 (1972).

21. K. E. Jeismann, 'Gymnasium, Staat und Gesellschaft in Preußen. Vorbemerkung der politischen und sozialen Bedeutung der "höheren Bildung" im 19. Jahrhundert' in U. Herrmann (ed.), *Schule und Gesellschaft im 19. Jahrhundert* (Beltz, Weinheim, 1977), pp. 55ff.; Jarausch, 'German Student Unrest', pp. 551ff.; Zorn, 'Hochschule'; Müller, *Sozialstruktur und Schulsystem*; Ringer, 'Higher Education'; idem, *Education and Society*; Kocka, 'Bildung'; for the eighteenth century, see McClelland, 'The Aristocracy and University Reform', pp. 146–76.

22. Craig, 'Higher Education' (a study also very interesting for its methods).

23. N. Hans, *New Trends in Education in the 18th Century* (Routledge & Kegan Paul, London, 1951), pp. 43ff., 210ff.; B. Simon, *Studies in the History of Education 1780–1870* (Lawrence & Wishart, London, 1960), pp. 298ff.; Bamford, 'Public Schools and Social Class', pp. 119f.; Stone, 'Size and Composition', pp. 37ff.; Mathew, 'Glasgow Students'; see also F. M. L. Thompson, *English Landed Society in the Nineteenth Century* (Routledge & Kegan Paul, London, 1963), pp. 81ff.

24. R. D. Anderson, 'Secondary Education in Mid–Nineteenth Century France: Some Social Aspects', *Past and Present*, vol. 50 (1971), pp. 121–46; idem, *Education in France, 1848–1870* (Clarendon Press, Oxford, 1975); P. J. Harrigan, 'Secondary Education and the Professions in France during the Second Empire', *Comparative Studies in Society and History*, vol. 17 (1975), pp. 349–71; idem, 'Social Origins, Ambitions, and Occupations'; idem, *Mobility, Elites and Education*; T. Zeldin, 'Higher Education in France, 1848–1945', *Journal of Contemporary History*, vol. 2 (1967), pp. 53–98; Chevallier et. al. (eds.), *L'enseignement français*; Ringer, *Education and Society*; for strong similarities in French and German secondary school reforms. See Albisetti, 'French Secondary School Reform'.

25. See Zorn, 'Hochschule'; Ringer, 'Higher Education', pp. 337ff.; Jarausch, 'Die neuhumanistische Universität'; Jeismann, 'Gymnasium, Staat und Gesellschaft'; Müller, *Sozialstruktur und Schulsystem*, pp. 37ff.; R. Meyer, 'Das Berechtigungswesen in seiner Bedeutung für Schule und Gesellschaft im 19. Jahrhundert', *Zeitschrift für die gesamte Staatswissenschaft*, vol. 124 (1968), pp. 763–76; Lundgreen, 'Educational Expansion and Economic Growth', pp. 85ff.; idem, 'Historische Bildungsforschung' in R. Rürup

(ed.), *Historische Sozialwissenschaft* (Vandenhoeck & Ruprecht, Göttingen, 1977); H. J. Herrlitz and H. Titze, 'Überfüllung als bildungspolitische Strategie' in U. Herrmann (ed.), *Schule und Gesellschaft im 19. Jahrhundert (Beltz, Weinheim, 1977).*

26. M. Sanderson, 'The Grammar School and the Education of the Poor 1786–1840', *British Journal of Educational Studies*, vol. 11 (1962); idem, *Universities and British Industry*, pp. 97ff. (social structure of students outside Oxford and Cambridge); J. W. Adamson, *English Education 1789–1902*, (Cambridge UP, Cambridge, 1964), pp. 62ff., 258ff.; Bamford, 'Public Schools and Social Class' (social structure of the students); Simon, *Studies in the History of Education*; idem, *The Concept of Popular Education* (MacGibbon & Kee, London, 1965); L. Stone, 'Japan and England: A Comparative Study', in P. W. Musgrave (ed.), *Sociology, History and Education* (Methuen, London, 1970), pp. 101–14; idem, 'Size and Composition', pp. 60ff.

27. For England see Stone, 'Size and Composition'; for France see Toutain, *La population de la France*; Weisz, *The Emergence of Modern Universities*, p. 225 (with reservations); for Germany see H. Kaelble, 'Sozialer Aufstieg in Deutschland 1850–1914' in K. H. Jarausch (ed.), *Quantifizierung in der Geschichtswissenschaft* (Droste, Düsseldorf, 1976), pp. 282ff.; for the business élite, see Chap. 3; J. Kocka, 'Entrepreneurs and Managers in the German Industrial Revolution' in P. Mathias and M. M. Postan (eds.), *Cambridge Economic History of Europe*, vol. 7 (Cambridge UP, Cambridge, 1978); Jarausch, 'Higher Education', p. 17; H. Titze, 'Enrolment Expansion and Academic Overcrowding in Germany', in Jarausch (ed.), *Transformation.*

28. Stone, 'Size and Composition'; Ringer, *Education and Society*; Jarausch, 'Social Transformation of the University'; Jarausch, 'Higher Education'.

29. Weisz, *The Emergence of Modern Universities*, pp. 227ff.

30. France: Anderson, 'Secondary Education'; G. Duveau, *La pensée ouvrière sur l'éducation pendant la Seconde République et le Second Empire* (Gallimard, Paris, 1947); Germany: Müller, *Sozialstruktur und Schulsystem*; Herrlitz and Titze, 'Überfüllung als bildungspolitische Strategie'.

31. Statistical surveys only exist, however, on the number of school pupils and students and on relative attendance at school and in higher education. See P. Flora, *Indikatoren der Modernisierung* (Westdeutscher Verlag, Opladen, 1975) (numbers of students in the USA, Russia, Japan, Germany, France and Great Britain); idem, *Quantitative Historical Sociology* (Mouton, The Hague, 1977), pp. 56ff. (for relative higher education attendance for Western Europe excepting Spain, Portugal, Greece); idem, *State, Economy and Society in Western Europe 1815–1970*, 2 vols. (Campus Verlag, Frankfort, 1984, 1985); Mitchell, *European Historical Statistics* pp. 749–78 (numbers of school pupils and students in all European countries excepting Russia/USSR); cf. the older statistical survey, still useful for some aspects (among others, women students and investments in education) by Edding, *Internationale Tendenzen* (numbers of students in the USA, Japan, Great Britain, Sweden, France, Holland and Germany). None of these surveys treats of the social, ethnic, religious or regional distribution of educational opportunities. The definitions of secondary and higher education vary considerably. Almost none of the data collections include all European countries. Aggregate data are given neither for Europe nor for Western Europe.

32. For comparative studies on historical developments: Ringer, *Education and Society*; Heidenheimer, 'Education and Social Security'; Premfors, *The Politics of Higher Education* (on the postwar period only); A. H. Passow et. al., *The National Case Study: an Empirical Comparative Study of 21 Educational*

Systems (Almqvist & Wiksell, Stockholm, 1976) (deals only with secondary schools in the postwar period); R. L. Geiger, *Two Paths to Mass Higher Education: Issues and Outcomes in Belgium and France* (Yale Higher Education Research Group, Working Paper, YHERG 34, 1979); idem, 'The Changing Demand for Higher Education in the Seventies: Adaptations within Three National Systems', *Higher Education*, vol. 9 (1980), pp. 255–76; (on the postwar period only); B. Williamson, *Education, Social Structure and Development* (Macmillan, London, 1979), pp. 47–88 (England, Germany and cases outside Western Europe, mainly twentieth century; however, this is more a collection of studies than a strict comparison); H. Levin, 'Educational Opportunity and Social Inequality in Western Europe', in *Social Problems*, vol. 24 (1976); Jarausch (ed.), *Transformation* (comparative introduction by the editor, otherwise individual studies on the USA, USSR, England and Germany).

33. The *relative* figures for attendance of women at institutions of higher education have not been calculated, since in some cases — for example in Switzerland — they were heavily affected by the intake of foreign female students and would thus give a false impression of the actual educational opportunities of Swiss women.

34. Armstrong, *The European Administrative Elite*; cf. also Chapter 3.

35. M. Weber, *Wirtschaft und Gesellschaft* (1921; repr. Kiepenhueur & Witsch, Cologne, 1964), vol. 2, p. 735.

36. Since the standard of the American college diploma lies between the university degrees and secondary school leaving certificates of many European countries, one ought also to draw a comparison with the latter, to provide as it were a minimal proof of this argument. However, no data collections on secondary school leavers exist. But in his study on the USA, France, England and Germany, Ringer does show that since the beginning of the twentieth century, the American lead is also clearly evident in a comparison of college and secondary school leavers. One may assume that this conclusion also applies to most other West European countries (Ringer, *Education and Society*, p. 251ff.).

37. The variation coefficient of educational opportunities in these four countries (France, Great Britain, Italy and Germany) was 21 per cent in 1890, 20 per cent in 1900, 26 per cent in 1910 (calculations based on Flora, *Quantitative Historical Sociology*, p. 57f. The variation coefficient calculated on the basis of Table 2.2 is considerably lower).

38. Cf. Ringer, *Education and Society*, passim; B. Simon, *Education and the Labour Movement* (Lawrence & Wishart, London, 1965); D. Rubinstein and B. Simon, *The Evolution of the Comprehensive School, 1926–1972* (Routledge & Kegan Paul, London, 1969); A. H. Halsey, 'Educational Opportunities and Social Selection in England', in *Transactions of the 2nd World Congress of Sociology*, vol. 2 (London, 1954), p. 196ff.; J. E. Talbott, *The Politics of Educational Reform in France 1918–1940* (Princeton UP, Princeton, 1969); S. F. Müller, *Die höhere Schule Preußens in der Weimarer Republik* (Beltz, Weinheim, 1977); M. Kater, 'Die Krisis des Frauenstudiums in der Weimarer Republik', *Vierteljahresschrift für Sozial- und Wirtschaftsgeschichte*, vol. 59 (1972); cf. also the literature cited in Kaelble, *Soziale Mobilität*, pp. 127ff.; A. Elmiro, 'Italian Education from 1859 to 1923', PhD thesis, Univ. of Pennsylvania (1975).

39. Calculations based on Table 2.2. for 1890–1910 and 1920–40.

40. Calculations based on Table 2.2.

41. The variation coefficient of educational opportunities in these four countries is 23 per cent for 1920, 19 per cent for 1930 (calculations based on Flora,

Quantitative Historical Sociology, p. 57f.).

42. Cf. on Germany: Müller, *Die höhere Schule Preußens*; Ringer, *Education and Society*, pp. 90ff.; on France: Talbott, *Politics of Educational Reform*; Ringer, *Education and Society*, pp. 180ff.; on Italy: Barbagli, *Disoccupazione intelletuale*, pp. 157ff., 195ff.; Kaelble, *Soziale Mobilität*, pp. 139ff.

43. Cf. together with Table 2.11 on the USA: Edding, *Internationale Tendenzen*, statistical appendix.

44. On Germany, cf. Kaelble, *Soziale Mobilität*, pp. 139ff.; on Italy: Barbagli, *Disoccupazione intelletuale*, pp. 212ff., 228ff..

45. Cf. the literature cited in note 38 above.

46. Like Switzerland, Scotland belongs to the leading group according to Flora's data, which — as has been emphasised — are based on a different definition and which should therefore also be taken into consideration alongside Table 2.2 in connection with such statements on the order of precedence among European countries. See on the high proportion of foreigners in Austria, for example: *Statistisches Handbuch für die Republik Österreich*, vol. 9 (1928), p. 170 (foreign students at Austrian institutions of higher education in 1927: 37 per cent). However, the extent of educational opportunities in Austria was quite considerable before 1914, when the proportion of foreigners was still very small. In comparison with other European countries, it seems that the determining factors were the low school fees, the fact that certain occupations were reserved for university graduates to a particularly great extent and the low occupational and advancement opportunities in non-graduate posts in the economy. See H. Haas, 'Statistische Streiflichter zur österreichischen Hochsschulstatistik', *Statistische Monatsschrift*, vol. 22 (1917), p. 165ff.; on the proportion of foreign students in Switzerland (22 per cent in 1935/6) see. *Die Studierenden an schweizerischen Hochschulen. Sondererhebung 1936* (Eidgen. Stat. Amt, Bern, 1938), p. 67.

47. This is clearly shown in Table 2.2. Similar results are also reached using Flora's data which — as we have said — are based on a somewhat different definition of higher education. If one calculates the variation coefficients for Western European countries on the basis of Flora's data *without* his leading group (Scotland, Switzerland, Austria — the latter except in 1940), one arrives at lower values which indicate a very great similarity: 1910: 15 per cent; 1920: 12 per cent; 1930: 8 per cent; 1940: 8 per cent (calculations based on Flora, *Quantitative Historical Sociology*, pp. 57f.). It is one of the characteristics of this indicator that individual cases, e.g. Germany, can alter very drastically without this having an effect on the coefficients.

48. For the calculation of the variation coefficients for Western Europe, a variant without the purely Mediterranean countries of Spain, Portugal and Greece was computed, since, as Table 2.2 shows, they also do not follow the West European pattern. On growth rates cf. *Higher Education in Europe: Problems and Prospects, Statistical Study* (UNESCO, Paris, 1973), p. 10.

49. See together with the studies named in notes 54, 55 and 57: H. Titze, 'Überfüllungskrisen in akademischen Karrieren: Eine Zyklustheorie', *Zeitschrift für Pädagogik*, vol. 27 (1981).

50. Variation coefficient of per capita product in Western Europe can be calculated on the basis of: P. Bairoch, 'Europe's Gross National Product: 1800–1975', *Journal of European Economic History*, vol. 5 (1976), pp. 281, 195, 303 (GNP in $US); variation coefficient of occupational structure (share of workforce employed in industry); 1900: 46 per cent; 1920: 30 per cent; 1950: 28 per cent; 1970: 17 per cent; cf. Kaelble, 'Prometheus Most Unbound?'

51. See P. Flora, 'Krisenbewältigung oder Krisenerzeugung? Der Wohl-

156   *Notes to pages 78–90*

fahrtsstaat in historischer Perspektive' in J. Matthes (ed.), *Sozialer Wandel in Westeuropa* (Campus Verlag, Frankfurt, 1979); H. Kaelble, *Sozialgeschichte Europas, 1880–1980*. *Gemeinsamkeit und Angleichung der Westeuropäischen Gesellschaften* (Suhrkamp, Frankfurt, 1986), Chap. 2.

52. For a more recent comparison which draws attention to the growing divergences during the educational crisis of the past few years, see Premfors, *Higher Education*, pp. 97ff.

53. No attempt has been made here to calculate the opportunities of working-class children in relation to the opportunities of the offspring of other occupational groups. Definitions both of salaried employees and of the professions vary so greatly that it is seldom possible to draw conclusions from such calculations; it is for this reason that they have not been made here.

54. See, as examples of a pessimistic conclusion: R. Boudon, *Education, Opportunity and Social Inequality* (Wiley, New York, 1974); W. Müller and K. U. Mayer, *Chancengleichheit durch Bildung?* (Klett-Cotta, Stuttgart, 1976); Bourdieu and Passeron, *Les héritiers*; Halsey et al., *Origins and Destinations*; Geiger, *Two Paths to Mass Higher Education*, pp. 25ff. For a comparison of the educational opportunities of graduates' children and working-class children: *Education, Inequality and Life Chances*, vol. 1, pp. 168ff.

55. See W. Müller, *Familie — Schule — Beruf* (Westdeutscher Verlag, Opladen, 1975); ibid. and Mayer, *Chancengleichheit durch Bildung?*; P. Bourdieu, 'Cultural Reproduction and Social Reproduction' in J. Karabel and A. H. Halsey (eds.), *Power and Ideology in Education* (Oxford UP, New York, 1977); Goldthorpe et al., *Social Mobility and Class Structure*; Halsey et. al., *Origins and Destinations*.

56. A compilation based on the narrowest possible definition of higher education (universities), not included here for reasons of space, is to be found in H. Kaelble, 'Abweichung oder Konvergenz? Soziale Mobilität in Frankreich und Deutschland während des 19. und 20. Jahrhunderts' in G. A. Ritter and R. Vierhaus (eds.), *Aspekte der historischen Forschung in Frankreich und Deutschland* (Vandenhoeck & Ruprecht, Göttingen, 1981), p. 129. A very differentiated compilation for the period 1960–70, which could not be included here for reasons of space, in: *Second Conference of Ministers of Education of European Member States, Bucharest 26.11–3.12.1973. Appendix: statistical tables* (UNESCO, Paris, 1973), p. 6–8 (without distinguishing the types of higher educational institutions in, for example, France and Italy). On the percentages of trainee primary school teachers in some countries, see the note to Table 2.2. above.

57. Premfors, *Higher Education*, pp. 97ff. (his analysis is considerably more detailed than the main argument presented here and also deals with the great differences between France and Sweden in the phase of retarded expansion in the 1970s); Geiger, *Mass Higher Education*, pp. 22ff; Ringer, *Education and Society*, pp. 151–6, 211ff., 230f., 244ff. (this aspect, however, is only touched on in passing. Ringer concentrates on the period before 1945).

58. A similar development is shown by local studies on secondary schools in J. E. Floud and A. H. Halsey, 'Social Class, Intelligence Tests and Selection for Secondary Schools' in Halsey et. al. (eds.), *Education, Economy and Society* (Glencoe Free Press, New York, 1961).

59. Ringer, *Education in Society*, pp. 216ff., 242ff.; Floud and Halsey, 'Social Class'; J. Vaizey and J. Sheehan, *Resources for Education. An Economic Study of Education in the United Kingdom 1920–1965* (Allen & Unwin, London, 1968), pp. 12ff.; very sceptical of this view, but without presenting new material:

Williamson, *Education*, pp. 62–4; on postwar institutional reforms: Rubinstein and Simon, *Evolution of the Comprehensive School*; J. G. K. Fenwick, *The Comprehensive School. The Politics of Secondary School Reorganisation* (Methuen, London, 1976); Halsey et. al., *Origins and Destinations*.

60. B. Nilsson, 'Study Financing and Expansion of Education', in *Economy and History*, vol. 20 (1977), pp. 92ff.; R. Torstendahl, 'The Social Relevance of Education. Swedish Secondary Education during the Period of Industrialization', *Scandinavian Journal of History*, vol. 6 (1981).

61. For Finland, percentage of working class children (23 per cent in 1935), see Anderson, 'Access to Higher Education', p. 256. It is not clear, however, from where Anderson derives these figures. There appears to be a lack of historical research on distribution of opportunities at institutions of higher education. See M. T. Kuikka, 'Die Erforschung der Geschichte der Erziehung in Finnland 1945–1975' in *Die historische Pädagogik in Europa und den USA* (Klett-Cotta, Stuttgart, 1979), pp. 44ff.

62. See Ringer, *Education and Society*, pp 180ff.; J. Schriewer, *Die französischen Universitäten 1945–1968* (Klinkhardt, Heilbronn, 1972); Talbott, *Educational Reform*); Bourdieu, *Reproduction*.

63. See H. Becker, 'Bildungspolitik' in W. Benz (ed.), *Die Bundesrepublik Deutschland*, vol. 2 (Fischer Verlag, Frankfurt, 1983), pp. 324ff. (with further references).

64. See for the large differences in the relative attendance at institutions of higher education of the offspring of higher social strata and working-class children in the 'latecomer' countries' Austria, France, Federal Republic of Germany, the Netherlands and Spain: *Education, Inequality and Life Chances* vol. 1, p. 168.

Notes to Chapter 3

1. See Bendix and Howton, 'Social Mobility'.

2. Exceptions: Newcomer, 'The Big Business Executive'; H. G. Gutman, 'The Reality of the Rags–to–Riches "Myth"': The Case of the Paterson, New Jersey, Locomotive, Iron and Machinery Manufacturers, 1830–1880' in S. Thernstrom and R. Sennet (eds.), *Nineteenth-Century Cities* (Yale, New Haven, 1969); J. N. Ingham, 'Rags to Riches Revisited: The Effect of City Size on the Recruitment of Business Leaders', *Journal of American History*, vol. 62 (1976); idem, *The Iron Barons* (Greenwood Press, Westport, 1978); P. R. Decker, *Fortunes and Failures. White-Collar Mobility in 19th-Century San Francisco* (Harvard UP, Cambridge, 1978).

3. National level: Bendix and Howton, 'American Business Elite'; C. W. Mills, 'The American Business Elite in the 1870s' in W. Miller (ed.), *Men in Business* (Harper & Row, New York, 1962); Lévy-Leboyer, 'Le Patronat Français, 1912–1973'; C. Charles, 'Les milieux d'affaires dans la structure de la classe dominante vers 1900', *Actes de la recherche en sciences sociales*, no. 20–21 (1978); Torstendahl, 'Les chefs d'entreprise'; W. Stahl, *Der Elitekreislauf in der Unternehmerschaft* (Deutsch, Frankfurt, 1973); Kaelble, 'Sozialer Aufstieg'; H. Perkin, 'The Recruitment of Elites in British Society since 1880', unpubl. paper (1976) (abbrev. version: 'The Recruitment of Elites in British Society since 1880', *Journal of Social History*, vol. 12 (1978/9)); steel: F. W. Gregory and J. D. Neu, 'The American Industrial Elite in the 1870s', in W. Miller (ed.), *Men in Business* (Harper & Row, New York, 2nd ed. 1962);

Erickson, *British Industrialists*; Ingham, 'Rags to Riches Revisited'; T. Pieren-
kemper, *Die westfälischen Schwerindustriellen 1852–1913* (Vandenhoeck &
Ruprecht, Göttingen, 1979); idem, 'Entrepreneurs in Heavy Industry: Upper
Silesia and the Westphalian Ruhr Region, 1852–1913', *Business History
Review*, vol. 53 (1979); textiles: Gregory and Neu, 'American Industrial Elite';
Erickson, *British Industrialists*; O. Dascher, *Das Textilgewerbe in Hessen-Kassel
vom 16. bis 19. Jahrhundert* (Elwert, Marburg, 1968); W. Huschke, *Forschungen
über die Herkunft der thüringischen Unternehmerschicht des 19. Jahrhunderts* (Lutzeyer, Baden-Baden, 1962); Kaelble, *Berliner Unternehmer*, pp. 30ff.; idem,
Historical Research: published thereafter: H. Henning, 'Soziale Verflechtung
der Unternehmer in Westfalen 1860–1914', *Zeitschrift für Unternehmensgeschichte*, vol. 1 (1978); a comparative article focusing upon entrepreneurial
behaviour rather than upon the recruitment of business leaders: J. Hirschmeier, 'Entrepreneurs and the Social Order: America, Germany and
Japan 1879–1900' in K. Nakagawa (ed.), *Social Order and Entrepreneurship*
(Univ. of Tokyo Press, Tokyo, 1977), pp. 10ff.; research surveys covering
other studies as well: J. Kocka, 'Entrepreneurs and Managers'; pp. 516ff.;
idem, 'Entrepreneurship in a Late–Comer Country: The German Case' in
Nakagawa (ed.), *Social Order*, pp. 157ff.
4. National level is not included in Tables 3.1–3.4; Perkin, *Elites*, Table 5 (repr.
   in Kaelble, *Historical Research*, p. 96); Charles, 'Milieux d'affaires', pp. 86f.;
   individual branches: Erickson, *British Industrialists*, pp. 11ff., 79ff.; Ingham,
   'Rags to Riches', p. 634; Gregory and Neu, 'American Industrial Elite', p.
   202; Pierenkemper, *Schwerindustrie*, pp. 117ff.; Kaelble, *Unternehmer*, p.99.
5. For the British, American, French, Swedish and German cases, see the
   above studies and Tables 3.1–3.4.
6. Gutman, 'Reality of the Rags-to-Riches "Myth" '; A. Schröter and W.
   Becker, *Die deutsche Maschinenbauindustrie in der industriellen Revolution* (Akademie Verlag, Berlin, 1962), p. 65. The exceptional recruitment pattern of the
   machine-building manufacturers seems to have been due to two reasons:
   Firstly, ownership of large amounts of capital was not necessary, since
   capital intensity was low until about the middle of the century, while profits
   were high. Secondly, the marketing of the as yet unstandardized products
   did not require the special skills of a merchant, whose social origins would
   have been much more exclusive during the nineteenth century.
7. See Table 3.5; Mills, 'American Business Elite', pp. 33ff.; H. Beau,
   *Das Leistungswissen des frühindustriellen Unternehmertums in Rheinland und
   Westfalen* (Rheinisch-Westfäl. Wirtschaftsarchiv, Cologne, 1959), pp. 66ff.;
   Kocka, 'Entrepreneurs), pp. 533; idem, 'Entrepreneurship', pp. 174ff.; Charles,
   'Milieux d'affaires', p. 87; Torstendahl, 'Chefs d'entreprise', p. 47.
8. In Britain even at the end of the nineteenth century we may observe that 10
   per cent of the business leaders had this background (cf. Perkin, 'Elites',
   Table 5).
9. See H. Rosenberg, 'Die Pseudodemokratisierung der Rittergutsbesitzer-
   lasse' in H.-U. Wehler (ed.), *Moderne deutsche Sozialgeschichte* (Kiepenheuer
   & Witsch, Cologne/Berlin, 1970); R. Braun, 'Zur Einwirkung sozio-
   kultureller Umweltbedingungen auf das Unternehmerpotential und das
   Unternehmerverhalten' in W. Fischer (ed.), *Wirtschafts- und sozialgeschichtliche Probleme der frühen Industrialisierung* (Colloquium, Berlin, 1968); J. J.
   Sheehan, 'Conflict and Cohesion among the German Elites in the Nineteenth Century', in R. J. Bezucha (ed.), *Modern European Social History*
   (Heath, Lexington, 1972); D. S. Landes, *The Unbound Prometheus* (Cambridge UP, Cambridge, 1969), pp. 128ff.

10. P. Bairoch, 'Niveaux de développement économique de 1810 à 1910', in *Annales*, vol. 20 (1965), pp. 1091–117; idem, 'Agriculture and Industrial Revolution' in C. M. Cipolla (ed.), *Fontana Economic History of Europe* (Fontana, London, 1973).

11. Kocka, 'Entrepreneurs', pp. 514f.; Ringer, 'Higher Education in Germany'; idem, *The Decline of the German Mandarins* (Harvard UP, Cambridge, Mass., 1969); D. Rueschemeyer, *Lawyers and their Society* (Harvard UP, Cambridge, Mass., 1973), pp. 160ff.

12. J. P. Cullity, 'The Growth of Governmental Employment in Germany, 1882–1950', *Zeitschrift für die gesamte Staatswissenschaft*, vol. 123 (1967), pp. 210–17; H.–J. Puhle, 'Vom Wohlfahrtsstaat', in G. A. Ritter (ed.), *Vom Wohlfahrtsausschuss zum Wohlfahrtsstaat* (Mankus, Cologne, 1973), pp. 29ff.; F. Zunkel, 'Beamtenschaft und Unternehmertum beim Aufbau der Ruhrindustrie 1849–1880', in *Tradition*, vol. 9 (1964); Braun, 'Unternehmerpotential'; J. Kocka, 'Family and Bureaucracy in German Industrial Management', in *Business History Review*, vol. 45 (1971); idem, *Unternehmer in der deutschen Industrialisierung* (Vandenhoeck & Ruprecht, Göttingen, 1975), pp. 85ff.; Kaelble, *Unternehmer*, pp. 236ff. For the recruitment of the French business élite see, apart from Table 3.3: Charles, 'Milieux d'affaires', p. 87.

13. For the steel and textile industries: Gregory and Neu, 'Industrial Elite', p. 202; Ingham, 'Rags to Riches', p. 634; Erickson, *British Industrialists*, pp. 12, 93; Pierenkemper, *Schwerindustriellen*, p. 119; Kaelble, *Berliner Unternehmer*, p. 99.

14. Very well described in: L. Bergeron, *Banquiers négociants et manufacturiers parisiens du Directoire à l'Empire*, 2 vols. (Écoles des hautes étudesen sciences sociales, Paris, 1975); idem, 'Familienstruktur und Industrieunternehmer in Frankreich (18. bis 20. Jahrhundert)', in W. Bulst, J. Goy and J. Hook (eds.), *Familie zwischen Tradition und Moderne* (Vandenhoeck & Ruprecht, Göttingen, 1981); Germany: Kocka, 'Family and Bureaucracy'; idem, 'Familie, Unternehmer und Kapitalismus an Beispielen aus der frühen deutschen Industrialisierung', *Zeitschrift für Unternehmensgeschichte*, vol. 24 (1979).

15. For a comparative approach to the social approval of entrepreneurial activity see A. Gerschenkron, 'Social Attitudes, Entrepreneurship, and Economic Development' in idem (ed.), *Economic Backwardness in Historical Perspective* (Belknap, Cambridge, Mass., 1962); Landes, *Unbound Prometheus*, pp. 128ff.; L. O'Boyle, 'The Middle Class in Western Europe 1815–1848', *American Historical Review*, vol. 71 (1966), pp. 826–45; see also Kocka, 'Entrepreneurs', pp. 515ff.

16. W. D. Rubinstein, 'Men of Property: Some Aspects of Occupation, Inheritance and Power among Top British Wealthholders' in P. Stanworth and A. Giddens (eds.), *Elites and Power in British Society* (Cambridge UP, Cambridge, 1974), p. 163; Germany: data from a current project on the German multi-millionaires prior to 1914.

17. Flora, *Indikatoren*; Ringer, *Education and Society*; see also Chapter 2.

18. See Armstrong, *European Administrative Elite*, with references to further literature; for the combination of administrative and business careers in modern France, see P. Bourdieu and M. de Saint Martin, 'Le patronat', *Actes de la recherche en sciences sociales*, no. 20/21 (1978)

19. For the American research, see the survey by Bendix and Howton which covers the studies of Newcomer, Miller, Keller, Mills, Warner and Abegglen. For later research see n. 3 above. British: Erickson, *British Industrialists*; Perkin, 'Elites'; P. Stanworth and A. Giddens, 'An Economic Elite: A Demographic Profile of Company Chairmen' in idem (eds.), *Elites and Power*; T. R. Gourvish, 'A British Business Elite: The Chief Executive

Managers of the Railway Industry, 1850–1922', in *Business History Review*, vol. 47 (1973): French: Charles, 'Milieux d'affaires'; Lévy-Leboyer, *Patronat*; Bourdieu and de Saint Martin, 'Patronat'; German: Kocka, 'Entrepreneurs'; Kaelble, *Soziale Mobilität*, Chap. 2.2; idem, 'From the Family Enterprise to the Professional Manager: the German Case', in L. Hannah (ed.), *From the Family Enterprise to the Professional Manager*, Eighth International Economic History Congress, Theme 139, Budapest, 1982; Sweden: Torstendahl, 'Chefs d'entreprise'.

20. Some additional evidence and remarks. Great Britain: the study by Clements does not support this argument; the proportion of businessmen from business families does not indicate any clear trend (Clements, *Managers*, p. 186). The study covers about 650 rather loosely defined executives in twenty-eight large and middle–sized firms in the Manchester area (idem, pp. 17ff.). USA: Newcomer, *Big Business Executive*, pp. 52ff. (study of the largest railroad, public utility, and industrial corporations, with assets of more than $25 million (1900), more than $50 million (1925), and more than $75 million in 1950); Warner and Abegglen, *Occupational Mobility*, pp. 44ff. (for 1952, based on a sample of 7,300 American business and industrial leaders; for 1928, based on a comparable investigation by Taussig and Joslyn). The conclusions of Bendix and Howton contradict the data of both Newcomer and also Warner and Abegglen. Bendix and Howton cover a much smaller section of the top business positions, not exceeding 400 individuals. Their results are organised according to birth cohorts and not according to periods of occupational activity (Bendix and Howton, 'American Business Elite', p. 131); France: The 1912 findings are at variance with a tendency towards a decline in self–recruitment. However, the author of the study does not think that the information for 1912 is as good as for the subsequent period (cf. Lévy-Leboyer, *Patronat*). Moreover Bourdieu, in a study on the presidents of the 100 largest French enterprises, has demonstrated a reversal of the trend between 1952 and 1972, the proportion of presidents from business families (industrialists and bankers) rising from 31 per cent to 44 per cent. To Bourdieu, this is due to changes in the leading group of enterprises in France as well as to a more elitist education of French business leaders (Bourdieu and de Saint Martin, 'Patronat', pp. 46ff.); Sweden: Torstendahl, 'Chefs d'entreprise', pp. 45ff.; Germany: see Notes to Table 3.2.

21. Lévy-Leboyer, *Patronat*; Kocka, 'Entrepreneurs', pp. 582f.; Stahl, 'Elitenkreislauf', pp. 87ff.; Kaelble, *Soziale Mobilität*, p. 104; see also Table 3.2. More generally on the rise of large corporations: L. Hannah, *The Rise of the Corporate Economy* (Methuen, London, 1976); S. J. Prais, *The Evolution of the Giant Firms in Britain: A Study of the Growth of Concentration in Manufacturing Industry in Britain 1909–1970* (Cambridge UP, Cambridge, 1976); A. D. Chandler and L. Galambos, 'The Development of Large-Scale Economic Organization in Modern America', *Journal of Economic History*, vol. 30 (1970), pp. 210–221; A. D. Chandler, *The Visible Hand* (Harvard UP, Cambridge, Mass., 1977); W. Fischer and P. Czada, 'Wandlungen in der deutschen Industriestruktur um 20. Jahrhundert' in G. A. Ritter (ed.), *Entstehung und Wandel der modernen Gesellschaft* (de Gruyter, Berlin, 1970); R. Tilly, 'The Growth of Large-Scale Enterprise in Germany since the Middle of the 19th Century' in H. Daems and H. van der Wee, *The Rise of Managerial Capitalism* (Nijhoff, The Hague, 1974); Kocka, 'Entrepreneurs', pp. 555ff.; J. Kocka and H. Siegrist, 'Die hundert größten deutschen Industrieunternehmen im späten 19. und frühen 20. Jahrhundert' in W. Horn and J. Kocka (eds.), *Law*

and *Formation of the Big Enterprises in the Late 19th and Early 20th Centuries*
(Vandenhoeck & Ruprecht, Göttingen, 1979); Hannah (ed.), *Family Enterprise*.

22. Newcomer, *Big Business Executive*, p. 53; Perkin, 'Elites', Table 5; Erickson,
British Industrialists, p. 12; Lévy-Leboyer, *Patronat*, Table 1; for Germany,
see Table 3.2 above.
23. Bendix and Howton, 'American Business Elite', pp. 139ff.; Newcomer, *Big Business Executive*, p. 53; see also Lévy-Leboyer, *Patronat*; Bourdieu and de
Saint Martin, 'Patronat'; Torstendahl,'Chefs d'entreprise', p. 46.
24. USA: Bendix and Howton, 'American Business Elite', pp. 126ff.; Mills,
'American Business Elite', pp. 34ff.; Newcomer, 'Big Business Executive',
pp. 34, 68ff.; Warner and Abegglen, *Occupational Mobility*, pp. 108ff.; Great
Britain: Perkin, 'Elites', Table 5; Erickson, *British Industrialists*, pp. 30ff.;
France: Charles, 'Milieux d'affaires', p. 87; Lévy-Leboyer, *Patronat*, Table 5;
Bourdieux and de Saint Martin, 'Patronat', pp. 46ff.; Germany: Kocka,
'Entrepreneurs', pp. 582f.: Kaelble, 'Family Enterprise'; cf. also Table 3.5
above.
25. Erickson, *Industrialists*, pp. 25ff., 79ff., 188ff.; Perkin, 'Elites'; Lévy–
Leboyer, *Patronat*; Kaelble, *Historical Research*, pp. 82ff.; idem, 'Social Mobility
in Germany', pp. 454ff.

Notes to Chapter 4

1. K. Hopkins, 'Elite Mobility in the Roman Empire', in M. I. Finley (ed.),
Studies in Ancient Society (RKP, London, 1974); H. Castritius, 'Die Gesellschaftsordnung der römischen Kaiserzeit und das Problem der sozialer
Mobilität', *Mitteilungen der Technischen Universität Braunschweig*, 8 (1973), pp.
38–45; K. Hopkins, 'Mobility in the Later Roman Empire: the Evidence of
Ausonius', *Classical Quarterly*, vol. 55 (1961) — A general remark: eras of
educational opportunities and eras of social mobility as proposed here differ
in two respects. Firstly, the impact of the industrial revolution is often
pronounced for social mobility and very weak for educational opportunities; hence the era of charitable opportunities in education persists during
parts of the industrial revolution. Secondly, the effect of the rise of organised capitalism may be observed less distinctly in education than in social
mobility. Organised capitalism does not substantially change the character
of education. We admit that it has some impact which we have dealt with
when discussing a later phase of competitive opportunities in education.
This later phase is mainly characterised by growth of educational opportunities and a slight change in the social and sexual distribution. Thus it
appears that the eras of welfare opportunities in education and postindustrial social mobility more or less coincide even though the determining
factors are not the same.
2. L. Stone, 'Social Mobility in England 1500–1700', *Past & Present*, vol. 33
(1966); Chartier and Revel, 'Université et société'; R. Grasky, 'Social Mobility and Business Enterprise in 17th Century England' in D. Pennington and
K. Thomas (eds.), *Puritans and Revolutionaries* (Clarendon Press, Oxford,
1978; I. Mieck (ed.), *Soziale Schichtung und Soziale Mobilität in der Gesellschaft
Alteuropas* (Historische Kommission zu Berlin, Berlin, 1984).
3. See F. F. Mendels, 'Social Mobility and Phases of Industrialization', *Journal
of Interdisciplinary History*, vol. 7 (1976).

4. See Bairoch (ed.), *The Working Population*, pp. 149, 178–9; Sylos Labini, *Saggio sulle classi sociali*, Table 1.2; G. Hardach, 'Klassen und Schichten in Deutschland 1848–1970', *Geschichte und Gesellschaft*, vol. 3 (1977).
5. See *Historical Statistics 1960–1980. OECD Economic Outlook* (OECD, Paris, 1978), p. 35; H. Kaelble, 'Der Mythos der rapiden Industrialisierung in Deutschland', *Geschichte und Gesellschaft*, vol. 9 (1983).
6. Evidence for the increase of life expectancy during the active period of the life cycle: A. E. Imhof, *Die gewonnenen Jahre* (Beck, Munich, 1981), pp. 79ff.
7. See Eriksson and Rogers, *Rural Labour*; L. Niethammer and F. Brüggemeier, 'Wie Wohnten die Arbeiter im Kaiserreich?', *Archiv für Sozialgeschichte*, vol. 16 (1976); the contributions by Dieter Langewiesche and Hedwig Schomerus in W. Conze and U. Engelhardt (eds.), *Arbeiter im Industrialisierungsprozeß* (Klett-Cotta, Stuttgart, 1979).
8. See, besides the articles by Kocka and by van Dijk, Visser and Wolst, 'Regional Differences'; Erikson and Rogers, *Rural Labour*; von Hippel, 'Industrieller Wandel'; Hubscher, *L'agriculture et la société rurale*; Söderberg, *Agrar fattigdom*.
9. Erickson, *British Industrialists*, pp. 11ff.; Lévy-Leboyer, 'Innovations and Business Strategies'; J. Kocka, 'Entrepreneurs and Managers'; Pierenkemper, 'Entrepreneurs in Heavy Industry'; Torstendahl 'Les chefs d'entreprise'; see also Chap. 3 above.
10. See Crossick, *An Artisan Elite*, p. 117; J. W. Scott, *The Glassworkers of Carmaux* (Harvard UP, Cambridge, Mass., 1974), pp. 35ff., 72ff., 129ff.; Y. Lequin, 'La formation du proletariat industriel dans la region lyonnaise au XIXe siècle', in *Le mouvement social*, no. 97 (1976), pp. 129ff.; D. Woronoff, 'Le monde ouvrier de la Sidérurgie ancienne: note sur l'exemple français', in *Le mouvement social*, no. 97 (1976), pp. 113ff.; K. Tenfelde, 'Bildung und sozialer Aufstieg im Ruhrbergbau vor 1914' in Conze and Engelhardt (eds.), *Arbeiter*, pp. 488ff.; Schomerus, *Die Arbeiter*, pp. 263ff.; F. D. Marquardt, 'Sozialer Aufstieg, sozialer Abstieg und die Entstehung der Berliner Arbeiterklasse, 1806–1848' in H. Kaelble (ed.), *Geschichte der sozialen Mobilitaet seit der industriellen Revolution* (Athenäum, Königstein, 1978); P. Borscheid, *Textilarbeiterschaft in der Industrialisierung* (Klett-Cotta, Stuttgart, 1978); H.-J. Rupieper, *Arbeiter und Angestellte im Zeitalter der Industrialisierung. Eine sozialgeschichtliche Studie am Beispiel der Maschinenfabrik Augsburg und Nürnberg (MAN) 1837–1914* (Campus Verlag, Frankfurt, 1982) pp. 85ff.
11. For the long-term change of social differentials of life expectancy, see Imhof, *Die gewonnenen Jahre*, pp. 119ff.
12. See D. Langewiesche, 'Mobilität in deutschen Mittel- und Großstädten. Aspekte der Binnenwanderung' in W. Conze and U. Engelhardt (eds.), *Arbeiter im Industrialisierungsprozess* (Klett-Cotta, Stuttgart, 1979).
13. See G. Kleining, 'Die Veränderung der Mobilitätschancen in der Bundesrepublik', *Kölner Zeitschrift für Soziologie und Sozialpsychologie*, vol. 23 (1971) (between the birth cohorts 1876–1895 and 1916–1925, the white-collar workers from children of unskilled and skilled workers rose from 4 per cent to 19 per cent and from 9 per cent to 24 per cent respectively); Heath, *Social Mobility*, pp. 78ff.; less distinct: G. Pourcher, 'Un essai d'analyse par cohorte de la mobilité géographique et professionelle en France', *Acta sociologica*, vol. 9 (1965).
14. The most important studies putting forward these arguments are: Stearns, 'The Unskilled and Industrialization'; Scott, *Glassworkers of Carmaux*; Schomerus, *Arbeiter*; H. Zwahr, *Zur Konstituierung des Proletariats als Klasse* (Beck, Munich, 1981); K. Tenfelde, 'Der bergmännische Arbeitsplatz

während der Hochindustrialisierung (1890–1914)' in Conze and Engelhardt (eds.), *Arbeiter*; R. Vetterli, *Industriearbeit, Arbeiterbewußtsein und gewerkschaftliche Organisation* (Vandenhoeck & Ruprecht, Göttingen, 1978); R. Q. Gray, *The Labour Aristocracy in Victorian Edinburgh* (Clarendon Press, Oxford, 1976); J. Kocka, *Die Angestellten in der deutschen Geschichte 1850–1980* (Vandenhoeck & Ruprecht, 1981); G. Anderson, *Victorian Clerks* (Manchester UP, Manchester, 1976); for a summary of this research: Kaelble, *Industrialisierung*.

15. See for the long-term change of the recruitment of the business élite in the late nineteenth and early twentieth centuries: S. M. Lipset and R. Bendix, *Social Mobility in Industrial Society* (Univ. of Calif. Press, Berkeley, 1959), pp. 114ff.; J. Kocka, 'Entrepreneurship in a Late–Comer Country'; Lévy-Leboyer, 'Le patronat'; see also Chap. 3 above.

16. For one factor, the reduction of social differentials of life expectancy of children, see Imhof, *Die gewonnenen Jahre*, pp. 116ff.; R. Spree, *Soziale Ungleichheit vor Krankheit und Tod* (Vandenhoeck & Ruprecht, Göttingen, 1981), pp. 49ff.. On the social differentials of family size, direct evidence is rare; hence what is presented here is a hypothesis on a topic which needs investigation.

17. Langewiesche, 'Mobilität', pp. 76f.

18. The term 'post–industrial society' is used since it is more comprehensive than 'tertiary society', which refers mainly to employment, or 'corporate pluralism', concerned mainly with political decision–making and interest groups. The danger of an ideological bias seems small since the term has been used by such very different scholars as Daniel Bell and Alain Touraine (cf. D. Bell, *The Coming of Post–Industrial Society: a Venture in Social Forecasting* (Heinemann, London, 1974); A. Touraine, *La société post–industrielle* (Denoël, Paris, 1969).

19. See J. Fourastié, *Le grand espoir du XIXe siècle* (Presses univ. de France, Paris, 1963); Singelmann, *Agriculture to Services*; Flora, *Quantitative Historical Sociology*, pp. 48ff.;) R. Fuchs, *The Service Economy* (National Bureau of Economic Research, New York, 1968); Kaelble, 'Prometheus'.

20. *Historical Statistics 1960–1980. OECD Economic Outlook* (OECD, Paris, 1982), p. 35 (covers the European member states of the OECD). In the decade between 1950 and 1960, the growth of the service sector was lower: cf. Kaelble, 'Prometheus', appendix. Growth rates of the industrial sector before the First World War can also be calculated from that article.

21. See, as examples, Goldthorpe et al., *Social Mobility*, pp. 68ff.; Darbel, 'L'evolution'; Blau and Duncan, *American Occupational Structure*, pp. 428ff.

22. A recent comparative article referring to further studies: P. Flora and J. Alber, 'Modernization, Democratization and the Development of the Welfare State in Modern Europe', in P. Flora and A. J. Heidenheimer (eds.), *The Development of the Modern Welfare States in Europe and America* (Transaction Books, New Brunswick, 1981); dealing more directly with the relationship between welfare states and social mobility: K. U. Mayer and W. Müller, 'Historical Changes in Life-Course Processes and the Role of the State', an unpublished paper given at a session of the American Social Science Research Council, Committee on Life-Course Perspectives on Human Development, in 1982 (to be published).

23. For access to higher education, see Jarausch (ed.), *Higher Learning*; also Chap. 2 above. For access to the professions, information is more scattered. See, above all, the studies by Goldthorpe, Heath and Darbel mentioned above.

24. Mayer and Müller, 'Life-Course Processes'.
25. For initial comparative studies on the shift in political goals in Europe, see Ringer, *Education and Society*; Armstrong, *European Administrative Elite*. For a sceptical approach to the effects on the actual distribution of opportunities, a major example is Goldthorpe, *Social Mobility*.
26. Some scattered information on the purely hypothetical argument: Halsey, *Change in British Society*, p. 99; Spree, *Soziale Ungleichheit*, p. 180.

Bibliography

Adamson, J. W., *English Education 1789–1902* (Cambridge Univ. Press, Cambridge, 1964)

Akerman, S., 'Swedish Migration on Social Mobility: the Tale of Three Cities', *Social Science Hist.*, vol. 1 (1977)

Albers, J., 'Die Entstehung der westeuropäischen Sozialversicherungssysteme im Kontext von Industrialisierung und Demokratisierung', unpubl. art. (1980)

Albisetti, J. C., 'French Secondary School Reform in German Perspective, 1850–1914', in D. K. Müller, F. K. Ringer and B. Simon (eds.), *The Rise of the Modern Educational System. Structural Change and Social Reproduction, 1820–1920* (1985)

Allerbeck, K. R. and H. R. Stock, 'Soziale Mobilität in Deutschland 1833–1970', *Kölner Zeitschrift für Soziologie und Sozialpsychologie*, vol. 32 (1980)

Aminzade, R. and R. Hodson, 'Social Mobility in a mid–19th-Century French City', *American Sociological Review*, vol. 47 (1982)

Anderson, C. A. and M. Schnaper, *School and Society in England: Social Background of Oxford and Cambridge Students* (Public Affairs Press, Washington, D.C., 1952)

————, 'Access to Higher Education and Economic Development', in A. H. Halsey et al. (eds.), *Education, Economy and Society* (Glencoe Free Press, New York, 1965)

Anderson, G., *Victorian Clerks* (Manchester Univ. Press, Manchester, 1976)

Anderson, R. D., 'Secondary Education in Mid-Nineteenth-Century France: Some Social Aspects', *Past and Present*, vol. 50 (1971)

————, *Education in France, 1848–1870* (Clarendon Press, Oxford, 1975)

————, *Education and Opportunity in Victorian Scotland* (Clarendon Univ. Press, Oxford, 1983)

Armstrong, J. A., *The European Administrative Elite* (Princeton Univ. Press, Princeton, 1973)

Bairoch, P., 'Niveaux de développement économique de 1810 à 1910', *Annales*, vol. 20 (1965)

————— (ed.), *The Working Population and its Structure* (Université libre de Bruxelles, Brussels, 1968)

————— and J. M. Limbor, 'Changes in the Industrial Distribution of the World Labour Force by Region, 1880–1960', *International Labour Review*, Vol. 98 (1968)

————, 'Agriculture and Industrial Revolution', in C. M. Cipolla (ed.), *Fontana Economic History of Europe* (Fontana, London, 1973)

————, 'Europe's Gross National Product: 1800–1975', *Journal of European Economic History*, vol. 5 (1976)

Baker, D. N. and P. J. Harrigan (eds.), *The Making of Frenchmen: Current Directions in the History of Education in France, 1679–1979* (Historical Reflections Press,

Waterloo, 1980)

Bamford, T. W., 'Public Schools and Social Class 1801–1850', *British Journal of Sociology*, vol. 12 (1961)

Barbagli, M., *Disoccupazione intelletuale e sistema scolastico in Italia* (Il Mulino, Bologna, 1974)

Beau, H., *Das Leistungswissen des frühindustriellen Unternehmertums in Rheinland und Westfalen* (Rheinisch–Westfäl. Wirtschaftsarchiv, Cologne, 1959)

Becker, H., 'Bildungspolitik' in W. Benz (ed.) *Die Bundesrepublik Deutschland*, vol. 2 (Fischer, Frankfurt, 1983)

Bell, D., *The Coming of Post–Industrial Society; a Venture in Social Forecasting* (Heinemann, London, 1974)

Bendix, R. and W. F. Howton, 'Social Mobility and the American Business Elite', in S. M. Lipset and R. Bendix (eds.), *Social Mobility in Industrial Society* (Univ. of Calif. Press, Berkeley, 1959)

Bergeron, L *Banquiers, négociants et manufacturiers parisiens du Directoire à l'Empire*, 2 vols. (Écoles des hautes études en sciences sociales, Paris, 1975)

————, 'Familienstruktur und Industrieunternehmen in Frankreich (18. bis 20.Jh.)', in W. Bulst, J. Gay and J. Hook (eds.), *Familie zwischen Tradition und Moderne* (Vandenhoeck & Ruprecht, Göttingen, 1981)

Bezucha, R. J. (ed.), *Modern European Social History* (Heath, Lexington, 1972)

Bishop, J. G. and R. Wilkinson, *Winchester and Public School Elite. A Statistical Analysis* (Faber, London, 1967)

Blau, P. M. and O. D. Duncan, *The American Occupational Structure* (John Wiley & Sons, New York, 1967)

Blumin, S., 'Mobility and Change in Ante–bellum Philadelphia', in S. Thernstrom and R. Sennet (eds.), *Nineteenth Century Cities* (Yale Univ. Press, New Haven, 1969)

Bodnar, J., *Immigration and Industrialization. Ethnicity in an American Mill Town, 1870–1940* (Univ. of Pittsburgh Press, Pittsburgh, 1977)

Borscheid, P., *Textilarbeiterschaft in der Industrialisierung* (Klett-Cotta, Stuttgart, 1978)

Boudon, R., *Education, Opportunity and Social Inequality* (Wiley, New York, 1974)

Bourdieu, P., 'Cultural Reproduction and Social Reproduction', in J. Karabel and A. H. Halsey (eds.), *Power and Ideology in Education* (Oxford Univ. Press, New York, 1977)

———— and J.-C. Passeron, *Les Héritiers*, (Ed. de Minuit, Paris, 1964)

———— and M. de Saint Martin, 'Le patronat', *Actes de la recherche en sciences sociales*, no. 20/21 (1978)

Braun, R., 'Zur Einwirkung sozio–kultureller Umweltbedingungen auf das Unternehmerpotential und das Unternehmerverhalten' in W. Fischer (ed.), *Wirtschafts- und sozialgeschichtliche Probleme der frühen Industrialisierung* (Colloquium, Berlin, 1968)

Broadman, A. E. and M. P. Weber, 'Economic Growth and Occupational Mobility in Nineteenth–Century Urban America', *Journal of Social History*, vol. 11 (1978–79)

Bühl, W. L., *Schule und gesellschaftlicher Wandel* (Klett-Cotta, Stuttgart, 1968)

Bulst, W. G., J. Gay and J. Hook (eds.), *Familie zwischen Tradition und Moderne* (Vandenhoeck & Ruprecht, Göttingen, 1981)

Burke, C. B., 'The Expansion of American Higher Education', in K. H. Jarausch (ed.), *The Transformation of Higher Education 1860–1936* (Klett-Cotta, Stuttgart, 1983)

————, *American Collegiate Populations* (New York Univ. Press, New York, 1982)

Carlsson, G., *Social Mobility and Class Structure* (Gleerup, Lund, 1958)

Carter, E. C., R. Forster and J. N. Moody (eds.), *Enterprise and Entrepreneurs in 19th and 20th Century France* (Johns Hopkins Univ. Press, Baltimore, 1976)

Castritius, H., 'Die Gesellschaftsordnung der römischen Kaiserzeit und das Problem der sozialen Mobilität', *Mitteilungen der Technischen Universität Braunschweig*, 8 (1973)

Chandler, A. D. and L. Galambos, 'The Development of Large-Scale Economic Organization in Modern America', *Journal of Economic History*, vol. 30 (1970)

_____, *The Visible Hand* (Harvard Univ. Press, Cambridge, Mass., 1977)

Charles, C., 'Les milieux d'affaires dans la structure de la classe dominante vers 1900', *Actes de la recherche en sciences sociales*, nos. 20–21 (1978)

Chartier, R. and J. Revel, 'Université et société dans l'Europe nouvelle', *Revue d'histoire économique et sociale*, 25 (1978)

Chevallier, P. (ed.), *La scolarisation en France depuis un siècle* (Mouton, Paris, 1974)

Chudacoff, H. P., *Mobile Americans* (Oxford Univ. Press, N.Y., 1972)

_____ and T. K. Hareven, 'Family Transitions into Old Age', in T. K. Hareven (ed.), *Transitions, Family and Life Course in Historical Perspective* (Academic Press, New York, 1978)

Clements, R. V., *Managers: a Study of Their Careers in Industry* (Allen & Unwin, London, 1958)

Conference on Policies for Educational Growth, Background study No. 4: Group Disparities in Educational Participation (OECD, Paris, 1970)

Conze, W. and U. Engelhardt (eds.), *Arbeiter im Industrialisierungsprozeß* (Klett-Cotta, Stuttgart, 1979)

Craig, J. E., 'Higher Education and Social Mobility in Germany', in K. H. Jarausch (ed.), *The Transformation of Higher Learning 1860–1930* (Klett-Cotta, Stuttgart, 1983)

Crew, D., 'Definitions of Modernity: Social Mobility in a German Town, 1880–1901', *Journal of Social History*, vol. 7 (1973/74)

_____, *Town in the Ruhr. The Social History of Bochum 1860–1914* (Columbia Univ. Press, New York, 1979)

Crossick, G. (ed.), *The Lower-Middle Class in Britain 1870–1914* (Croom Helm, London, 1977)

_____, 'The Emergence of the Lower-Middle Class in Britain: a Discussion', in idem, op.cit.

_____, *An Artisan Elite in Victorian Society. Kentish London 1840–1880* (Croom Helm, London, 1978)

_____ and H.–G. Haupt (eds.), *Shopkeepers and Master Artisans in 19th-century Europe* (Methuen, London, 1984)

Cullity, J.P., 'The Growth of Governmental Employment in Germany, 1882–1950', *Zeitschrift für die gesamte Staatswissenschaft*, vol. 123 (1967)

Curti, M., *The Making of an American Community. A Case Study of Democracy in a Frontier Community* (Stanford U.P., Stanford, Ca., 1959)

Daheim, H., 'Berufliche Intergenerationen-Mobilität in der komplexen Gesellschaft', *Kölner Zeitschrift für Soziologie*, vol. 16 (1964)

Darbel, H., 'L'évolution récente de la mobilité sociale', *Économie et statistique*, vol. 71 (1975)

Dascher, O., *Das Textilgewerbe in Hessen-Kassel vom 16. bis 19. Jahrhundert* (Elwert, Marburg, 1968)

Day, C. R., 'Making Men and Training Technicians, Boarding Schools of the Écoles des Arts et Métiers during the 19th Century', in D. N. Baker and P. J.

Harrigan (eds.), *The Making of Frenchmen: Current Directions in the History of Education in France, 1679–1979* (Historical Reflections Press, Waterloo, 1980)
Decker, P. R., *Fortunes and Failures. White-Collar Mobility in 19th-Century San Francisco* (Harvard Univ. Press, Cambridge, Ma. 1978)
van Dijk, H., *Rotterdam 1810–1880* (Interbook International, Schiedam, 1976)
————, S. Visser and E. Wolst, 'Regional Differences in Social Mobility Patterns in the Netherlands between 1830 and 1940', *Journal of Social History*, vol. 17 (1984)
Duveau, G., *La pensée ouvrière sur l'éducation pendant la Seconde Republique et le Second Empire* (Gallimard, Paris, 1947)

Edding, F., *Internationale Tendenzen in der Entwicklung der Ausgaben für Schulen und Hochschulen* (Kiel, 1958)
Ehmer, J., 'Zur Stellung alter Menschen in Haushalt und Familie', in H. Konrad (ed.), *Der alte Mensch in der Geschichte* (Verlag für Gesellschaftskritik, Vienna, 1982)
Elmıro, A., 'Italian Education, 1859–1923', PhD thesis, U. of Pennsylvania (1975)
Englis, K., 'Eine Erhebung über die Lebensverhältnisse der Wiener Studentenschaft', *Statistische Monatsschrift*, vol. 20 (1915)
Erickson, C., *British Industrialists, Steel and Hosiery 1850–1950* (Cambridge Univ. Press, Cambridge, 1959)
————, *Invisible Immigrants* (Weidenfeld & Nicolson, London, 1972)
Erikson, R., J. H. Goldthorpe and L. Portocarero, 'Intergenerational Class Mobility and the Convergence Thesis', *British Journal of Sociology*, vol. 34 (1983)
Erikson, J. and J. Rogers, *Rural Labor and Population Change. Social and Demographic Developments in East-Central Sweden during the 19th Century* (Almquist & Wiksell, Uppsala, 1978)
Esslinger, D. R., *Immigrants and the City* (Kennikat Press, Port Washington, N.Y., 1975)

Fenwick, J. G. K., *The Comprehensive School. The Politics of Secondary School Reorganisation* (Methuen, London, 1976)
Finley, M. J., *Studies in Ancient Society* (Routledge & Kegan Paul, London, 1974)
Fischer, W. (ed.), *Wirtschafts- und sozialgeschichtliche Probleme der frühen Industrialisierung* (Colloquium, Berlin, 1968)
———— and P. Czada, 'Wandlungen in der deutschen Industriestruktur im 20. Jahrhundert', in G.A. Ritter (ed.), *Entstehung und Wandel der modernen Gesellschaft* (de Gruyter, Berlin, 1970)
Flora, P., 'Die Bildungsentwicklung. Eine vergleichende Analyse', in P.C. Ludz (ed.), *Soziologie und Sozialgeschichte* (Westdeutscher Verlag, Opladen, 1973)
————, *Indikatoren der Modernisierung* (Westdeutscher Verlag, Opladen, 1975)
————, *Quantitative Historical Sociology* (Mouton, The Hague, 1977)
————, 'Die Entwicklung sozialer Sicherungssysteme im Licht empirischer Analysen', in H.–F. Zacher (ed.), *Bedingungen für die Entwicklung und Entstehung von Sozialversicherung* (Duncker & Humblot, Berlin, 1979)
————, 'Krisenbewältigung oder Krisenerzeugung? Der Wohlfahrtsstaat in historischer Perspective', in J. Matthes (ed.), *Sozialer Wandel in Westeuropa* (Campus, Frankfurt, 1979)
———— and A. J. Heidenheimer (eds.), *The Development of the Welfare State* (Transaction Books, New Brunswick, 1981)
————, *State, Economy and Society in Western Europe 1815–1970*, 2 vols. (Campus Verlag, Frankfurt, 1984, 1985)

_____ and J. Alber, 'Modernization, Democratization, and the Development of the Welfare State in Modern Europe' in P. Flora and H. J. Heidenheimer (eds.), *The Development of the Modern Welfare States in Europe and America* (Transaction Books, New Brunswick, 1981)

Floud, J. E. and A. H. Halsey, 'Social class, Intelligence Tests and Selection for Secondary Schools', in A. H. Halsey et al. (eds.), *Education, Economy and Society* (Glencoe Free Press, New York, 1961)

Fourastié, J., *Le grand espoir du XXC siècle* (Presses universitaires de France, Paris, 1963)

Friis, F. T. B., 'De studerende ved Københavns universitet', *Nationalokomisk Tideskrift*, vol. 57 (1919)

Fuchs, R., *The Service Economy* (Nat. Bureau of Econ. Research, New York, 1968)

Geiger, R. L., *Two Paths to Mass Higher Education: Issues and Outcomes in Belgium and France* (Yale Higher Education Research Group, Working Paper, YHERG 34, 1979)

_____, 'The Changing Demand for Higher Education in the Seventies: Adaptations within Three National Systems', *Higher Education*, vol. 9 (1980), pp. 255–76;

Geiger, T., *De danske studenters social oprindelse* (Gads, Copenhagen, 1950)

Gerschenkron, A., 'Social Attitudes, Entrepreneurship, and Economic Development', in A. Gerschenkron (ed.), *Economic Backwardness in Historical Perspective* (Belknap, Cambridge, Mass., 1962)

Gildea, R., 'Education and the Classes Moyennes in the 19th Century', in D. N. Baker and P. J. Harrigan (eds.), *The Making of Frenchmen: Current Directions in the History of Education in France, 1679–1979* (Historical Reflections Press, Waterloo, 1980)

Gitelman, H. M., *Workingmen of Waltham: Mobility in American Urban Industrial Development 1850–1890*, (Johns Hopkins U.P., Baltimore, 1974)

Goldthorpe, J. H., C. Llewellyn and C. Payne, *Social Mobility and Class Structure in Britain* (Clarendon Press, Oxford, 1980)

Gourvish, T. R., 'A British Business Elite: The Chief Executive Managers of the Railway Industry, 1850–1922', *Business History Review*, vol. 47 (1973)

Grasky, R., 'Social Mobility and Business Enterprise in 17th-Century England', in D. Pennington and K. Thomas (eds.), *Puritans and Revolutionaries* (Clarendon Press, Oxford, 1978)

Gray, R. Q., *The Labour Aristocracy in Victorian Edinburgh* (Clarendon Press, Oxford, 1976)

Gregory F. W. and J. D. Neu, 'The American Industrial Elite in the 1870s', in W. Miller (ed.), *Men in Business* (Harper & Row, New York, 2nd ed., 1962)

Griffen, C. and S., *Natives and Newcomers: The Ordering of Opportunities in Mid–Nineteenth–Century Poughkeepsie* (Harvard Univ. Press, Cambridge, Mass., 1978)

Grusky, D. B. and R. M. Hauser, 'Comparative Social Mobility Revisited: Models of Convergence and Divergence in 16 Countries', *American Sociological Review*, vol. 49 (1984)

Gutman, H. G., 'The Reality of the Rags–to–Riches "Myth": The Case of the Paterson, New Jersey, Locomotive, Iron and Machinery Manufacturers, 1830–1880', in S. Thernstrom and R. Sennett (eds.), *Nineteenth–Century Cities* (Yale Univ. Press, New Haven, 1969)

Haas, H., 'Statistische Streiflichter zur österreichischen Hochschulstatistik', *Statistische Monatsschrift*, vol. 22 (1917)

Habakkuk, H. S., *American and British Technology in the Nineteenth Century* (Cambridge U.P., Cambridge, 1962)

Halsey, A. H., 'Educational Opportunities and Social Selection in England', in *Transactions of the 2nd World Congress of Sociology*, vol. 2 (London, 1954)

————— et al. (eds.), *Education, Economy and Society* (Glencoe Free Press, New York, 1965)

————— (ed.), *Trends in British Society since 1900* (Macmillan, London, 1972)

—————, *Change in British Society* (Oxford Univ. Press, Oxford, 1980)

————— et al., *Origins and Destinations* (Oxford Univ. Press, Oxford, 1980)

Hannah, L., *The Rise of the Corporate Economy* (Methuen, London, 1976) .

—————, L. (ed.), *From the Family Enterprise to the Professional Manager*, Eighth International Economic History Congress, Theme 139, (Budapest, 1982)

Hans, N., *New Trends in Education in the 18th Century* (Routledge & Kegan Paul, London, 1951)

Hardach, G., 'Klassen und Schichten in Deutschland 1848–1970', *Geschichte und Gesellschaft*, vol. 3 (1977)

Hareven, T. K., (ed.) *Anonymous Americans* (Prentice-Hall, Englewood Cliffs, N.J., 1971)

—————, 'The Last Stage of Adulthood and Old Age', *Daedalus*, vol. 60 (1976)

————— (ed.), *Transitions, Family and the Life course in Historical Perspective* (Academic Press, New York, 1978)

—————, 'From Empty Nest to Family Dissolution: Life Course and Transition into Old Age', *Journal of Family History*, vol. 1 (1979)

Harrigan, P. J., 'Secondary Education and the Professions in France during the Second Empire', *Comparative Studies in Society and History*, vol. 17 (1975)

—————, 'The Social Origins, Ambitions and Occupations of Secondary Students in France during the Second Empire', in L. Stone (ed.), *Schooling and Society* (Johns Hopkins Univ. Press, Baltimore, 1976)

Harrigan, P. S., *Mobility, Elites and Education in Second Empire France* (Laurier, Waterloo, 1980)

Hartmann, K., *Hochschulen und Wissenschaft in Polen* (Metzner, Frankfurt/Berlin, 1962)

Hauser, R. M. et al., 'Structural Changes in Occupational Mobility among Men in the United States', *American Sociological Review*, vol. 40 (1975)

—————, *Comparative Social Mobility Revisited: Models of Convergence and Divergence in 16 Countries* (Univ. of Wisconsin, Madison, 1983)

Heath, A., *Social Mobility* (Fontana, London, 1981)

Heclo, H., 'Toward a New Welfare State' in P. Flora and A. J. Heidenheimer (eds.), *The Development of the Welfare State* (Transaction Books, New Brunswick, 1981).

Heidenheimer, A. J., 'Education and Social Security Entitlements in Europe and America', in P. Flora and A. J. Heidenheimer (eds.), *The Development of the Welfare State* (Transaction Books, New Brunswick, 1981)

Henning, H., 'Soziale Verflechtung der Unternehmer in Westfalen 1860–1914', *Zeitschrift für Unternehmensgeschichte*, vol. 1 (1978)

Herrlitz, H. J. und H. Titze, 'Überfüllung als bildungspolitische Strategie', in U. Herrmann (ed.), *Schule und Gesellschaft im 19. Jahrhundert* (Beltz, Weinheim, 1977)

Higher Education in Europe: Problems and Prospects, Statistical Study (UNESCO, Paris, 1973)

von Hippel, W., 'Regionale und soziale Herkunft der Bevölkerung einer Industriestadt', in W. Conze and U. Engelhardt (eds.), *Arbeiter im Industrialisierungsprozeß* (Klett-Cotta, Stuttgart, 1979)

————, 'Industrieller Wandel im ländlichen Raum', *Archiv für Sozialgeschichte*, vol. 14 (1979)

Hirschmeier, J., 'Entrepreneurs and the Social Order: America, Germany and Japan 1879–1900', in K. Nakagawa (ed.), *Social Order and Entrepreneurship* (Univ. of Tokyo Press, Tokyo, 1977)

Hofbauer, H. and H. Kraft, 'Materialien zur Statusmobilität bei männlichen Erwerbspersonen in der Bundesrepublik Deutschland', *Mitteilungen der Berufs- und Arbeitsmarktforschung*, 5 (1972)

Hopkins, K., 'Mobility in the later Roman Empire: the Evidence of Ausonius', *Classical Quarterly*, vol. 55 (1961)

————, 'Elite Mobility in the Roman Empire', in M. J. Finley (ed.) *Studies in Ancient Society* (Routledge & Kegan Paul, London, 1974)

Hopkins, R. J., 'Occupational and Geographical Mobility in Atlanta, 1870–1896', *Journal of Southern History*, vol. 34 (1968)

Hubbard, W. H., 'Social Mobility and Social Structure in Graz, 1875–1910', *Journal of Social History*, vol. 17 (1984)

Hubscher, R., *L'agriculture et la société rurale dans le Pas-de-Calais*, 2 vols. (Commission département de monuments historiques du Pas-de-Calais, Arras, 1980)

Huschke, W., *Forschungen über die Herkunft der thüringischen Unternehmerschicht des 19. Jahrhunderts* (Lutzeyer, Baden-Baden, 1962)

Imhof, A. E., *Die gewonnenen Jahre* (Beck, Munich, 1981)

Ingham, J. N., 'Rags to Riches Revisited: The Effect of City Size on the Recruitment of Business Leaders', *Journal of Amer. History*, vol. 62 (1976)

————, *The Iron Barons* (Greenwood Press, Westport, Conn., 1978)

Isambert Jamati, V., *Crises de la société, crises de l'enseignement* (Presses Universitaires de France) Paris, 1970

Jarausch, K. H., 'The Sources of German Student Unrest 1815–1848' in L. Stone (ed.), *The University in Society*, vol. 2 (Princeton Univ. Press, Princeton, 1974)

————, 'Die neuhumanistische Gesellschaft, 1800–1870' in C. Probst (ed.), *Darstellungen und Quellen zur Geschichte der deutschen Einheitsbewegung im 19. und 20. Jahrhundert* (Winter, Heidelberg, 1978)

————, 'The Social Transformation of the University. The Case of Prussia 1865–1914', *Journal of Social History*, vol. 12 (1979)

————, (ed.), *The Transformation of Higher Learning 1860–1930* (Klett-Cotta, Stuttgart, 1983)

————, 'Higher Education and Social Change: Some Comparative Perspectives', in K. H. Jarausch (ed.), *The Transformation of Higher Learning 1860–1930*, (Klett-Cotta, Stuttgart, 1983)

Jeismann, K. E., 'Gymnasium, Staat und Gesellschaft in Preußen. Vorbemerkung der politischen und sozialen Bedeutung, der "höheren Bildung" im 19. Jahrhundert', in U. Herrmann (ed.), *Schule und Gesellschaft im 19. Jahrhundert* (Beltz, Weinheim, 1977)

Jenkins, H. and D. C. Jones, 'Social Class of Cambridge University Alumni of the 18th and 19th Centuries', *British Journal of Sociology*, vol. 1 (1950)

Jenks, C., and D. Riesman, *The Academic Revolution*, (Garden City, 1968)

Jörberg, L., 'Some Notes on Education in Sweden in the 19th Century', *Annales Cisalpines d'Histoire sociale*, vol. 2 (1971)

Kaelble, H., *Berliner Unternehmer während der frühen Industrialisierung* (de Gruyter, Berlin, 1972)

——————, 'Long-term Changes in the Recruitment of the Business Elite: Germany Compared to the US, Britain and France since the Industrial Revolution', in *Journal of Social History*, 13, 1979/80, pp. 404–23 (French version in M. Lévy-Leboyer (ed.), *Le patronat pendant la deuxième industrialisation*, (Éditions Ouvrières, Paris, 1979, pp. 15–36)

——————, 'Social Mobility in Germany 1900–1960', *Journal of Modern History*, vol. 50 (1978)

——————, 'Sozialer Aufstieg in Deutschland 1850–1914', in K. H. Jarausch (ed.), *Quantifizierung in der Geschichtswissenschaft* (Droste, Düsseldorf, 1976)

——————, 'Abweichung oder Konvergenz? Soziale Mobilität in Frankreich und Deutschland während des 19. und 20. Jahrhunderts', in Ritter, G. A. and R. Vierhaus (eds.), *Aspekte der historischen Forschung in Frankreich und Deutschland* (Vandenhoeck & Ruprecht, Göttingen, 1981)

——————, 'Educational Opportunities and Government Policies in Europe in the Period of Industrialization', in P. Flora and A. Heidenheimer (eds.), *The Development of the Welfare State in Europe* (Transaction Books, New Brunswick, 1981, pp. 235–64)

——————, *Historical Research on Social Mobility. Western Europe and the USA in the 19th and 20th Centuries* (Croom Helm, London, 1981)

——————, 'Social Mobility in America and Europe: A Comparison of 19th Century Cities', in *Urban History Yearbook*, 1981, pp. 24–38

——————, 'From the Family Enterprise to the Professional Manager: The German Case', in L. Hannah (ed.), *From the Family Enterprise to the Professional Manager*, Eighth International Economic History Congress, Theme 139 (Budapest, 1982)

——————, *Industrialisation and Social Inequality in 19th-Century Europe*, Berg Publishers, Leamington Spa, 1986

——————, 'Der Mythos der rapiden Industrialisierung in Deutschland', *Geschichte und Gesellschaft*, vol. 9 (1983)

——————, Chapter 3.3 in *Soziale Mobilität und Chancengleichheit im 19. und 20. Jahrhundert. Deutschland im internationalen Vergleich* (Vandenhoeck & Ruprecht, Göttingen, 1983)

——————, 'Eras of Social Mobility in 19th and 20th Century Europe', in *Journal of Social History*, 17, 1983/84, pp. 489–504

——————, 'Was Prometheus most Unbound in Europe? Labour Force in Europe during the late 19th and 20th Centuries', *Journal of European Economic History*, vol. 14 (1985)

Karabel, J. and A. H. Halsey (eds.), *Power and Ideology in Education* (Oxford Univ. Press, New York, 1977)

Karady, V., 'Normaliens et autres enseignants à la belle epoque', *Revue française de sociologie*, vol. 13 (1972)

Kater, M., 'Die Krisis des Frauenstudiums in der Weimarer Republik', *Vierteljahresschrift für Sozial– und Wirtschaftsgeschichte*, vol. 59 (1972)

Katz, M. B., *The People of Hamilton, Canada West: Family and Class in a Mid-Nineteenth Century City* (Harvard Univ. Press, Cambridge, Ma., 1975)

Kearns, D. T., *The Social Mobility of New Orleans Laborers 1870–1900* (Ph.D. thesis, Tulane Univ., 1977)

Kleining, G., 'Die Veränderung der Mobilitätschancen in der Bundesrepublik', *Kölner Zeitschrift für Soziologie und Sozialpsychologie*, vol. 23 (1971)

——————, 'Soziale Mobilität in der Bundesrepublik Deutschland II: Status- oder Prestigemobilität', *Kölner Zeitschrift für Soziologie*, vol. 27 (1975)

——————, 'Struktur- und Berufsmobilität in der Bundesrepublik Deutschland',

Kölner Zeitschrift für Soziologie, vol. 23 (1971)

Knights, P.R., *The Plain People of Boston, 1830–1860* (Oxford Univ. Press, New York, 1971)

Kocka, J., 'Family and Bureaucracy in German Industrial Management', *Business History Review*, vol. 45 (1971)

————, 'Organisierter Kapitalismus oder staatsmonopolistischer Kapitalismus', in H. A. Winkler (ed.), *Organisierter Kapitalismus* (Vandenhoeck & Ruprecht, Göttingen, 1974)

————, *Unternehmer in der deutschen Industrialisierung* (Vandenhoeck & Ruprecht, Göttingen, 1975)

————, *Angestellte zwischen Faschismus und Demokratie* (Vandenhoeck & Ruprecht, Göttingen, 1977)

————, 'Entrepreneurship in a Late–Comer Country: The German Case', in K. Nakagawa (ed.), *Social Order and Entrepreneurship* (Univ. of Tokyo Press, Tokyo, 1977)

————, 'Bildung, soziale Schichtung und soziale Mobilität im Deutschen Kaiserreich am Beispiel der gewerblich-technischen Ausbildung', in B. J. Wendt, D. Stegmann and P. C. Witt (eds.), *Industrielle Gesellschaft und politisches System* (Neue Gesellschaft, Bonn, 1978)

————, 'Entrepreneurs and Managers in German Industrialization', in P. Mathias and M. M. Postan (eds.), *Cambridge Economic History of Europe*, vol. 7, part 1 (Cambridge Univ. Press, Cambridge, 1978)

————, 'Familie, Unternehmer und Kapitalismus am Beispiel aus der frühen deutschen Industrialisierung', *Zeitschrift für Unternehmensgeschichte*, vol. 24 (1979)

———— and H. Siegrist, 'Die hundert größten deutschen Industrieunternehmen im späten 19. und frühen 20. Jahrhundert', in W. Horn and J. Kocka (eds.), *Law and Formation of the Big Enterprises in the Late 19th and Early 20th Centuries* (Vandenhoeck & Ruprecht, Göttingen, 1979)

————, 'The Study of Social Mobility and the Formation of the Working Class in the Nineteenth Century', *Le mouvement social*, vol. 111 (1980)

————, K. Ditt, H. Moser, J. Reif, and R. Schüren, *Familie und soziale Plazierung* (Westdeutscher Verlag, Opladen, 1980)

————, *Die Angestellten in der deutschen Geschichte 1850–1980* (Vandenhoeck & Ruprecht, 1981)

————, 'Family and Class Formation: Intergenerational Mobility and Marriage Patterns in 19th-Century Westphalian Communities', *Journal of Social History*, vol. 17 (1984)

Kraul, M., 'Untersuchungen zur sozialen Struktur der Schülerschaft des preußischen Gymnasium im Vormärz', *Bildung und Erziehung*, vol. 29 (1976)

————, *Gymnasium und Gesellschaft im Vormärz* (Vandenhoeck & Ruprecht, Göttingen, 1980)

Kuikka, ·M. T., 'Die Erforschung der Geschichte der Erziehung in Finnland 1945–1975', in *Die historische Pädagogik in Europa und den USA* (Klett-Cotta, Stuttgart, 1979)

Landes, D. S., *The Unbound Prometheus* (Cambridge UP, Cambridge, 1970)

Langewiesche, D., 'Mobilität in deutschen Mittel– und Großstädten. Aspekte der Binnenwanderung', in W. Conze and U. Engelhardt (eds.), *Arbeiter im Industrialisierungsprozeß* (Klett-Cotta, Stuttgart, 1979)

Lequin, Y., 'La formation du prolétariat industriel dans la région Lyonnaise au XIXe siècle', *Le mouvement social*, no. 97 (1976)

Levin, H., 'Educational Opportunity and Social Inequality in Western Europe',
    Social Problems, vol. 24 (1976)
Lévy-Leboyer, M., 'Le patronat française a-t-il été malthusien?', Le mouvement
    social, no. 88 (1974)
_____, 'Innovation and Business Strategies in 19th- and 20th-Century France',
    in E. G. Carter et al. (eds.), Enterprise and Entrepreneurs in 19th and 20th Century
    France (Johns Hopkins Univ. Press, Baltimore, (1976)
_____, 'Le patronat français, 1912-1973', in M. Lévy-Leboyer (ed.), Le patro-
    nat dans la seconde industrialisation (Éd. Ouvrières, Paris, 1979)
_____ (ed.), Le patronat dans la seconde industrialisation, Éditions Ouvrières,
    Paris, 1979
Lipset, S. M. and R. Bendix (eds.), Social Mobility in Industrial Society (Univ. of
    Calif. Press, Berkeley, 1959)
_____, The First New Nation (Basic Books, New York, 1963)
Little, A. and J. Westergaard, 'The Trend of Class Differentials in Educational
    Opportunity in England and Wales', British Journal of Sociology, vol. 15 (1964)
Ludz, P. C. (ed.), Soziologie und Sozialgeschichte (Westdeutscher Verlag, Opladen,
    1973)
Lundgreen, P., 'Educational Expansion and Economic Growth in Nineteenth-
    Century Germany: a Quantitative Study', in L. Stone (ed.), Schooling in
    Society (Johns Hopkins Univ. Press, Baltimore, 1976)
Lundgreen, D., 'Historische Bildungsforschung', in R. Rürup (ed.), Historische
    Sozialwissenschaft (Vandenhoeck & Ruprecht, Göttingen, 1977)

Maddison, A., Phases of Capitalist Development (Oxford UP, 1982)
Maier, C. S., Recasting Bourgeois Europe: Stabilization in France, Germany and Italy
    in the Decade after World War I (Princeton Univ. Press, Princeton, 1975)
Maillet, J., 'L'évolution des effectifs de l'enseignement secondaire de 1803 à
    1961', in La scolarisation en France depuis un siècle (Mouton, Paris, 1974)
Marquardt, F. D., 'Sozialer Aufstieg, sozialer Abstieg und die Entstehung der
    Berliner Arbeiterklasse, 1806-1848', in H. Kaelble (ed.), Geschichte der sozialen
    Mobilität seit der industriellen Revolution (Athenäum, Königstein, 1978)
Mathew, W. M., 'The Origins and Occupations of Glasgow Students, 1740-1839', Past
    and Present, vol. 33 (1966)
Mayer, K. U., 'Gesellschaftlicher Wandel und soziale Struktur eines Lebens-
    laufs', in G. Matthes (ed.), Lebenswelt und soziale Probleme (Campus, Frank-
    furt, 1981)
Mayer, K. M. and W. Müller, 'Historical Changes in Life-Course Processes and
    the Role of the State', unpubl. paper given at a conference of the American
    Social Science Research Council, Committee on Life-Course Perspectives on
    Human Development in 1982
Mayntz, R., Soziale Schichtung und sozialer Wandel in einer Industriegemeinde (Enke,
    Stuttgart, 1958)
McLachlan, J., 'The American College in the 19th Century. Towards a Reappraisal',
    Teachers College Record, vol. 80, 1980
McClelland, C. E., 'The Aristocracy and University Reform in Eighteenth-
    Century Germany', in L. Stone (ed.), Schooling and Society (Johns Hopkins
    Univ. Press, Baltimore, 1976)
Mendels, F. F., 'Social Mobility and Phases of Industrialization', Journal of
    Interdisciplinary History, vol. 7 (1976)
Meyer, R., 'Das Berechtigungswesen in seiner Bedeutung für Schule und Gesell-
    schaft im 19. Jahrhundert', Zeitschrift für die gesamte Staatswissenschaft, vol. 124
    (1968)

Mieck, I. (ed.), *Soziale Schichtung und soziale Mobilität in der Gesellschaft Alteuropas* (Historische Kommission zu Berlin, Berlin, 1984)
Mills, C. W., 'The American Business Elite: A Collective Portrait', *Journal of Economic History*, vol. 5 (1945), supplement
Mitchell, B. R., *European Historical Statistics 1750–1970* (Macmillan, London, 1975)
Moberg, S., *Vem blev Student och vad blev Student* (Iduns, Malmö, 1951)
Moltmann, G. (ed.), *Deutsche Amerikaauswanderung im 19. Jahrhundert* (Metzler, Stuttgart, 1976)
Mouton, M.-R. 'L' enseignement supérieur en France de 1890 à nos jours', in P. Chevallier (ed.), *La scolarisation en France depuis un siècle* (Mouton, Paris, 1974)
Müller, D. K., *Sozialstruktur und Schulsystem. Aspekte zum Strukturturwandel des Schulwesens im 19. Jahrhundert* (Vandenhoeck & Ruprecht, Göttingen, 1977)
Müller, S. F., *Die höhere Schule Preußens in der Weimarer Republik* (Beltz, Weinheim, 1977)
Müller, W., *Familie — Schule — Beruf* (Westdeutscher Verlag, Opladen, 1975)
_____ and K. U. Meyer, *Chancengleichheit durch Bildung?* (Klett-Cotta, Stuttgart, 1976)

Nakagawa, K. (ed.), *Social Order and Entrepreneurship* (Univ. of Tokyo Press, Tokyo, 1977)
Newcomer, M., 'The Big Business Executive/1964: A Study of his Social and Educational Background', unpubl. paper (1965)
Niethammer, L. and F. Brueggemeier, 'Wie wohnten die Arbeiter im Kaiserreich?', *Archiv für Sozialgeschichte*, vol. 16 (1976)
Nilsson, B., 'Study Financing and Expansion of Education', *Economy and History*, vol. 20 (1977)

O'Boyle, L., 'The Middle Class in Western Europe 1815–1848', *American Historical Review*, vol. 71 (1966)
_____, 'A Possible Model for the Study of 19th-Century Secondary Education in Europe', *Journal of Social History*, vol. 12 (1978)

Papp. D. ,and B. Oehngren, *Arbeterna vid Oskarshamus varv kring sekeskiftet* (Sjöhistorika Museet, Stockholm, 1973)
Passow, A. H. et al., *The National Case Study: an Empirial Comparative Study of 21 Educational Systems* (Almquist & Wiksell, Stockholm 1976)
Perkin, H., 'The Recruitment of Elites in British Society, since 1880', unpubl. paper (1976)
_____, 'The Recruitment of Elites in British Society since 1880', *Journal of Social History*, vol. 12 (1978/9) (abbrev. version of above)
Pierenkemper, T., 'Entrepreneurs in Heavy Industry: Upper Silesia and the Westphalian Ruhr Region, 1852-1913', *Business History Review*, vol. 53 (1979)
_____, *Die westfälischen Schwerindustriellen 1852–1913* (Vandenhoeck & Ruprecht, Göttingen, 1979)
Pourcher, G., 'Un essai d'analyse par cohorte de la mobilité géographique et professionelle en France', *Acta sociologica*, vol. 9 (1965)
Prais, S. J., *The Evolution of the Giant Firms in Britain: A Study of the Growth of Concentration in Manufacturing Industry in Britain 1909–1970* (Cambridge Univ. Press, Cambridge, 1976)
Premfors, R., *The Politics of Higher Education in a Comparative Perspective. France, Sweden, United Kingdom* (Gotob, Stockholm, 1980)
Probst, C. (ed.), *Darstellungen und Quellen zur Geschichte der deutschen Einheitsbewe-*

gung im 19. und 20. Jahrhundert (Winter, Heidelberg, 1978)
Pross, H. and K. W. Boetticher, *Manager des Kapitalismus* (Suhrkamp, Frankfurt, 1971)
Puhle, H.-J., 'Vom Wohlfahrtsstaat', in G. A. Ritter (ed.), *Vom Wohlfahrtsaus-schuss zum Wohlfahrtsstaat* (Mankus, Cologne, 1973)

Reinhardt, A., *Das Universitätsstudium der Württemberger seit der Reichsgründung*, (Tübingen, 1918)
Revel, J., 'Université et société dans l'Europe Nouvelle', *Revue d'histoire moderne et contemporaine*, vol. 25 (1978)
Ringer, F. K., 'Higher Education in Germany in the 19th Century', *Journal of Contemporary History*, vol. 2 (1967)
————, *The Decline of the German Mandarins* (Harvard Univ. Press, Cambridge, Ma., 1969)
————, 'The Education of Elites in Modern Europe', *History of Education Quarterly* (1978)
————, *Education and Society in Modern Europe* (Indiana Univ. Press, Bloomington, 1979)
————, 'Bildung, Wirtschaft und Gesellschaft in Deutschland, 1800–1960', *Geschichte und Gesellschaft*, vol. 6 (1980)
————, 'On Segmentation in Modern European Educational Systems', in Müller et. al. (eds.), *The Rise of the Modern Educational System* (1985)
Rishoy, T., 'Metropolitan Social Mobility, 1850-1950: The case of Copenhagen', *Quantity and Quality*, vol. 5 (1971)
Ritter, G. A. (ed.), *Vom Wohlfahrtsausschuss zum Wohlfahrtsstaat* (Mankus, Cologne, 1973)
———— and R. Vierhaus (eds.), *Aspekte der historischen Forschung in Frankreich und Deutschland* (Vandenhoeck & Ruprecht, Göttingen, 1981)
Rosenberg, H., 'Die Pseudodemokratisierung der Rittergutsbesitzerklasse', in H.–U. Wehler (ed.), *Moderne deutsche Sozialgeschichte* (Kiepenheuer & Witsch, Cologne, 1970)
Rubinstein, D. and B. Simon, *The Evolution of the Comprehensive School, 1926–1972* (Routledge & Kegan Paul, London, 1969)
Rubinstein, W. D., 'Men of Property: Some Aspects of Occupation, Inheritance and Power among Top British Wealthholders', in P. Stanworth and A. Giddens (eds.), *Elites and Power in British Society* (Cambridge Univ. Press, Cambridge, 1974)
Rueschemeyer, D., *Lawyers and their Society* (Harvard Univ. Press, Cambridge, Ma., 1973)
Runblom, H. and H. Norman (eds.), *From Sweden to America* (Univ. of Minnesota Press, Minneapolis, 1976)
Rupieper, H.-J., *Arbeiter und Angestellte im Zeitalter der Industrialisierung. Eine sozialgeschichtliche Studie am Beispiel der Maschinenfabrik Augsburg und Nürnberg (MAN) 1837–1914* (Campus, Frankfurt, 1982)

Samuel, R., 'The Workshop of the World: Steam Power and Hand Technology', *History Workshop*, vol. 3 (1977)
Sanderson, M., 'The Grammar School and the Education of the Poor 1786–1840', *British Journal of Educational Studies*, vol. 11 (1962)
————, *The Universities and British Industry 1850-1870* (Routledge & Kegan Paul, London, 1972)
Saul, S.B. (ed.), *Technological Change, the United States and Britain in the Nineteenth Century* (Methuen, London, 1970)

Schneider, R., 'Die Bildungsentwicklung der westeuropäischen Staaten, 1870–1979', *Zeitschrift für Soziologie*, vol. 10 (1982)

Schneider, W., 'Die soziale Bedingtheit der Ausbildungschancen', in F. Hess et al. (eds.), *Die Ungleichheit der Bildungschancen* (Walter, Olten, 1966)

Schomerus, H., *Die Arbeiter der Maschinenfabrik Eßlingen* (Klett-Cotta, Stuttgart, 1977)

Schriewer, J., *Die französische Universitäten 1945–1968* (Klinkhardt, Heilbronn, 1972)

Schröder, W. H., *Arbeitergeschichte und Arbeiterbewegung* (Campus Verlag, Frankfurt, 1978)

Schröter, A. and W. Becker, *Die deutsche Maschinenbauindustrie in der industriellen Revolution* (Akademie Verlag, Berlin, 1962)

Schüren, R., 'Familie und soziale Plazierung in einer durch Landwirtschaft, Heimgewerbe und Industrialisierung geprägten Gemeinde am Beispiel des Kirchspiels Borghorst im 19. Jahrhundert', in J. Kocka et al., *Familie und soziale Plazierung* (Westdeutscher Verlag, Opladen, 1980)

Scott, J. W., *The Glassworkers of Carmaux* (Harvard UP, Cambridge, Mass., 1974)

Second Conference of Ministers of Education of European Member States, Bucharest 26.11.–3.12.1973 (UNESCO, Paris, 1973)

Sewell, W. H., 'Social Mobility in a Nineteenth-Century European City', *Journal of Interdisciplinary History*, vol. 7 (1976)

Sheehan, J. J., 'Conflict and Cohesion among the German Elites in the Nineteenth Century', in R. J. Bezucha (ed.), *Modern European Social History* (Heath, Lexington, 1972)

————, *Structure and Mobility: The Men and Women of Marseilles, 1820–1870* (CUP, Cambridge, 1985)

Shergold, P. R., *Working Class Life. The "American Standard" in Comparative Perspective 1899–1913* (Univ. of Pittsburgh Press, Pittsburgh, 1982)

Simon, B., *Studies in the History of Education 1780–1870* (Lawrence & Wishart, London, 1960)

————, *The Concept of Popular Education* (MacGibbon & Kee, London, 1965)

————, *Education and the Labour Movement* (Lawrence & Wishart, London, 1965)

Singelmann, J., *From Agriculture to Services. The Transformation of Industrial Employment* (Sage, London, 1978)

Skovgaard-Petersen, V., 'Towards an Educational Policy in Denmark', *Scandinavian Journal of History*, vol. 6 (1981)

Söderberg, J., *Agrar fattigdom i Sydswerige under 1800-talet* (Almqvist & Wiksell, Stockholm, 1978)

Sorokin, P. A., *Social and Cultural Mobility* (Harper, 1927; repr. Free Press of Glencoe, London, 1964)

Spree, R., *Soziale Ungleichheit vor Krankheit und Tod* (Vandenhoeck & Ruprecht, Göttingen, 1981) (transl. as *Social Inequality in Illness and Death*, Berg Publishers, Leamington Spa, 1986)

Stahl, W., *Der Elitekreislauf in der Unternehmerschaft* (Deutsch, Frankfurt, 1973)

Stanworth, P. and A. Giddens, 'An Economic Elite: A Demographic Profile of Company Chairmen', in P. Stanworth and A. Giddens (eds.), *Elites and Power in British Society* (Cambridge Univ. Press, Cambridge, 1974)

Stearns, P. N., 'The Unskilled and Industrialization. A Transformation of Consciousness', *Archiv für Sozialgeschichte*, vol. 16 (1976)

————, *Old Age in European Society* (Croom Helm, London, 1977)

Stone, L., 'Social Mobility in England. 1500–1700', *Past & Present*, vol. 33 (1966)

————, 'Japan and England: A Comparative Study', in *History and Education*

(Methuen, London, 1970)

———— (ed.), *The University in Society*, vol. 2, (Princeton UP, Princeton, 1974)

————, 'The Size and Composition of the Oxford Student Body, 1580–1910', in L. Stone (ed.), *The University in Society*, vol. 1 (Princeton Univ. Press, Princeton, N.J., 1975)

————, *Schooling and Society* (Johns Hopkins Univ. Press, Baltimore, 1976)

Sylos Labini, P., *Saggio sulle classi sociali* (Laterza, Rome, 1978)

Synnot, M. G., *The Half–Opened Door. Discrimination and Admission at Harvard, Yale and Princeton, 1900–1970* (Greenwood Press, Westport, 1979)

Talbott, J. E., *The Politics of Educational Reform in France 1918–1940* (Princeton UP, Princeton, 1969)

Tenfelde, K., 'Der bergmännische Arbeitsplatz während der Hochindustrialisierung (1890–1914)', in W. Conze and U. Engelhardt (eds.), *Arbeiter im Industrialisierungsprozeß* (Klett-Cotta, Stuttgart, 1979)

————, 'Bildung und sozialer Aufstieg im Ruhrbergbau vor 1914', in W. Conze and U. Engelhardt (eds.), *Arbeiter im Industrialisierungsprozeß* (Klett-Cotta, Stuttgart, 1979)

Thélot, C., *Tel père tel fils? Position sociale et origine familiale* (Dunod, Paris, 1982)

Thernstrom, S., *Poverty and Progress: Social Mobility in a Nineteenth-Century City* (Harvard U.P., Cambridge, Ma., 1964)

————. and R. Sennett (eds.), *Nineteenth-Century Cities* (Yale Univ. Press, New Haven, 1969)

————, *The Other Bostonians* (Harvard Univ. Press, Cambridge, 1973)

Thompson, F. L. *English Landed Society in the Nineteenth Century* (Routledge & Kegan Paul, London, 1963)

Tilly, R., 'The Growth of Large–Scale Enterprise in Germany since the Middle of the 19th Century', in H. Daems and H. van der Wee, *The Rise of Managerial Capitalism*, (Nijhoff, The Hague, 1974)

Titze, H. *Die Politisierung der Erziehung* (Athenäum, Frankfurt, 1973)

————, 'Überfüllungskrisen in akademischen Karrieren: Eine Zyklustheorie', *Zeitschrift für Pädagogik*, vol. 27 (1981)

————, 'Enrolment Expansion and Academic Overcrowding in Germany' in K. Jarausch (ed.) *The Transformation of Higher Learning 1860–1930* (Klett-Cotta, Stuttgart, 1983)

Torstendahl, R., 'Les chefs d'entreprise en Suède de 1880 à 1950: sélection et milieu social', in M. Lévy-Leboyer (ed.), *Le patronat dans la seconde industrialisation* (Ed. Ouvrières, Paris, 1979)

————, 'The Social Relevance of Education. Swedish Secondary Education during the Period of Industrialization', *Scandinavian Journal of History*, vol. 6 (1981)

Touraine, A., *La société post-industrielle* (Denoë, Paris, 1969)

Toutain, J.-C., *La Population de la France de 1700 à 1959* (ISEA, Paris, 1963)

van Tulder, J. J. M., *De beroepsmobiliteit in Nederland van 1919 tot 1954* (H. E. Stenfert Kroese, Leiden, 1962)

Tully, J. C. et. al., 'Trends in Occupational Mobility in Indianapolis', *Social Forces* vol. 49 (1970–71)

Vaizey, J. and J. Sheehan, *Resources for Education. An Economic Study of Education in the United Kingdom 1920–1965* (Allen & Unwin, London, 1968)

Vetterli, R., *Industriearbeit, Arbeiterbewußtsein und gewerkschaftliche Organisation* (Vandenhoeck & Ruprecht, Göttingen, 1978)

Vidalenc, J., *La société française de 1815 à 1848*, 2 vols. (Ed. M. Rivière, Paris, 1970,

1973)
Walker, M., *Germany and the Emigration 1816–1885* (Harvard Univ. Press, Cambridge, Mass., 1964)
Warner, W. L. and J. O. Low, *The Social System of the Modern Factory* (Greenwood Press, Westport, Cn., 1976)
——— and J. C. Abegglen, *Occupational Mobility in American Business and Industry, 1928–1952* (Univ. of Minnesota Press, Minneapolis, 1955)
Weber, M., *Wirtschaft und Gesellschaft* (1921; repr. Kiepenheuer & Witsch, Cologne, 1964)
Weber, M. P., 'Economic Growth and Occupational Mobility in Nineteenth–Century Urban America', *Journal of Social History*, vol. 11 (1977–78)
Wehler, H.-U., 'Der Aufstieg des organisierten Kapitalismus und Interventionsstaates in Deutschland', in H. A. Winkler (ed.), *Organisierter Kapitalismus* (Vandenhoeck & Ruprecht, Göttingen, 1974)
Weisz, G., *The Emergence of Modern Universities in France, 1863–1914* (Princeton Univ. Press, Princeton, 1983)
Weschler, H. S., *The Qualified Student. A History of Selective College Admission in America* (Wiley, New York, 1977)
Williamson, B., *Education, Social Structure and Development* (Macmillan Press, London, 1979)
Winkler, H. A. (ed.), *Organisierter Kapitalismus* (Vandenhoeck & Ruprecht, Göttingen, 1974)
Woronoff, D., 'Le monde ouvrier de la sidérurgie ancienne: note sur l'exemple français', *Le mouvement social*, no. 97 (1976)
Worthmann, P. B., 'Working Class Mobility in Birmingham, Alabama, 1880–1914', in T. K. Hareven (ed.), *Anonymous Americans* (Prentice-Hall, Englewood Cliffs, N.J., 1971)

Yellowitz, I., *Industrialization and the American Labor Movement, 1850–1900* (Kennikat Press, Port Washington, N.Y., 1977)
———, 'Skilled Workers and Mechanization: The Lasters in the 1800's', *Labor History*, vol. 8 (1977)

Zacher, H. F. (ed.), *Bedingungen für die Entwicklung und Entstehung von Sozialversicherung* (Dunker & Humblot, Berlin, 1979)
Zapf, W., 'Die deutschen Manager', in W. Zapf (ed.), *Beiträge zur Analyse der deutschen Oberschicht* (Piper, Munich, 1965)
Zapf, W. (ed.), *Beiträge zur Analyse der deutschen Oberschicht* (Piper, Munich, 1965)
Zeldin, T., 'Higher Education in France, 1848–1945', *Journal of Contemporary History*, vol. 2 (1967)
———, *France 1848–1945*, vol. 2 (Clarendon Press, Oxford, 1977)
Zorn. W., 'Hochschule und höhere Schule in der deutschen Sozialgeschichte der Neuzeit', in K. Repgen and S. Skalweit (eds.), *Spiegel der Geschichte*, Festgabe Braubach (Aschendorff, Münster, 1964)
Zunkel, F., 'Beamtenschaft und Unternehmertum beim Aufbau der Ruhrindustrie 1849–1880', *Tradition*, vol. 9 (1964)
Zwahr, H., *Zur Konstituierung des Proletariats als Klasse* (Beck, Munich, 1981)

Subject Index

Aarhus (Denmark) 28
aristocracy 41, 48, 56ff, 107
army officers 101
artisans (also craftsmen) 5, 67, 71, 103, 105, 107, 122, 127
Atlanta (USA) 17f
Austria 16, 40, 66–69, 71, 76, 78, 81, 86f, 90, 93

Baden 41f, 44, 49
Bavaria 54
Belgium 39f, 57f, 89, 84, 86f, 90, 93
Berlin 9f, 12f, 41, 48, 98
Bielefeld (Germany) 9f, 13, 26f
Birmingham (USA) 17, 19
Bochum (Germany) 6, 13, 16, 19, 27, 44
Borghorst (Germany) 1, 6, 9f, 13, 27
Boston 6, 9f, 15ff, 23, 284
Breslau 44
Bulgaria 46
bureaucracy 1, 37
business elite 33, 61, 94–103, 114f, 119, 126, 139ff
businessmen (also business leaders, entrepreneurs, business elite: cf. also managers) 22, 33, 36, 42, 46, 51f, 54, 61, 67, 71, 94, 119, 126, 139ff
businessmen, education 49, 98, 104, 113f
businessmen, family 97, 104, 113, 117
businessmen, owner 101, 105, 111, 114, 118

Cambridge 31, 48, 60
Canada 9f, 12
capital 104, 112, 124, 127, 129
capitalism, organised 126–131, 135
career mobility 15f, 18, 26, 132, 139
cities, industrial 6f, 14, 124, 128, 137
civil servants 36f, 44–48, 52f, 55, 65, 73, 102, 128f
civil servants, higher 42, 49ff, 54f, 67, 71, 101ff

civil servants, lower 43f, 49, 51, 54, 57, 67, 71, 101, 117
class, upper see upper class
classes, lower see lower classes
clergy 50, 56
Copenhagen 9f, 12f, 28
Cologne 9f, 12f, 27
Czechoslovakia 47, 123

demographic development (also demographic transition population growth) 2f, 13, 125, 129, 133
Denmark 8, 39f, 46, 58, 67f, 80, 83f, 86f, 90

école centrale 48, 50, 54
école des arts et métiers 48, 50, 54
école normale 67
école polytechnique 48, 50, 54, 67
écoles grandes 31, 58, 62, 66
education 121, 127, 132
education, eras of 34ff, 65ff, 69ff, 75ff
education, higher 31f, 35–41, 48–55, 58, 60–66, 79–93, 114, 141
education, investment in 81, 88
educational expansion 3, 33, 36, 62f, 65ff, 86, 81, 114
educational opportunities, magnitude (cf. also student ratio, university attendance) 34f, 38ff, 53, 56, 61, 65ff, 70ff, 75f, 84–92, 139, 141
educational opportunities, definition 34f, 63f
educational opportunities, distribution 2, 33–56, 62, 65f, 75ff, 78ff, 88–93, 140f
educational policies (also educational reforms, school reforms, scholarship) 33, 36ff, 58f, 62ff, 69, 73–76, 79–82, 91ff, 108
Eindhoven (Netherlands) 9f, 16, 19, 26f
elite 24, 50, 61, 94, 107, 127
England 32, 39, 42, 51, 60, 67ff, 71, 73,

180

Name Index

Anderson R. D. 48, 53, 58
Angelo R. 53

Bamford T. W. 41, 57
Bendix R. 6, 15, 96, 99, 104, 113, 158ff
Beveridge W. 76
Borsig E. v. 95

Carnegie A. 95
Craig J. 57 .
Gentile G. 74f
Geiger T. 88

Hans N. 57
Harrigan P. 58

Jarausch K. H. 57
Jeismann E. -K. 57
Jenks Ch. 53

Katz M. 15
Kraul M. 41

Lipset S. M. 6, 15, 138ff

Lundgreen P. 59

Mendels W. 96
Müller W. 22
Mathew W. D. 48

Premfors 85f, 88

Riesmann D. 53
Ringer F. 32, 38, 57, 66, 88f, 141

Simon B. 57
Sombart W. 24
Sorokin P. 53
Stone L. 48, 58

Tocquille de A. 1, 6, 11, 14f, 20, 136, 138ff

Warner W. L. 25
Weber M. 59
Wilkinson W. 95

Zeldin T. 41, 58

This volume forms the culmination of the author's works on social mobility which have already established him in the Anglo-Saxon world as one of the leading historians in the field. This collection presents a number of theses advanced on the basis of a very wide reading of printed primary and secondary literature; the author sets his own German research very firmly in the context of British, French and American work in the same area which allows him to make some interesting international comparisons.

CONTENTS: Periods of Social Mobility — The Recruitment of the Business Elite since the Industrial Revolution — Social Mobility in 19th-Century Cities — Opportunities in 19th-Century Higher Education — Conclusion — Bibliography

[Hartmut Kaelble] is one of the few historians to have attempted comparative history on a systematic basis . . . and deserves full credit for tackling what many less courageous historians would regard as an impossible task.
Richard Evans, Professor of History, University of East Anglia